FACING TOUGH
CHOICES

FACING TOUGH CHOICES

Balancing Fiscal
and
Social Deficits

Steven R. Eastaugh

PRAEGER

Westport, Connecticut
London

Library of Congress Cataloging-in-Publication Data

Eastaugh, Steven R.
    Facing tough choices : balancing fiscal and social deficits /
Steven R. Eastaugh.
        p.   cm.
    Includes bibliographical references and index.
    ISBN 0–275–94747–5 (acid-free paper).—ISBN 0–275–94748–3 (pbk.
: acid-free paper)
    1. Budget deficits—United States.   2. Fiscal policy—United
States.   3. United States—Social policy—1993– .   I. Title.
HJ2051.E25   1994
339.5′23′0973—dc20   93–5443

British Library Cataloguing in Publication Data is available.

Library of Congress Catalog Card Number: 93–5443
ISBN: 0–275–94747–5
        0–275–94748–3 (pbk.)

First published in 1994

Praeger Publishers, 88 Post Road West, Westport, CT 06881
An imprint of Greenwood Publishing Group, Inc.

Printed in the United States of America

The paper used in this book complies with the
Permanent Paper Standard issued by the National
Information Standards Organization (Z39.48–1984).

10 9 8 7 6 5 4 3 2 1

This book is dedicated to Paul E. Tsongas. In his public life he offered innovative policy options, took a stand against unrealistic assumptions, and forced some members of the public to face the costs, risks, and benefits of making tough choices. Paul was fond of the observation by Thomas Jefferson that "the principle of spending money to be paid by posterity, under the name of deficit funding, is but swindling futurity on a large scale." As to futurity, this book is also dedicated to my newborn son Robert.

Contents

Preface

Cogitate, an old-fashioned word for think, originally meant to "shake up." Hopefully, this book will shake up some preconceptions concerning our struggle with "the deficit." Today America is facing a number of critical financial and social deficits. Our problems are interconnected, and there is no single solution, no "silver bullet" cure. In writing this I have intentionally cast a wide net over seven basic problems: the fiscal deficit (chapter 1; the $4 trillion national debt), tax equity and economic growth issues (chapter 3), the trade deficit (chapter 4), the productivity deficit (chapter 5), the education deficit (chapter 6), and the health care access deficit (chapter 7). The deficits are interrelated; for example, an education deficit in one decade can cause sluggish productivity in future decades. Reducing the federal deficit in one year can help reduce the trade deficit the next year. Our economic cup is 80 percent full; the cup is leaking. We know how to mend it, but do we have the will? The approach taken in this book is essentially positive, presenting 49 basic policy proposals by which America can mend or reduce these multiple deficits.

The root cause for all seven socioeconomic problems revolves around special interest politics, discussed in chapter 2. Special interest politics allowed bankers to urge politicians to deregulate banks and pressure federal bank regulators to go easy on savings and loan (S&L) institutions in financial trouble. The banks were deregulated in 1980 by the Democratic congressional banking committees during President Carter's last year in office. Members of Congress were "money in the bank" for any bank manager furious over scrutiny from federal bank examiners trying to do their job. Congressmen would intervene on a bank's behalf in the name of "harassment." The resulting bailout of S&Ls will cost the taxpayer $350 to $390 billion over three decades and add substantially to our federal deficit. The S&L bailout is the only continuing government program paid for solely by increasing the nation's debt. The government borrows funds needed to close bankrupt thrifts and pays them back, with interest, over three decades. Democrats and Republicans both got the government off the back of irresponsible bankers, running the S&Ls like a casino.

Given that federal taxes are up from 19.4 to 20.5 percent of the GNP (gross national product) since 1979, but federal spending has grown to almost 24 percent of the GNP, our primary problem therefore is excessive federal spending. John Stuart Mill wrote that "the despotism of custom is everywhere a standing hindrance to human advancement." Chapter 2 argues that the despotism of special interest politics must be eliminated. For example, the special interests that cause 20 percent of health care dollars to be spent on paperwork are opposed to reform that would reduce these costs to only 7 to 8 percent (chapter 7).

Four central points run through the text: (1) There is no painless way to trim the deficit. (2) Congress is an overindulgent parent that tells the public twin lies (the dentist is painless, and you do not need a dentist for current levels of rot and decay). (3) A deficit plan is not a total economic plan; it is only a component. (4) The deficits are multiple in nature and interlinked. Any effective solutions to our problems will produce disharmony among special interest groups. Hopefully, calls for common sacrifice and cooperation will not be met with apathy and inaction.

Our problems are indeed substantial, but our growth capacity to mend our problems and enhance our standard of living is up to the task. The challenge of national economic growth presents positive sides to every crisis. The S&L crisis helped to reduce debt, as banks had less to lend, thus keeping a partial lid on inflation. The budget crisis helps keep Congress from inventing new "pork" programs, that is, wasteful expenditures that have no cost-benefit for society. The health care cost crisis creates the climate to trim overutilization and wasteful paperwork.

Our fiscal situation, however, grows more unforgiving each year. Congress continues to pay out absurdly generous entitlement benefits and pension checks. For example, in 1993 the cost to the taxpayers of civil service pensions will be $37 billion, while actual contributions to this trust fund by employees were only $5.1 billion. The military pension funds and Social Security trust fund are equally overgenerous, paying out 2- to 3-fold more than an actuarial fair amount. The very term "trust fund" does not have the same meaning as in the private sector; it is merely a federal bookkeeping tool set up to record earmarked income and spending. Any excess money in the trust funds is spent annually to pay the salaries of bureaucrats and cover other operating expenses within the government. The trust funds are not as trustworthy as having the funds in the hands of an honest banker in Zurich.

To be sure, there are no quick and easy solutions. The only way to make American leaders behave as if they are fiscally literate is to confront them with more literate and less passive voters. In the spirit of Newton's principle of parsimony, I have intentionally limited the number of chapters and the number of tables and have anticipated that a wide audience is more interested in a synthesis of currently available information and potential policy ramifications than econometric details or financial analysis. This book is a blend of positive economics (description and prediction) and normative economics (prescriptions for what the nation ought to do). The boundaries of possibility are expanding for American society, but the outcome depends on how we solve nine basic problems—the federal deficit, excessive special interest group power, ineffective tax incentives, trade deficits, poor productivity, education system reform, health care reform, eco-smart economic growth, and Social Security reform.

The author must apologize in advance for writing in idiomatic "Americanese," but this is the only way to identify broad themes and translate the theoretical into the world of the practical. I have depended on the assistance and ideas of others in writing this book, including Jack Rodgers, Warren Greenberg, Sachin Diwan, Susan Labovich, Amy Smereck, Richard Southby, Barbara Boykin, Haviland Wallace, Ascanio Terracciano, and Bonnie Horvath. I acknowledge the invaluable help of the editors, Margaret A. Hogan and Peter Simon. For any errors in the book I am, of course, responsible.

FACING TOUGH
CHOICES

1

Deficits as Financial Dreamland

Balancing the budget is like going to heaven: everybody wants to balance the budget, but nobody wants to do what you have to do to balance the budget.
                                   —Senator Phil Gramm (R–Tex.), 1990

We have excess domestic spending in the federal government because of the power of the middle class. Federal policy follows what I label Director's Law, in that most government programs benefit the middle class.
                                   —George J. Stigler, 1980

Stop financing long-term projects with short-term debt. This is a primary rule of finance. Yet 68 percent of our $4.4 trillion national debt comes due in the next five years. We cannot live on hope that foreigners keep showing up at Treasury auctions with what used to be our money.
                                   —H. Ross Perot, 1992

The economics profession generally accepts a federal deficit over 3 percent of gross national product (GNP) as "excessively high." In 1994 over 22 percent of every federal dollar will be borrowed. This deficit should not be viewed as a progressive redistribution of funds. For example, families making $15,000 to $50,000 a year pay taxes, and one-sixth of the proceeds of these tax collections go to pay the debt service on our deficit. The primary beneficiary of printing more bonds as the IOU for our government is the bondholder elite: rich Americans, rich foreign citizens, and foreign governments. In some sense deficits are a luxury good, or at least they lead to more luxury for certain investors. Yet, most Democrats support deficit spending. Why? Because excess deficits result from excess spending to voting blocks that reelect the most free-spending politicians. No politicians ever lost office because they rechanneled too much spending to their home districts or too much federal largesse to the middle class. We enact programs for the poor, but we do not restrict channeling most of the benefits to the middle class. A classic example of "naming the poor to get money for the middle class" was presented during the day-care subsidy debates of 1989–1990. President Bush declared day care the single most important issue arising from changes in the work force (more working mothers). At a cost of $2.24 billion, the Bush $1,000-per-child tax credit plan would limit the subsidy to families earning under $20,000 by 1994. The Democrats proposed a program that was $0.5 billion more expensive, but channels 70 percent of the benefit to families earning $18,000–70,000. In other words, the Democrats' proposal was good for the middle class, in the name of doing something for the poor.

Some may consider it heresy to suggest that citizens should pay today for the way they live today. Expanding federal spending creates visible winners (special interests) and invisible victims (the poor that need it more and future generations of taxpayers). Reducing the deficits will create invisible winners (the public, the future) and visible victims carping for restored funding levels for their pet projects or personal tax subsidy. The 1992 House check-bouncing scandal offers a metaphor for what the public has come to hate: those who seek a seemingly endless supply of funds by writing bad checks. There is too much at stake here, namely the future of a nation, to delay real action on the deficits and to continue playing accounting games to make the problem disappear on paper.

Our biggest deficit problem may be the honesty deficit politicians exhibit in "informing" the public. Uncontrolled fiscal and social deficits narrow choices, making solutions increasingly difficult over time. A glossary of 75 basic terms, from budget deficit to trust fund, is included at the end of the text.

UBIQUITOUS DEFICITS: SLOW DAMAGE AHEAD

In seeking a balance between tax hikes and cost cutting in any deficit reduction plan our leaders should consider a few basic facts. In 1954 private investment was four times larger than the federal budget, but in 1994 investment is projected to be half the size of federal spending. Total spending by federal, state, and local government was 19 percent of the gross domestic product (GDP) in 1954, but it will equal 45 percent of the economy in 1994. What is the most reliable and stable source of deficit reduction? Cost cuts. When government raises the taxes on luxury items over $30,000 or hikes sin taxes, the revenues are often a fraction of the civil servants' expectations. In summary we need a larger dosage of cost reduction and government downsizing. Congress and the Clinton administration compromised on a five year plan (1994–1998) for deficit reduction including: the second largest tax increase in history ($294 billion), $325 billion in reduced spending and entitlement payments, and $124 billion in new spending on domestic programs (net impact on the deficit, a $495 billion reduction over five years).

The reductions on spending are not that difficult to impose, or they frequently represent taxation in sheep's clothing. The largest cost reduction is the $105 billion in defense spending relative to the bloated budget proposed by the Bush administration for 1994–1998. The Pentagon will produce almost all of the 1994 savings ($10.9 billion) by speeding up personnel reductions planned for 1995. Some line items are stretched out to produce ersatz economy; to save a few million in 1993 the Super Collider project is expanded in life cycle costs by $2.1 billion by stretching the completion date from 1999 to 2003. In other cases the cost cuts are, in fact, tax hikes (e.g., increased taxes on Social Security benefits for couples earning over $44,000 and individuals earning over $34,000 was labeled "a spending cut," not a tax hike, yielding $24 billion of spending reduction over 1994–1998 by taxing the elderly more). The Clinton administration also labeled $3.2 billion in user fees for parks and home loans as spending cuts. One Clinton administration official explained: "If you pay an extra dollar at the park gate it's a cost cut by government because you're really paying an offsetting receipt."

Cost cutting is a foreign concept for many in government, judging by the local reaction to Vice President Gore's Commission on Reinventing Government in 1993. One civil servant announced that "we can meet President Clinton's goal of downsizing by 100,000 workers by 1996 if we cut the number of authorized people in the department, never lay off a single member on the roster of current employees, and label this theoretical cost savings a benefit for the American people." Streamlining is a fiction if the workers trimmed never existed or received any salary. The government should begin to treat the public with respect and taxpayers as customers. Good public relations is a nice thing, but firing anti-productive federal workers is a much better objective. In private industry one reads of layoffs of 74,000 or 200,000, across-the-board pay cuts of 22 percent, and pension cutbacks of 50 percent. Federal employees are lucky to have avoided this real world of the private sector worker for so long. If real world workers face true cost cutting, so should government.

The general proposition put forth in much of this chapter is that deficits are like liquor during prohibition. As we shall observe in chapter 2, politicians can get reelected by special interest groups when they deliver the liquor of deficit spending. The public is as full of hypocrisy as our elected officials. Too many citizens will eagerly criticize deficit spending while drinking its byproducts. The public asks for more pork spending while condemning pork spending. General public opinion suggests that government spends too carelessly, except when it spends on me. The "me generation" does not want to be taxed more, but it feels that government should do more. Fiscal conservatives are disliked by many voters because "pay now, fly now" is not as enticing as "deficit spend now, let someone else pay later." Borrowing amounts to 22 percent of federal revenues, and net interest equals 15 percent of federal expenses. Social insurance payroll receipts are 29.4 percent of federal revenues, while entitlement payments to individuals are 45 percent of federal expenses.

The interest expenses on the $4.36 trillion national debt is expected to be $4,300 per family in 1993, compared with $1,146 per family in 1980. Those wishing to minimize the damage of a large national debt emphasize that 12 percent of the debt is owned by foreign hands and has to be paid out of export earnings (see chapter 4). This fund flow is a drag on the American economy. Since 88 percent of the debt is not a burden, but only a transfer between current and future generations, "don't worry, be happy" has become the philosophy of choice. The future gets higher taxes and lower benefit levels (e.g., Social Security, chapter 8). The hot button for a campaign to make Americans more concerned about the future involves bringing forth the twin fears of a rapidly declining standard of living and a rising rate of child poverty. As a result, the future may be a radical departure from the American tradition that each generation should inherit a higher standard of living.

Is the size of the federal deficit fiscally prudent? In 1993 net public debt for all levels of government represented 41 percent of the gross domestic product. With a debt ratio of 41 percent and nominal GDP growth of 2.5 percent, America can afford a deficit of only 1 percent of the GDP to keep the debt ratio constant. America should trim excess spending not simply to stabilize the debt ratio, but to aim for a balance sheet target to maintain net worth (i.e., total fixed and financial assets less liabilities). While recognizing that accounting studies valuing assets at replacement costs overstate true value, the American government's capital stock eroded from 70 percent of the GDP in 1976 to 50 percent in 1993. While 80 percent of educational expenses and 50 percent of health care expenditures should be relabeled as an investment in human capital, and not as current spending, the trend is clear. The American foundation, or infrastructure, is eroding. If we invest in repairing the foundation, at best we can stabilize the deficit at 1 percent of the GDP. Therefore, abetment of deficits, not necessarily a zero deficit, should be a critical domestic policy goal. The Clinton administration goal of trimming the deficit to 1.9–2.1 percent of GDP is insufficient medicine for our disease ("swindling futurity on too large a scale," to paraphrase Paul Tsongas).

Other metaphors have been used to capture the long-run problems associated with deficit spending. Doom-and-gloom specialist Eliot Janeway (1989) makes it appear as if America is burning up the furniture to heat the house. Alternatively, high federal deficits are like termites or radiation, very pernicious because the damage is unheard and unseen for decades. By the time the damage becomes visible it will be very costly to repair. Politicians are familiar with more dramatic language, such as the deficit wolf is at the door. In fact, the damage of the deficits may cripple the patient or eat up our economic home in future years, unless we take action now.

Ideally, the public wants a more productive government that will do more with less. This chapter has three basic segments: cut the bureaucracy, reduce expenditures, and privatize certain government functions in the name of quality service delivery and productivity enhancement.

THE GRAMM-RUDMAN-HOLLINGS ATTEMPT

The Gramm-Rudman-Hollings (GRH) law, enacted in 1985 and replaced in 1990, had as its objective to reduce the deficit to zero. It provided the illusion of fiscal discipline, not the real thing. The sword of automatic spending reductions by formula, the so-called sequestration cuts, have been invoked three times. In the midyear of fiscal 1986 the GRH sword reduced spending projections by $11.7 billion to leave a deficit of $221 billion. This midyear cut was equivalent in percentage to a full-year cut of $23 billion. The second mandated GRH formula cuts occurred in the second month of fiscal year 1990. Real cuts of $12.6 billion were made after the initial projection of a $16 billion sequestration. The formula cuts in 1990 eliminated the inflation adjustment, so few program budgets declined from 1989 to 1990.

The 1990 incarnation of fiscal responsibility, the Budget Enforcement Act (BEA), designated a specific target amount of savings to be achieved each year, irrespective of the resulting deficit. The law still has a requirement that the administration's Office of Management and Budget (OMB) set deficit targets at the start of a fiscal year, but if it misses the target, the shortfall can be blamed on unexpected economic conditions. Congress is also assigned credit for the nonexistent savings. In 1991 the OMB forecast was for a $100.5 billion deficit, when, in fact, the deficit in twelve months expanded to $269 billion. Congress took credit for $42.2 billion in "savings," while it actually voted $2.6 billion in additional spending. (No, this is not a comedy sketch. It is your Congress at work.) Even if the deficit grows, the BEA guarantees that Congress receive credit for the $492 billion in savings for five years, through 1995. In summary, Congress can play with the forecasts to achieve "savings," while the deficit still grows (up from $162 billion in 1989 to $220 in 1990, $269 billion in 1991, and $290 billion in 1992).

Over 60 percent of the budget, entitlement and interest payments on the debt, are exempt from the BEA spending "caps." Firewalls were built into the law for the initial three years, whereby separate categories were built for military, domestic, and international spending. Until 1994 Congress may not produce a cost savings in the military to the benefit of a reallocation of funds for a domestic program. Only in 1994 and 1995 may savings be lumped together across the categories. Thus, in the early years of BEA, if spending in a category (e.g., domestic) exceeded the limit, all programs in that category were cut by an equal percentage to meet the target.

Members of the appropriations committees in the Senate and the House were the biggest supporters of the BEA. These powerful spenders disliked the two times the GRH produced equal percentage cuts in their favorite programs because of poor performance in the American economy (i.e., low tax receipts, high bank bailout costs). Any sequesters under the BEA have been small. Congress claims it is addressing the problem, but the deficit grows larger. A bitter Senator Ernest Hollings (D–S.C.) said the director of OMB is also a big BEA supporter because "armed with his fairy dust economic and technical misestimates he will now be in the driver's seat" (October 22, 1990). Being an enforcer is a great job if you do not do any enforcing, thus making no member of Congress unhappy.

Even the watered-down 1989 version of the GRH would have had more enforcement powers than the BEA. The GRH would have forced Congress to sequester $84.4 billion at the start of fiscal year 1991 and required at least another $110 billion in cuts over the rest of 1991. The only incentive for economizing in government, now partially preserved by the BEA, is the "pay-as-you-go" requirement for new program initiatives. Pay as you go requires that any new spending must be financed by a tax hike or spending cut so that the deficit does not increase. However, Congress has found many creative ways to avoid this requirement with sham "savings" claims. These sham savings were used to "finance" the expansion of unemployment benefits in 1992–1993.

SHAM BUDGETS

Our politicians from the don't-worry-be-happy school of public finance claim that a budget deficit equal to 3.8 percent of the GNP averaged over 1989–1993 should not be a cause for concern. Their argument by analogy goes as follows: the sky has not fallen yet, and the federal deficit as a fraction of the GNP has been equally high (3.4 percent in 1975). Our mounting problems are best summarized by the "wind chill theorem" of public finance: the temperature is the federal deficit, the wind chill adjusted temperature is the outstanding federal debt (soon to exceed $4.5 trillion), and the politicians are amateur weathermen. In the mid-1970s an annual deficit of 3.4 percent of GNP was not a problem because outstanding federal debt was less than one-third of GNP. Analogously, 34 mph winds on a warm summer day do not really make your body feel a wind chill adjusted by 30 degrees. Wind chill only counts if you are really cold. This means we are in for a cold end to the 1990s. We have already spent over $244 billion in 1993 on gross interest costs for the rental of money for our bloated government. To balance the budget without increases, we would have to cut out over 40 percent of current spending programs, excluding the debt service on which we cannot issue a stop payment.

An annual deficit of 5 percent of the GNP in 1998 will be a huge problem because outstanding federal debt from all sources already exceeds two-thirds of the GNP. Unfortunately, our problems are bigger than most people think because our political weathermen are prisoners to the liar's dilemma: they lie about the size of the deficit by over $130 billion because they borrow off the books. Many Republicans supported the last GRH cut (1990) because they were not as deep on the defense side. Defense programs experienced only a 3.4 percent cut against a budget baseline that includes a larger full adjustment for inflation, while nondefense programs were subjected to a 4.4 percent cut. There were no cuts in Social Security, Medicaid, or Supplemental Security Income for the aged, blind, and disabled. By law, Medicare was limited to a 2 percent cut, but program expenses increased by 5 percent due to inflation and the increased number of Medicare-eligible Americans.

Whether the reader thinks the GRH is good or bad, the formula has one critical virtue. The GRH process is the only public mechanism that generates embarrassment over huge federal deficits. Rather than repeat beautiful lies (e.g., Congress is becoming fiscally prudent), we must face four ugly truths. (1) The GRH requires only that the executive branch Office of Management and Budget *projections* of the deficit 15 days into the fiscal year will meet the law's target 12 months later. When the actual deficit swells in the last ten months of the fiscal year the law's penalties no longer apply. The actual deficit has never achieved the target figure (see Table 1.1), and Congress' own Congressional Budget Office (CBO) always presents more accurate projections (e.g., the CBO projected $117.8 billion in 1990 and $152.4 billion in 1989, closer to the actual figure than the OMB). (2) For the mutual convenience of Congress and the president, the OMB cooks the books and fudges the projections by understating spending (e.g.,

Table 1.1
Federal Deficits and the Gramm-Rudman-Hollings Targets

Year	1986	1987	1988	1989	1990	1991	1992
A. Federal Spending Outlays (%GNP)	4.8	24.1	24.4	24.8	25.2	25.0	24
B. Receipts (%GNP)	18.7	18.7	19.1	20.0	20.4	21.2	22
C. Deficit Forecast OMB (bill.$)	124	134	145	130	93	67	32
D. Gramm-Rudman Target+$10b	182	154[1]	154	146	110	74	38
E. National Economic Commission Forecast					136	131	126
F. Actual Deficit	221	150	155	162	220[2]	269[3]	290
G. Original GRH - 1985	172	144	108	72	36	0	0

[1] The original law was revised in 1987.

[2] The deficit would have been $277.5 billion if Congress had included the $57.2 billion for the savings and loan cleanup.

[3] The deficit would have been $331 billion if Congress had chosen to include the estimated $62.6 billion for the S&L cleanup in fiscal year 1991. The real deficit in 1991 would be closer to $435 billion if we excluded the raid on the trust funds (Social Security, etc.) from the official deficit.

pushing payroll payment six days ahead to the next fiscal year, or raiding funds from the three trust funds—highway, Social Security, and airport improvements) to achieve the paper goal of the GRH spending targets. (3) This game of annual evasion and convenient lying did not cover the fact that the actual deficit increased from 1987 ($149.7 billion) to 1992 ($290 billion). The BEA rewards certain behavior. In this context, a smashing success has been achieved in reducing deficit projections, but not actual deficits. (4) Congress will add anything into the budget with a surplus (e.g., without Social Security on-budget the deficit is $55.9 billion higher in 1990 and $68 billion higher in 1991) and subtract any program it can with a deficit off-budget (e.g., the Savings and Loan bailout or the post office going off-budget in 1990 because it was projected to lose $1.7 billion rather turn a profit). Someone should tell the members of Congress that by rearranging the categories one doesn't actually save real money. Cynics believe the public is only interested in the appearance of their government saving money, and if it ever did save money the losers would make life difficult for their elected officials. In summary, our current deficit reduction process has delusions of adequacy.

To live in a rich nation is sometimes to succumb to illusions. Too many Americans overlook the Perot-Tsongas viewpoint and engage in the grand debt illusion ("don't worry, be happy"). The illusionists overlook the future massive tax increases and spending cuts associated with our current policy of debt-financed big government and generous entitlement payouts. The most delusionary of the debt illusionists view government bonds as net wealth and see the deficit as a 100 percent investment in a better America. In point of fact, government overspending substitutes current taxes for future big tax hikes and bigger program cuts in present value terms.

Under public pressure Congress may place the three big trust funds off-budget as of fiscal 1994. In the period 1984–1993 the Social Security trust fund will have "paid" $566 billion of the accumulated official cook-the-books national debt. The highway and airport trust funds will have "paid" $672 billion to reduce the official operating deficit. But in real dollar terms future citizens will have to be taxed to pay for pensions, highways, and airports in the 21st century. These accounting games diminish the future financial position of the federal government. The critical issue goes beyond dollars. The consent of the governed is eroded when Uncle Sam labels a pile of unfolded IOUs as "trust funds." Over time fewer Americans will be stupid enough to believe that a pile of IOUs is trustworthy. The so-called trust funds are in fact unfunded liabilities; thus our $4.4 trillion national debt in 1993 will be effectively a $5.7 trillion debt. Understating a problem does not make that problem disappear.

The real annual deficit, without the accounting tricks, seems stuck above $300 billion. The GRH was revised (P.L. [Public Law] 100–119) in 1987 in response to calls for easier targets (Congress added a $10 billion cushion before the automatic cuts kick-in). Since the GRH targets proved difficult to achieve, Congress replaced them in 1990. The only positive thing one can say about the GRH is that it focused public attention on the deficit problem and stopped the deficit from ballooning over the $300 billion mark in 1989. The bottom line is that the federal government still has to borrow over $800 million every weekday to make the mortgage payment on our national debt.

Chapter 2 will ask why members of congressional committees feed like tribesmen at a common water hole. The budget process has increased the competition among committees to feed on the general revenues until the pool is exhausted and more federal borrowing is required. This was originally defined by Harold Demsetz (1967) as a common resource problem. In contrast to a tribe subject to natural selection, Congress can continue the abandonment of leadership in making difficult choices by avoiding the hard choices and borrowing money. Tribes in nature have no such federal credit card, such as our $4.4 trillion national debt in 1993. Who plays the role of enforcer in this modern fiscal tragedy? Judging by the 140 members of Congress out of work following the 1992 elections, the enforcer is the court of public opinion. This court sleeps, but it can also cut off heads.

Most readers are not familiar with data on the national debt as presented by the Treasury Department in monthly reports "Statement of the Public Debt" (SPD). SPD lists the face value for various types of debt. The federal government owns over one-fourth of the gross federal debt (e.g., this book covers in chapter 8 the way in which the Social Security fund loans all the surplus to other parts of the federal government). Table 1.2 indicates that debt held by such government accounts will be $1,417 billion by 1996. Debt held by the public in 1994 ($3.5 trillion) is simply what is left when government account holdings, from pensions to highways, are removed from the gross federal debt. The intragovernmental IOU of $1.23 trillion in 1994 involves interest payments that shift from one government account to another. In terms of economic impact on interest rates the debt held by the public is much more significant (column 4, table 1.2) than the gross debt. However, this book will continue the convention of summarizing the debt in terms of the gross debt, for the federal fiscal year (September 30), or the calendar year (December 31).

DOWNSIZE ENTITLEMENTS AND BUREAUCRACY

Domestic federal spending increased 10.6 percent annually during the four-year Bush administration (1988–1992), 2 points higher than under any president since 1946. Future presidents are caught in the entitlement trap whereby their budget is stuck on autopilot to spend more on nondiscretionary programs. Congress is of no help. It passes more generous entitlements each year to make voters happy and legislates federal mandates without funding that break the backs of state and local governments (Fix and Kenyon, 1992). Entitlements are automatically disbursed by formula and do not require congressional appropriations annually. Consider one example, the $588 billion budget for the Department of Health and Human Services (HHS) in 1993. The HHS budget is $43 billion higher than in 1992, but 96 percent of this increase goes to entitlement programs that assist 61 million citizens: Medicare ($144 billion), Social Security ($303 billion), Medicaid ($85.4 billion), AFDC (Aid to Families with Dependent Children, i.e., welfare—$15.8 billion), and Supplemental Security Income for the aged, blind, and disabled ($20 billion). The Public Health Service receives a $950 million budget increase and is hard-pressed to finance new programs in AIDS research or cancer prevention (Eastaugh, 1992). Entitlements could be rolled back to the benefit of the sick and the poor simply by

Table 1.2
Federal Debt by Fiscal Year (billions of dollars) Through September 30 (end federal fiscal year)

Year	Total Gross Debt	Debt Held by Government Accounts	Debt Held by the Public	Debt Held by the Public as a Percentage of GDP
1981	994	209	785	26.5%
1982	1,137	218	919	29.4
1983	1,371	240	1,131	34.1
1984	1,564	264	1,300	35.2
1985	1,817	318	1,499	37.8
1986	2,120	384	1,736	41.2
1987	2,346	458	1,888	42.4
1988	2,601	551	2,050	42.6
1989	2,867	678	2,189	42.4
1990	3,206	796	2,410	44.1
1991	3,599	911	2,688	47.7
1992	4,003	1,004	2,999	51.1
1993	4,361	1,116	3,245	54.2
1994	4,694	1,230	3,464	57.1
1995	5,001	1,326	3,675	59.9
1996	5,273	1,417	3,856	62.6

Source: Congressional Budget Office (1993).

repealing eligibility for the rich (e.g., family income over $120,000). Over 82 percent of entitlement expenses are not tested for income. We may also need to downsize entitlements provided to the middle class.

The phrase "downsizing" is popular but not very explicit. It means we need fewer and more productive bureaucrats. Functions could be merged between departments, and unnecessary activities could be abolished. Even the White House could use some downsizing. The White House crisis management of the Panamanian coup attempts did not benefit from a large staff. President Franklin Roosevelt ran a world war and numerous new domestic programs with a White House staff of only 35. The nation would not be able to observe a decline in "government service" if the average office reduced staff levels by 10 to 15 percent.

Most bureaus produce customary soothing reports that suggest that problems exist, studies will be commissioned, reports will be written—and little action will be taken. The dreams of the "Great Society" program planners of the 1960s never came to fruition. Robert Kennedy and Walter Heller envisioned the growth of federally funded, nonbureaucratic, flexible community action teams for solving our problems. Instead, we have experienced a doubling of the entrenched central bureaucracy. Bureaucrats tend to perpetuate themselves and do little in the national interest. Cost-reduction programs could reduce the deficit while at the same time redeploying some funds to more worthy federal programs (e.g., public health, education, Head Start, family support centers).

Regulators and their bureaucracy will not allow their numbers to dwindle without a fight. The Reagan administration fought to decrease the number of regulators from 111,000 to 103,000 by 1986. However, the tenacious federal regulators increased their ranks to over 110,000 by fiscal 1993. In the spirit of deregulation, President Reagan selected 44 major programs for termination but only 2 were terminated, and only 2 of the remaining 42 had their funding reduced. Moreover, the Reagan administration added a whole new cabinet-level bureaucracy for the Veterans Administration.

The Clinton administration's federal budget is honest on a number of fronts. First, the president argues that we must have no sacred cows except the abiding national interest of the American people. He is tactical when he states that he doesn't want to send up to Congress cost cuts that will be rejected immediately. The president also makes the honest argument that taxation is more generationally responsible than running up future debts for the young and unborn to pay. After 12 years of runaway federal budget growth, the first two Clinton budgets keep spending in line with inflation. However, these pieces of good news are to be weighed against two pieces of bad news. Clinton's deficit reduction plan is really a tax program, with Defense Department cuts and a lot of new spending initiatives. Social programs and bureaucracy are not to be trimmed at all in the initial three years (1994, 1995, 1996). Over 81 percent of the spending cuts are set to occur in the last two years of the plan (1997 and 1998). Do you trust Congress to keep its word and do all these cost cuts in the future? Or will Congress do what it did in the jump from 1990 to 1993, and get a deal of $2 of taxation for every $1 of repromised (but never delivered) spending cuts in the 1997 budget deal. Many voters trust Perot more than they trust Congress to make a cut it promises a cut. Even if the economy avoids a recession and grows as fast as President Clinton suggests, the years 1994 to 1998 will accrue an additional $.146 trillion onto the national debt (a $5.9 trillion sum by 1998).

We must avoid bureaucratic elephantiasis and actually cut costs. The general public is in a sour mood because the family budget must be squeezed, pension benefits diminished, and many workers demoted to temporary contingent employees. If private industry is shedding jobs, trimming pensions, and forcing workers into part-time slots, why can't government do the same thing to civil service employees? Not to cut government is to put government first, not the people. We need shared sacrifice, not big government with generous pensions. Paperwork growth must stop. Regulations to hire or fire a federal employee weigh 1,088 pounds. Comparable material at the Big 3 auto companies and IBM weigh one pound.

Federal workers enjoy better inflation adjustments, pensions, and vacations than workers in private firms. Federal workers receive 20 paid vacation days a year compared to 10 in large and medium-sized private firms. The cost of living inflation adjustments have been 1.9 points more generous over the last five years. Federal workers received a 4.2 percent across-the-board raise in January 1992 and a 3.7 percent raise in January 1993. Even with President Clinton's February 1993 announcement of a pay freeze, the freeze turned out to be a pay increase for the 1.1 million workers who received a promotion (average raise, 5.8 percent) or an automatic step/grade pay raise. The 158,000 federal middle managers do not receive step/grade increases, but a whopping 99.82 percent qualified for "top outstanding merit pay raises." The Clinton wage freeze also doesn't affect the 700,000 employees that earn one-time awards or bonuses paid for superior performance (average payout, $1,000 in 1993). The Clinton wage freeze had no negative impact on job retention, since fewer than 2.8 percent of federal workers quit before retirement age. Clinton likes a large, and well-paid, federal workforce. Less than one-fourth of federal workers experienced a cut in pay in real dollar terms in 1993, compared to 41 percent of private sector professionals and managers (who also have twice the prevalence of college and graduate degrees). Federal employee unions still claim to be paid 25 percent less than the private sector (if the private sector were composed entirely of professionals, doctors, lawyers, and accountants).

REBUILDING THE INFRASTRUCTURE

One major motivation for cutting the deficit down to size involves the necessity of rebuilding certain American institutions. We are beginning to realize the long-run costs associated with neglect of infrastructure public investments (e.g., schools, sewers, streets). Skimping on infrastructure may improve the annual deficit, but only by eroding assets. Assets range from our children to our buildings and transportation networks. It is absolutely necessary that America make the long-deferred investment in the future, so that a bridge does not collapse or a neighborhood die. In the mid-1960s we worried about heroin as a male addiction that caused poverty, one-parent families, and the death of neighborhoods. In the 1990s, however, our neighborhoods are dying from crack (producing no-parent families) and from public schools that do not educate.

Neighborhood family support centers could be constructed to provide the functional equivalent of one-stop shopping for the needy. Paperwork could be reduced 75 percent if a single center dispensed prenatal care, food programs, Head Start enrollment, drug-prevention information, parenting education, and adult education. The poor are always criticized for low usage rates of available services, but we should not blame the victim. If we make such service uniformly available at one central location, usage rates will increase and administrative costs will decline. Such investments in human capital shall reap long-run financial benefits. More Americans may come to realize that the pursuit of happiness is dependent on individual effort plus the smooth functioning of infrastructure institutions. If certain sectors of the infrastructure operate too smoothly, we often understate their value (e.g., we vote more money for bridges after a major accident). It is prudent to care about deficits and infrastructure.

WANTED: BUDGETMEISTER WITH GRIT

The BEA has been a limited success in trimming, spending, and raising taxes to yield a net $27.6 billion annual deficit reduction below baseline forecasts (see glossary at the end of the text). The Clinton administration's toughest proposal in 1993, never enacted by Congress, would have reduced the deficit only by $19.5 billion annually over the 1994–1998 period. Apparently, Congress and the administration are insufficiently concerned with the deficit problem. Otherwise, our national leaders would have suggested a tripling of annual deficit reduction to $57 billion, to balance the budget by the year 2000. In our huge economy there is no danger that we will balance the budget too quickly. Balancing the budget by the start of the 21st century would still leave the country with a $6.4 trillion national debt. These facts are well-known to our leaders, but they suffer from the most basic deficit, an honesty deficit.

Deficits purchase nothing for the future. Paying the tab on deficits merely props up the federal credit rating and makes rich bondholders richer. America needs to spend more on education and other infrastructure programs. Public works spending was 3.5 percent of the GNP in 1969, and it declined to 2.5 percent by 1993. We need to spend 1 percent more of the GNP on infrastructure. America needs $1.4 trillion from 1994 to 2005 just to make necessary infrastructure repairs. The American dream has two components: the materialistic need to have the best house and car and the dream to feel secure. We shall all feel more secure if our neighbors are better educated, if crime and drug usage are markedly reduced, and we can accomplish this task by investing a little more in infrastructure.

Infrastructure is like pipes in your home or seed corn on a farm. If the pipes rust out, you need new pipes. If the seed corn rots, you need new seed corn. If the infrastructure erodes, we need to spend more money. If the federal deficit is successfully reduced to 1 percent of the GNP, perhaps 100 percent of this $60 billion deficit should be invested on additional programs to repair the infrastructure. In other words, if the deficit must be slashed from over $300 billion to $60 billion, we may need $360 billion of deficit reduction to make room for $60 billion of necessary new spending. America can afford to spend an additional $60 billion each year on education and infrastructure repairs within the context of an economy that spends $4.4 trillion annually on private consumption.

The public has a dual perception of a deficit problem that is serious but manageable. Federal spending patterns need to reallocate resources from paperwork bureaus to real infrastructure programs. American politicians cannot make real cost reductions while the economy is not in crisis. Republican presidents have made the rational decision to concentrate on two real world numbers, inflation and unemployment, yet not eliminate the problems posed by a third number, the deficit. This has been smart politics because voters feel the impact of inflation and unemployment more directly. However, a simple $200 billion trimming of the deficit could yield a 1.6 to 1.9 percent reduction in the inflation rate and help reduce the federal debt service level from 15 to 13.2 to 13.5 percent of the federal budget (equal to $255 billion in 1993).

The 1990s require both optimism and grit. We need to coalesce behind a series of hard decisions. We need an uplifting financial John Wayne or New York Mayor Abe Beame. The challenge is to come together as Americans and show a willingness to be part of something larger than ourselves. Liberals and conservatives alike agree that we are in a state of crisis, but they disagree sharply about appropriate cures. But if local politicians, from the conservative governor of California, Pete Wilson, to the liberal Mario Cuomo in New York State, argue that strong action must be taken in these areas, maybe a congressional compromise will be achieved. A pessimist might counterargue, however, that behind the facts of pork barrel spending is human nature. The selfish objectives of greed, promotions, post-government employment, and reelection constitute a very important medium through which we see selfish values. To wean the federal government away from special interest corruption may be akin in difficulty to moving a graveyard. This viewpoint neglects the many victories state and local taxpayers have won in beating back, but not eliminating, nonfederal spending. Leaders should not underestimate the ability of the public to reverse the prevailing conventional wisdom and do the right thing. By a margin of 2 to 1 in a fall 1987 Mervin Field poll, California voters would have rather seen a 1988 $700 million state budget surplus be given to public schools than be rebated to the taxpayers. In the next section we survey how some state and local governments have licked the deficit monster.

LESSONS FROM STATE GOVERNMENT

Texas governor Ann Richards has a neat way of summarizing how Reagan-Bush "got governments off our backs by sending us back 50 percent less federal dollars." Cost controls and service reductions (e.g., California in 1993) have become critical to balancing state budgets since 1987. State and local governments had run at a financial surplus in the early 1980s. While federal general fund expenditures increased 3 to 5 percent, state expenditures increased only 1.5 to 2.5 percent per year (1986–1993). The gross sum for federal aid to state and local government peaked at $112 billion in 1986, in contrast to $6.8 billion in 1960 and 48 percent fewer real dollars in 1993. One constraint that proved effective in solving state and local fiscal problems of the 1980s and 1990s was the line-item veto. Currently 44 states allow their governor to exercise considerable authority in the name of cost control. Many states do not allow the legislature to create a bloated budget. The Maryland legislature can only subtract from, but not add to, the budget the governor proposes. In other words, the chief politician suggests maximum spending levels.

Democrats, when presented with a financial crisis, can also make difficult choices with a line-item veto. In the period 1988–1990 Democratic Governor Buddy Roemer abolished 98 of Louisiana's 414 boards and commissions and cut the number of people on the state payroll (74,890) by 17 percent. A number of practical policy proposals by which America could mend or reduce our social and fiscal deficits are suggested in this book. The following is the first of 49.

POLICY PROPOSAL No. 1: Provide the president with line-item veto power. This would give the chief executive the role of fiscal periodontic expert: to extract rotten or useless programs with a poor cost-benefit ratio which should not exist in our federal government.

State governors have a number of fiscal problems. They can only tax economic activity; they cannot print money like the federal government. In attempting to preserve or expand economic activity, the states sometimes overtrim corporate taxes. For example, in 1989 the state of Illinois lost $60 million in projected revenue from Sears in exchange for its retaining the corporate headquarters in the state. On the spending front, Medicaid is the most inflationary item in most state budgets. Medicaid cost the states $2.7 billion, or 2.96 percent, of state budgets in 1967. In 1993 Medicaid will rise to $57.5 billion, or 13 percent, of state budgets. By 1996 Medicaid will cost $73 billion, or 15.3 percent of state budgets.

To accommodate this inflationary expense, sales taxes may have to rise to 22 percent of state revenues (up from 18 percent), and a number of states may be forced to enact or expand lottery programs. In the past decade, 19 states have initiated a lottery to raise funds. Lotteries are a voluntary taxation of the gambler, allowing players the intangible benefit of dreaming they might become millionaires, even if the odds are 60 to 82 percent in favor of expanding the state treasury each time one bets. One could not imagine a more popular method of taxation.

If lotteries are a quick fix approach to government, reinventing government while implementing cost-reduction programs is the more effective long-run approach. President Clinton often points out that if the government's incentive is to spend, and not innovate, one gets a lot of fruitless spending. Clinton's most cited example of reinventing government from the bottom up is the Sunnyvale, California, city government. Sunnyvale is a city of 120,000 south of Palo Alto which operates on a ten-year budget plan (not a one-year budget). Fireman and policemen have had the same job since 1986. Many employees hold joint jobs, and all are eligible to earn annual incentive pay for cost-reduction efforts that work. The program has saved money. In the years 1985 to 1993, Sunnyvale has had 48 percent fewer employees and has spent 23 percent less money compared to comparable-sized American cities. However, President Clinton has been slow to broaden the concept of incentive pay and cost reduction to his ideal, the creation of a performance-based federal budget. The president will face civil service and congressional resistance to a new labor-management council trying to cut the federal bureaucracy by 220,000 jobs through attrition.

President Clinton campaigned as a supporter of the line-item veto in 1992. Passage of a line-item veto may have a maximum impact of only $4 to $9 billion per year on the federal deficit. Obvious examples of pork spending are in the aggregate a small fraction of the deficit according to the Congressional Budget Office. As Arkansas governor, Bill Clinton used the line-item veto only three times in the period 1989–1992. Congress will try to beat the line-item veto through appropriating large lump-sum amounts, instead of single items. The rules must be changed so that no expenditure falls outside of the range of our next president's blue pencil. Agents for pork spending could then point to the president as our national scapegoat and say, "We wanted to finance your boondoggle, but he called your project waste." Experience in a number of states indicates that cost reduction through the line-item veto will strengthen a bid for reelection. If no one person has responsibility to fight waste, special interest contributions remain the coin of the realm. The line-item veto may have a mainly symbolic value, but it may cleanse some of the pork out of the appropriations process. The current recision process is too slow, and a line-item veto would force Congress to respond quickly to executive action that wields the blue pencil.

Democratic critics of the line-item veto fear that an aggressive president could use the veto as an ax or carrot to threaten or lure members of Congress to his way of thinking. But only one study of the line-item veto has been negative. Richard Moe published a study of the line-item veto prospects in the winter of 1988 for the National Academy of Public Administration. He argued for a free-spending Congress and against the "increased political conflicts that are likely to be exacerbated by the item veto." One could counterargue that the president may become more responsible and in control of the budget process. Indeed, fewer conflicts would develop if the president were to accumulate sufficient political capital with legislators through not using the item-veto. Two things seem certain: (1) an item-veto would permanently alter the relationship between the president and Congress and (2) someone needs to exert fiscal control over federal spending to undo the damage of the 1974 Budget Act.

BUDGETS, POLITICS, AND TOUGH CHOICES

Congressional Democrats used the $105 billion in defense cuts for budget years 1994–1998 to justify enacting the Clinton program for $124 billion in new domestic spending. In public finance terms, spending the $105 peace dividend (doubly counting it as a cost cut and a chance to spend more on pork and valid social programs) amounts to a hidden tax increase to finance $124 billion in social spending. In summary, the bad news has three components: (1) 117 percent of the peace dividend is a hidden tax increase, (2) 28 percent of the cost cuts are, in fact, tax hikes and higher user fees, and (3) Congress may repeat this false economy two-step every five years until somebody makes it face the basic questions (How much government can we afford? How can we finance the existing mountain of debt?). The "planned" 1997 deficit is now set at $193 billion, compared to existing policies that would have kept the deficit at $327 billion.

Federal workers' numbers, benefits, and salaries have not been trimmed in proportion to the sacrifice experienced within the private sector. Congress should make the tough, real-world decisions of an employer and trim costs until the job-retention rates in the public sector equal those in the private sector. Federal job retention is very high because salaries and benefits are excessively generous. Timid solutions will have no impact.

POLICY PROPOSAL No. 2: The 2.1 million federal workers should receive an across-the-board 20 percent cut in pension benefits and a one-time 10 percent reduction in pay. It is time government does what the private sector has had to do over these last six years. Government must sacrifice all at once to match the shared sacrifice of the general public since 1988. The budget crisis must be faced. By 1995 60 cents of every dollar of income tax receipts will go to finance the gross interest payments on the national debt ($319 billion of interest from $534 billion of income taxes paid by individuals). Shared sacrifice means that federal employees must do more to bear the burden of necessary cost reduction. Chapters 2 and 8 will outline what the greedy beneficiary of government largesse can do in terms of a shared sacrifice.

CHANGES IN THE BUDGET PROCESS

In the Congressional Budget and Impoundment Control Act of 1974 (P.L. 93-344), the president lost the power to impound or withhold appropriate funds. The executive branch can only ask Congress for its assent to recessions or deferrals, that is, cancellations or postponements of federal spending. However, the president seldom gets recisions by Congress (under $100 million in 1987–89).

One suggested innovation from state and local government bookkeeping involves potential division of the federal budget into operating expenses versus long-term capital investments. Many county and municipal governments have five- to ten-year capital budgets and depreciation schedules for major nonrecurring investments. Initiating a federal capital budget would have the effect of dramatically reducing the apparent size of the federal government. Accurate treatment of a government budget in business balance-sheet terms would require not just the slow depreciation of capital assets, but the addition of unfunded liabilities to pensioners. Depreciation would deflate the budget, but future pension liabilities would more than compensate for this. In fact the federal budget deficit for 1992 would have rocketed to $459 billion under agreed business accounting principles. The real deficit that counts is the amount the government has to borrow. It matters not whether the deficit borrowing is financing monthly expenses or capital costs. Again, one innovation that might strengthen control over the federal debt monster is the line-item veto.

Some of the deferrals in the purchase of items have proved cost-ineffective. For example, the unit cost of the order is increased if the federal government avoids buying in bulk and extends the purchase over three to five years. Few government officials have any knowledge of life-cycle costing issues to hold down nonlabor expenses. One may save money through deferrals in one year, but the total cost to the public is driven up over the full multiyear life cycle of acquisition and replacement. Unnecessary items should be canceled, and necessary items should be purchased in bulk in the shortest period of time so as to minimize the total cost of purchase price and storage costs.

Ideally, the federal budget could be balanced within the 13 appropriations bills that need to be approved each year to finance federal activities. Unfortunately, since 1982 the federal government has run on continuous resolution bills because the individual appropriations bills have not been approved before the fiscal year begins. The continuing resolution (CR), once thought of as a short-term, stopgap spending bill, has become a new tradition. Congress has been wrapping multiple appropriations in a CR, which then becomes a budget-busting trillion dollar omnibus spending bill for the fiscal year. The challenge for budget makers is how to get off the omnibus. One suggested reform is to make the appropriations a two-year process, so that the Congress can have more time to investigate the cost-benefit ratio and the efficiency of a number of questionable programs. But if Congress lacks the will to cut costs, simply freeing up its workday to read more of the cost-benefit studies it currently ignores is not a workable reform idea. The worst element of the 1974 reform act was the incentive to delay making hard decisions. If Congress does not finish on time, simply plow everyone's favorite programs into a CR bill. We need to abolish the ability to issue large CRs and shift some of the budgetary power from Congress to the Chief Executive.

A TALE OF TWO BUDGETS

If the statistics on the net government deficit are misleading, the official statistics on the federal deficit are even more deceptive. The federal deficit is really the cross product of two budgets, one with a substantial surplus, the other with a much larger deficit. This tale of two budgets is a public policy issue for two reasons. The trust fund budget that is currently in the best shape (i.e., running at a surplus) is regressively financed, taking a higher proportion of income from the nonrich. Social Security is regressively financed because it does not tax income over a certain limit. But the Social Security tax also steals from the poor due to the expected work life of those who pay into the fund. For example, the average high school dropout is poorer and has, even after factoring in periods of unemployment, eight more years of paying taxes than the individual with a Ph.D. or M.D. degree. Social Security, like most liberal domestic ideals, has effects opposite of those presumptively intended by their sponsors. Social Security takes money from the poor and gives it to the professionals, from the black to the white, from the young to the old. Social Security checks should not merely depend on recent earnings and marital status, but also on how long the individual has paid into the fund. Increased taxes on Social Security payments to the rich elderly would reverse the regressive nature of the program and reduce the deficit.

Consider the magnitude of the two deficits. A $290 billion total federal deficit in 1992 consists of a $160 billion trust fund surplus plus a federal fund deficit of $494 billion. If the trust funds did not have the $160 billion to "lend," then more federal bonds would have to be sold to private investors and foreign governments, and the cost over the years of servicing that debt would have to be paid. In no sense are the trust funds acting as an insurance fund. America, in marked contrast to the Japanese or German experience, does not have the financial slack to build up a huge insurance fund. A true insurance fund would require a generation of citizens to pay into the fund before receiving any benefits. The trust funds do not save money; they lend money to the federal government to pay current expenses each week. The financial stream is pay as you go, in that the more than $3 billion collected for social insurance each week goes to pay for the Social Security check or school meal or government worker's current paycheck or a new tank. Politicians mislead the public when they claim Social Security and other trust funds are social insurance programs whereby we earmark some resources against the taxpayer's old age. Politicians can only say the trust funds are "safe" in the years 2000–2049 to the extent that they will be able to withdraw $13 trillion from young taxpayers in those years. Social Security as an unfunded liability, operated on a pay-as-you-go basis, was popular precisely because it granted windfall pensions to the first three generations of elderly recipients. But the bills come due in the 21st century. By adding more long-term care of home health benefits onto the trust fund, Congress may further destabilize this federal accountant's Ponzi scheme. None of the money is in the bank; it is simply on the books of IOUs for what the government owes. If there is a prolonged downturn in economic growth, and we cannot get the young to live up to the social contract, pensions will be as worthless as a German mark in 1930.

In 1983 Congress decided to put Social Security outside the official budget as of fiscal year 1993. This was a sort of false gesture to suggest that the politics of Social Security is above politics. But financial reality does not change, nor would it change if we instantly placed two-thirds of the Defense Department "off-budget." Yet by this accounting logic we would instantly create a federal budget surplus. This false bookkeeping, however, would do nothing for the nation in begging other countries to lend us money for American social spending.

How could Congress make the tax incidence more progressive? Decreasing the federal deficit would be a slightly progressive form of taxation if done by withdrawal of tax breaks for the nonpoor. An oil tax increase is obviously regressive, but at least it promotes conservation, energy independence, and financial independence. The regressive tax collections for the trust funds are being fattened on paper. But will these trust fund surpluses paid in one year merely go to finance the debt service, interest plus principal, to foreign investors that borrowed $50 to $100 billion per year in Uncle Sam's IOU? Federal trust funds exist for Social Security, civil service pensions, military pensions, unemployment insurance, highways, airports, and airways. But some trust fund proceeds flow to rich investors and foreign governments insofar as we keep the deficit too high. The trust fund budget represents 40 percent of the total federal $1.6 trillion budget in 1993.

Currently trust fund payments to beneficiaries are treated as entitlements, granted automatically and not requiring any annual reauthorization from Congress. Their protected status may not continue if the federal government's current levels of generosity and pork spending continue. For example, if we are experiencing hard financial times in 2025, we will have to go to the American people and say: the elderly get $30 billion less in pension checks, $9 billion less in medical care, $5 billion less in payments to the unemployed, and $6 billion less highway and airway safety, so that we may send a check for $50 billion to the Japanese. The fattening of trust funds is occurring only on the ledger books of Uncle Sam. In the real world all this money is utilized. The passbook is empty. When this dubious bookkeeping faces the day of reckoning in 25 to 35 years, a smaller proportion of Americans will be employed and able to support those retired.

Leadership can be the most creative or destructive element in human affairs. If leadership ignores making the hard decisions, it is very destructive. Such leaders on the right wing and the left wing are afflicted with a "pass-the-buck" form of financial cancer. The patient with the disease and bad living habits in this case experiences none of the consequences but passes on all the bills and all the pain to future generations.

BUDGET POLITICS

Deficits also have an emotional cost. They generate voter cynicism because our leaders will not lead. An approach like the 1990 Budget Enforcement Act (BEA) is an inferior substitute for strong presidential leadership exercised under a line-item veto. The equation is nonselective, equally trimming all programs a little, thus preserving the wasteful and harming the good government investments. Until the incentives are changed, our politicians will continue to eschew major repairs in favor of cosmetic changes. For example, our published federal deficit in 1987 declined from $221 billion (FY1986) to $148 billion (see Table 1.1). However, $37 billion of this deficit reduction was unreal or atypical: (1) $16.5 billion was "saved" through accounting tricks like pushing one payday into the new year (1988) and selling off loans and government assets (selling a loan to reduce the deficit is like selling a car to pay the Visa card; the gain is nonexistent) or (2) one-time windfall from 1986 tax reform, such as people cashing in their capital gains before the capital gains taxes increased.

Progressive Democrats are fond of taxing the fortunate top 10 percent of wage earners. Many claim that the tax changes in 1981 and 1986 were to the benefit of the rich. The Congressional Budget Office suggests that the fortunate tenth had their after-tax income improve by $23,000 from 1979 to 1992, and only 7.1 percent of that gain came from changes in the tax laws. In the period 1979 to 1992 the proportion of the country identified as middle class shrunk from 75 to 61 percent of taxpayers. Did most of the middle class go to the "forgotten fifth," the poorest segment of the public? No; for every one that got poorer, two became richer, thus making the 1979 fortunate fifth one quarter of the 1992 population. If talented people work harder and create jobs under lower effective tax rates, and the middle class shrinks because the membership gets rich, this may be a nightmare for socialists, but it is good for America. The income inequality boom of the 1980s and 1990s is a good thing because the spread between rich and poor became wider for good reasons such as innovation by the upper-middle class, small business, and the self-employed. The poorest fifth saw their after-tax incomes decline by less than 4.9 percent during the last decade, which is easily explained by hikes in regressive Social Security taxes, rising immigration, and drug usage. Tax policy will not stop people from smoking crack or teach English as a second language, but we have health programs and education programs that must do a better job of assisting these people.

The dilemma for social policy makers is that the new educational, vocational, and public health programs must be cost-beneficial. America is too mortgaged to afford cosmetic projects. If we continue to add more cosmetic programs without repairing the engine of economic growth, the American people will be going nowhere. The BEA equation is nice, fuzzy publicity to distract our attention. But ineffective parts of the federal budget must be discarded, and the engine must be rebuilt through better support for education and productivity enhancement, so that we can control our own destiny. Cynics confuse higher deficits with destiny. If we cut federal programs, increase consumption taxes, and invest more in education, we can solve our own problems. In theory, under Clinton economics, education and more American savings and investment will provide the bootstraps by which the nation can pull itself up. But in the short run, if we do not cut pork programs and excessive levels of generosity in federal spending, we will own neither our boots nor our bootstraps. Only when the public realizes that we face an international economic war will we develop the courage to first wage a domestic war against the tightly knit mafias of special interest.

THE OVERWEIGHT NEED DIETS, NOT TAX FEED

Academics often discuss the "dietary theory" of public finance: if there are no excess funds on the plate, the politicians cannot overindulge in well-meaning, daydreaming new programs. If the federal government is to go on a financial diet, cutting calories through spending reductions or burning calories by raising taxes will not be easy. Only in dreamland does billowing fat easily evaporate. There are no good taxes and few good program cuts, but choices must be made. Cuts will not be painless, just as surgery is not painless. But the surgery must be done if the American economic engine for growth and a high standard of living is to remain healthy. The American voter will have to be convinced that the cause is sufficiently noble and necessary. If we are to avoid a sickening slump in our standard of living, a spirit of sacrifice must be reborn. We must put some of our own sacred cows up for slaughter and jettison the selfish mindset that Senator Russell Long (D–La.) lampooned with the slogan: "don't cut you, don't cut me, cut the other fellow behind the tree."

Some politicians collect political action committee (PAC) money from special interests amounting to $5,000 to $10,000 per month just to have lunch with the politician. Some churlish journalists have suggested that lobbyists would pay an extra $25,000 apiece to kiss a politician on both cheeks. Perhaps the voting public will begin to dump selfish, isolationist, special interest clans, jettison sleazy habits of allegiance and behavior, and demand sacrifice in the name of the national interest. We currently live in the world of Garrett Hardin's classic 1968 essay "The Tragedy of the Commons." Hardin described a community in which the people share a pasture where all their cattle graze. All voters feel that it will not hurt society and will benefit their household if they add extra animals to the pasture. But when everyone does this, overgrazing by special interest destroys the economy. And our political "leaders" add to this collective insanity with the full-throated slogan: "Got mine, get yours." What is in it for me? If we are to avoid a slow, steady decline in living standards, we must reclaim the traditional role of community sacrifice to build the Clinton-Reagan "city-on-the-hill" ideal society.

The 1970s phrase "limousine liberal" has been replaced by the 1990s phrase "reactionary liberal." Liberals want multiple new programs, but not the bill. Examples abound. There is the congressperson from the nation's capital who did not file her taxes for eight years in the 1980s because, as a lawyer and member of the Georgetown Law School faculty, she did not feel that filing was necessary. When the catastrophic health insurance act was passed in 1988, it was repealed in 1989 because the rich elderly making over $70,000 a year did not want to pay higher Medicare Part B premiums. Reactionary liberalism caused repeal of a health program that would have been cost-beneficial for 85 percent of the nonrich elderly. The rich like the concept of aid for the homeless, but only if it is not in their neighborhood. The New York City Alternative Pathways program to assist 40,000 poor families was closed down in 1992, and 5,000 of these families were homeless and in shelters within eight months. The program had an operating budget of only $26 million in 1991, but this was judged too expensive to maintain. How many more of these families with unpaid rent are homeless but not in shelters (Kryder-Coe, 1992) and not surveyed in 1993? Our wallet is big, but our effectiveness is low. In 1993 we will spend $167 billion on 102 different federally funded, antipoverty programs. We must get rid of the 95-plus program bureaucracies that "help the poor through paperwork." Whether in poverty programs or the Defense Department, if a sufficient number of programs are superimposed on top of each other, bureaucrats can make sure that failure is not left to chance. Professor James Q. Wilson (1989) suggests this red tape is an essential outgrowth of our mistrust of power and explains why governmental reforms seldom bring their intended results.

The American spirit of progress and development will wither unless we learn how to pay bills and cut waste. We cannot continue to steal public resources from the future, as if our children were a colony of animals we planned to starve. The radical right is already willing to suggest that the starvation process start with the eradication of public schools and public health programs. Such action would not be cost-beneficial, as it ignores all the external benefits we reap from an educated workforce and a clean environment. Such shortsighted cost reductions would produce social turmoil, resulting in an expansion of the distance between the powerful and the poor.

The question for public policy is, what balance of tax reduction and revenue enhancement is best for the nation? This mix may not be best for traditional pork barrel politicians, but as a more educated populace generates the will to make tough choices, hack politicians may be voted out of office. The lament of Senator Barry Goldwater (R–Ariz.) on retiring in the fall of 1986 may not always prove true: "The average member of Congress today puts more importance on his district or his state than he does on his country" (September 24, 1986).

If voters wish to prevent an erosion in their standard of living, they will have to accept the notion that the free lunch is over. We cannot order $110 worth of government when only $100 is needed; we cannot pay the credit card tax bill with only 75 cents on the dollar. In the recent past voters liked to reelect cowards that bowed to every special interest. Politicians diligently attend to protection of current special interests and ignore the future because we "will not work in it." The reason for the growth in support of special interest politics was summarized by President Roosevelt's aide Harry Hopkins: "tax and tax, spend and spend, elect and elect." We could afford the pork programs prior to the 1990s; now we cannot.

In 1964 President Lyndon Johnson agonized that something must be done for the country's "forgotten fifth," and the "fortunate fifth," the richest 20 percent, must pay the bill. The middle class three-fifths ended up paying for the majority of Johnson's Great Society initiative. Harvard professor Robert Reich, labor secretary for President Clinton, resurrects the language of Johnson and argues for progressive taxation on the fortunate fifth to benefit the other four-fifths of the American public. Reich and Clinton face three essential points. First, the real rich (top 1 percent) can avoid tax hikes by taking more income as perks rather than cash, working less, and sheltering assets. Second, the middle class has realized that each and every tax-the-rich scheme has resulted in a hike in their own taxes. Third, poverty is not caused by an insufficient supply of program bureaucrats. Currently, we have one million starving in the streets, and our demanding welfare system treats the poor as irretrievably crippled wards of the state. The nation requires welfare reform to help reverse the demoralization of the poor. A 1990s President John Kennedy might suggest that we need a society where the most gifted may strive and the weak need not feel fear or complacency. After finishing this book some readers may be left with fewer gnawing doubts that America can unleash the power in people, enhance productivity, and improve the American standard of living.

Federal subsidies are often at cross-purposes: we would help food shoppers if we eradicated sugar price supports and let the price drop 84 percent. Consider an example from the author's main area of research, health care. With Hill-Burton in 1948, we identified the need for a federal program to increase the supply of hospital beds in rural areas, but urban members of Congress would not allow this. Congress permitted 90 percent of the funds to be spent on adding hospital beds to urban areas during the period 1949 to 1981. Consequently, Congress initiated programs to contain health care costs in 1982 to cover the cost expansion that their Hill-Burton program created. Success has been limited in closing beds, and now almost 300,000 empty hospital beds still add to the fixed cost of medical care in 1993.

Better cost-benefit calculus can more efficiently allocate resources among infrastructure domestic programs or defense programs. Former representative William Gray (D–Pa.) has suggested redistributing unnecessary mass transit funds to inner-city public schools. As a leading responsible liberal on budget issues, Gray has stated that he "would rather have my son walk to school than ride to nowhere."

In the private sector special interest usually leads to the best allocation of resources in business, but the proposition is not true in politics. Special interests force our elected leaders into what game theory texts call the "prisoner's dilemma." Self-interests lead the majority of politicians to what becomes the worst possible outcome for the nation. Those who vote to waste public funds get reelected precisely because they waste. Such politicians are financial vacationers who feel obliged to offer indignation about the deficit crisis but take no specific action against their sacred cows or programs with a very poor cost-benefit ratio.

There are two basic schools of thought for deficit reduction: mostly raise taxes (the Democratic option of Governor Babbit and Walter Mondale) versus mostly cut spending (with few Republican details as to what is to be cut). We shall survey each of these options.

DEFICITS—NO PROBLEM, RAISE TAXES

This school of thought was defeated in the 1984 presidential election and the 1988 Democratic primary. Some proponents still argue that federal spending patterns are in control and our taxing patterns are too low. Summers (1990) and Jencks and Peterson (1991) argued for substantial tax hikes. Democrats believe that federal spending should remain unchanged, but some billions should be reallocated to domestic programs. They argue that inflation in the 1970s frightened voters into closing their wallets to the tax collector and closing their minds to unmet social needs. Measured in inflation-adjusted real dollars, discretionary domestic federal spending from 1981 to 1993 has declined 16.9 percent, while interest on the federal debt has risen 86 percent. Only in 1987–1988 did the federal government experience a −0.07 percent dip as a fraction of the GNP. However, the discretionary domestic federal budget is at a 40-year low, having fallen from 5.75 percent of the GNP in 1981 to 3.65 percent in 1993. In plain language, one cannot balance the budget by taking stereos away from college students, abolishing food stamps for the hungry, or denying welfare mothers necessary medical care. Items such as these are a small portion of our spending problem.

What evidence suggests that we are undertaxed? The link between taxing and spending trends is very weak. If Social Security contributions are excluded, other revenues raised by the federal government have declined to 11.9 percent of the GNP in 1993, in contrast to 13.51 percent of the GNP in 1979 under the Carter administration.

TAXPAYER EQUITY

Mavens of fairness often cite economist Wallace Peterson's phrase "silent depression" to suggest that the American standard of living has been eroded because wives and mothers now have to work (and yet family income has not kept pace with inflation). This author admits there is a social cost of unshared family dinners but prefers to avoid buzzword phrases like "declining supply of quality time." The fortunate fifth's family earnings improved over the last decade because of the rise in working spouses, sometimes stimulated by better tax policies. Progressives seeking to find fault suggest statistics for a silent depression. Example one: In 1971 married couples with children claimed 51 percent of household income, but in 1992 they accounted for only 34 percent. Are things that bad? No, married couples with children were 41 percent of 64 million households in 1971, and they were 26 percent of 97 million households in 1992. In point of fact, married couples with children have seen their income improve by $11,700 (in 1992 dollars) since 1979. Example two: Mavens of fairness use Labor Department figures to claim that hourly worker's average earnings, in real terms, have declined by 6.9 percent from 1979 to 1992. We could improve the statistic by banning students from taking jobs or preventing vocational education students from working 10 to 20 hours per week. That would be a better statistical artifact, but would it also be poor social policy? Moreover, the Labor Department figures are for only 60 percent of the population and exclude all managerial jobs and self-employed computer contractors, whose wages improved 8.1 percent since 1979 in inflation-adjusted terms. Progressive Democrats, too quick to criticize President Clinton, claim that the new "fortunate fourth" of society is quietly seceding from the rest of America, but such class warfare is statistically incorrect and ineffective politics. They should not make a direct connection between tax rates and tax progressivity. Under President Kennedy tax rates for the richest 1 percent of the public declined from 91 to 27 percent, and yet their tax share increased from 11 percent to 15 percent. President Reagan was equally effective at making the richest citizens bear a higher fraction of our tax burden by trimming the tax rates from 1970s levels. How does this magic occur? The rich pay a smaller fraction but they pay more? Easy; since the rich have more control over their compensation, now they have less incentive to avoid taxes by taking perks and are receiving more money as cash. All benefit and none are harmed in the society, which is "pareto optimal" in every sense.

Lindsey (1990) provides strong evidence for this reallocation of pay from perks to wages. What if we expand the definition of "rich" to include more people? The fortunate fifth paid 55.6 percent of our taxes in 1979 and 59 percent in 1992. They would have paid $38 billion more in 1992 if they had been taxed at 1979–1980 rates. However, they would have hired fewer people if taxed at 1980 rates (trimming annual economic growth by 0.09 points), and they would have collected more perks as a replacement for heavily taxed cash income. Summing the benefits to the rich over the tax-cut years since 1981, the fortunate fifth may have gained over $210 billion in reduced taxes, but the middle class (middle 60%) gained $131 billion, and everyone stayed silent as the federal deficit expanded by $3.2 trillion. All classes of Americans benefited from expansion of the deficit, which is why it will be so difficult to trim it in the 1990s. It's a short-run bargain to pay $73 for each $100 of government; the deficit gap must be reduced.

The poorest half of the public saw their incomes decline by $23.6 billion from 1979 to 1992 thanks to hikes in payroll taxes for financing Social Security. In other words, the progressive Democrats made a defacto rise in the taxes for 58 million Americans earning less than the median wage. In 1984 and 1992, these working Americans could have made a cost-beneficial decision by rejecting liberal Democrats that vote to enhance the generosity of Social Security, while balancing the benefit on the backs of the nonrich. However, one could counterargue that the effective tax rates for the unfortunate fifth have increased little since 1979 because Congress did raise the earned income tax credit for the poor.

The federal deficits have an air of unreality, hence the title for this chapter. Unrealistic members of Congress try to enact new programs and back-door taxes. Politicians tend to act like dream solvers, saying yes to the dreams of each special interest group while we, the taxpayers, pay for it. We will have to face some modest increases in tax rates, but we also must decrease the administrative economy. Budget shortfalls will draw an ever tightening noose around our domestic policy options. More government is the problem. The rhetoric of demagogues, such as "tax the rich," will not help. If we confiscated 100 percent of the earnings of those making over $90,000 per year, it would only be enough to fuel the federal government for nine days. One sage politician from Vienna once suggested that governments will "actually do the right thing after everything else has been tried."

MORAL AND FISCAL DEFICITS

On March 26, 1992, Senator John C. Danforth (R–Mo.) said, "We know that we have bankrupted America and that we have given our children a legacy of bankruptcy." Can the federal deficit be viewed in such moral terms? In 1932 conservatives fought the idea of a mere $2 million deficit as a moral issue. To ignore the building deficit crisis is akin to a moral felony, doing harm to the young and unborn. Programs that increase the deficit operate as Robin Hood in reverse; they take money from average citizens and pay debt service to rich Americans, rich foreign investors, and foreign governments.

Some pensioners are uneasy with the legacy of huge bills for their children and grandchildren. Parents want a house better than the one they were brought up in but know that future generations will have to accept downgraded expectations. Dreams are either downsized or eliminated, and the most disillusioned turn to drugs. In the jargon of economics, the current generation in control is enjoying public consumption that ensures the imposition of misery on future generations of taxpayers.

The interest expense on the federal deficit in 1993 is $430 per second. The national debt is a stack of $100 bills 3,002 miles high. This should be seen in the context of the gross national product, which is a stack of $1000 bills 4,090 miles high. Awash in mediocre times, we do not like to think about our mountain of debt. The debt service accounts for more than 15 percent of federal spending. Ignoring the future appears to be our number one public program. Many people have the spending philosophy of football great Bobby Lane: "the secret of life is to run out of cash and air at the same time." Unfortunately, the federal deficit is in worse shape, dumping all the unpaid bills on future generations.

The foregoing introduction in no way denigrates the taxpayer revolt on behalf of tax reduction. People feel they are not getting value for their tax contributions. Many Americans know firsthand the pain of Alice, in Lewis Carroll's *Alice's Adventures in Wonderland,* when she is offered a job that pays only every other day. Each year average Americans have to work from January 2 to May 8 to pay their federal taxes and then another three to five weeks to pay state and local taxes. If we were to balance the budget without spending reductions, "tax freedom day" would be July 3 of each year. We must cut federal spending. Spending reduction can occur without doing damage to the poor and the truly needy.

Annual federal deficits adding to the national debt are important because they soak up private capital for investment, research, development, and economic growth. Also, as the Perot quote at the beginning of this chapter indicates, deficits make the American people dependent on imports of foreign capital.

MAKE VIRTUE A NECESSITY: GENERATE A REAL BUDGET

Cost control requires a more rational federal budget, free of gimmicks and fraudulent assumptions. In 1967 President Johnson's Commission on Budget Concepts introduced the idea of a unified budget. Now is the time for even more basic, systematic reform of the federal budget with three basic components (trust funds, general funds, and enterprise funds like the Tennessee Valley Authority), subdivided into capital accounts and operating expenses. Rather than continue to let deceptive accounting generate deceptive management practices, the nation needs accurate current and future capital budgets. In addition, our budget should reflect more conservative assumptions with higher projected default rates than are presently in use. An accurate budget should separate current operational expenses and record at true cost the net impact of federal credit programs (i.e., loans plus loan guarantees). According to the January 25, 1992, *Economist*, New Zealand became the most recent nation to produce accounts on commercial accounting principles, including a full balance sheet of its assets and liabilities, and an operating statement, which changes depreciation on the capital assets.

Why are arcane issues like discounting important in the budget? Our current budget concentrates only on annual cash flow (e.g., a $5 million loan is treated as a full expenditure for one year, overstating the deficit since some fraction of the loan will be paid back). Loan guarantees do not raise the deficit, even though they create future liabilities that will have to be paid by the taxpayer. Under the strain of the GRH Congress converted $176 billion in loan/expenditures into off-budget loan guarantees from 1985 to 1990. Direct federal loans outstanding declined by $52 billion through 1992. This strategy is attractive if one admires creative lies. Congress is happy because the action of relabeling a loan as a "guarantee" creates the same cash flow to special interest groups and voters, while reducing the current paper deficit. Keeping a bad set of books for the official budget is dangerous for a number of reasons, not least of which is that it leads to self-deceit. We must avoid the "new investment budget," an artful dodge that allows big federal deficits as long as they are labeled "investments in the nation's future growth." A rose by any other name is an expense, whether it is labeled an investment or a future chunk of national debt. An investment budget deficit may not shrink substantially if the government has to start setting aside reserves to pay off the loans. Many in Congress would be surprised to discover that from 1980 to 1991 the federal government borrowed as much money as it lent. In a hypothetical world, no federal deficit would have existed if the poor claimants of dollars from Uncle Sam had borrowed from the buyer of Treasury Bills. In the period 1980 to 1993 the federal deficits equalled $2.9 trillion, while the same government issued $1.2 trillion in new primary loan guarantees (61.6 percent Federal Housing Administration, 29 percent VA, and 9.3 percent student loans) and $506 billion in new direct loans (37 percent Farmers Home Administration, 21 percent Rural Electrification, 14 percent military sales, 14 percent Commodity Credit Corporation, and 14 percent miscellaneous smaller programs). Our borrowing will outstrip our lending by over $75 billion annually in 1993.

PORK AND PORKERS

Members of Congress often have reputations as earmarkers or non-earmarkers. The earmarkers are always looking for opportunities to inject their pork spending programs, like the Republican from New York nicknamed "Senator Pothole." The earmarkers are subdivided into a second, extra-aggressive member of Congress: "the unauthorized earmarker." A senior member of Congress can act as an unauthorized earmarker by going into a joint conference (designed to iron out differences between Senate-passed and House-passed versions of a bill) and add new pork spending programs without telling any original authorizer or sponsor of the bill about these additions. Such last-minute, unauthorized earmarkers are members of two very powerful committees (Rules and Appropriations). Under an informal quid pro quo deal the members of the Rules Committee extend waivers to unauthorized pork programs to prevent non-earmarkers from eliminating them from the spending bills. In return members of the Appropriations Committee almost always pass pork projects requested by members of the Rules Committee (Gross, 1992; Galbraith, 1992).

Pork is spending with a zip code attached; the politician gets the funds for his or her home district. According to the 1992 report of the Congressional Budget Tracking System (CBTS), House members backed proposals calling for $18 of spending increases for every dollar of spending reduction. Politicians fight to control the national deficit as a lofty abstraction—but not in their local districts. In most cases political considerations outweigh macroeconomic general considerations. Only in the 1990s has the deficit issue become so critical as to begin to outweigh petty local political concerns (Kelly 1992). The more important the issues, the less important the political considerations. One can think of many obvious examples that transcend the dictum of former House Speaker Tip O'Neill that "all politics are local." These include foreign affairs, the AIDS epidemic, and now the federal deficit.

Congress has three lines of defense for explaining why it listens to special interest groups. First, modern society is so complex that it needs advice from specialists on how its industries should be financed and regulated. Second, the special interest groups are needed to finance expensive reelection campaigns. Third, few people come to Congress and testify against spending more money. According to Professor James L. Payne (1991), Congressional witnesses oppose spending only 1 time out of 150. The Beltway firms consulting for government seldom testify against the federal agencies that pay them, and few university professors have the stomach for cost containment. Consequently, one wins more friends and funding if the constant message, given to Congress 99.4 percent of the time, is spend more. It is not surprising that Congress voted (with 45 Democrats in the Senate) to fund two unnecessary Seawolf submarines in May 1992. Democrats proposed the notion that you could cut defense forever and incur no damage—just eliminate those $600 toilet seats and $500 hammers. Republicans put forth the comforting notion that you could cut domestic spending forever and never touch bone—just catch the welfare cheats and rich students with invalid educational loans. In point of fact, the correlation between political party and the pork barrel is imperfect.

It is not surprising that Congress seldom stops a scandal or fraud in the early stages. Congress does not look for fraud because it indirectly profits from claiming to micromanage so it can optimize contributions from PACs. Its source of PAC money would dry up if fraud was really found. No wonder the congressional public approval rating fell from 24 to 15 percent from 1990 to 1992. The next chapter will survey the nature of special interest politics in America today.

REFERENCES

Aaron, H., and Schultze, C., eds. (1992). *Setting Domestic Priorities: What Can Government Do?* Washington, DC: Brookings.

Bailey, M., and Winston, C., eds. (1990). *Microeconomics.* Washington, DC: Brookings.

Demsetz, H. (1967). "Toward a Theory of Property Rights," *American Economic Association Papers and Proceedings* 57:2, May, 347–59.

Eastaugh, S. (1992). *Health Care Finance: Economic Incentives and Productivity Enhancement.* Westport, CT: Auburn House.

————. (1981). *Medical Economics and Health Finance*. Boston: Auburn House.

Feldstein, M., and Elmendorf, D. (1990). "Government Debt, Government Spending, and Private Sector Behavior," *American Economic Review* 80:3, June, 589–99.

Fitzgerald, R. (1988). *When Government Goes Private: Successful Alternatives to Public Services*. New York: Universe.

Fix, M., and Kenyon, D. (1990). *Coping with Mandates: What Are the Alternatives?* 2nd ed. Washington, DC: Urban Institute.

Galbraith, J. (1992). *The Culture of Contentment*. Boston: Houghton Mifflin.

Gross, M. (1992). *The Government Racket: Washington Waste from A to Z*. New York: Bantam Books.

Gueron, J. (1990). "Work and Welfare: Lessons on Employment Programs," *Journal of Economic Perspectives* 4:1, Winter, 79–98.

Horner, C. (1988). "Beyond Mr. Gradgrind: The Case for Deregulating the Public Sector," *Policy Review* 44, Spring, 34–39.

Janeway, E. (1989). *The Economics of Chaos*. New York: Dutton Penguin.

Jencks, C., and Peterson, P., eds. (1991). *The Urban Underclass*. Washington, DC: Brookings.

Kelly, B. (1992). *Adventures in Porkland: How Washington Wastes Your Money*. New York: Villard.

Kryder-Coe, J., Salamon, L., and Molnar, J. (1991). *Homeless Children and Youth: A New American Dilemma*. New Brunswick, NJ: Transaction Press.

Lindsey, L. (1990). *The Growth Experiment: How Tax Policy Is Transforming the U.S. Economy*. New York: Basic Books.

Oding-Smee, J., and Jiley, C. (1985). "Approaches to Public Sector Borrowing Ratio: Net Worth," *National Institute for Economic Review* 113, August, 65–80.

Organization for Economic Cooperation and Development (OECD). (1993). "Public Debt in Perspective." Paris: OECD.

Payne, J. (1991). *The Culture of Spending: Why Congress Lives Beyond Our Means*. San Francisco: ICS Press.

Perot, H. R. (1992). *United We Stand: How We Can Take Back Our Country*. Dallas: Hyperion.

Rauch, J. (1989). "Is the Deficit Really So Bad?" *The Atlantic* 263, February, 36–42.

Reich, R. (1991). *The Work of Nations: Preparing Ourselves for the 21st-Century Capitalism*. New York: Knopf.

Rogoff, K. (1990). "Equilibrium Political Budget Cycles," *American Economic Review* 80:2, March, 21–36.

Schick, A. (1990). *The Capacity to Budget*. Washington, DC: Urban Institute.

Stigler, G. (1982). *Economists and Public Policy*. Washington, DC: American Enterprise Institute.

Summers, L. (1990). *Understanding Unemployment*. Cambridge: MIT Press.

Tavellini, G., and Alesina, A. (1990). "Voting on the Budget Deficit," *American Economic Review* 80:2, March, 21–36.

Thurow, L. (1992). *Head to Head: The Coming Economic Battle among Japan, Europe, and America*. New York: Morrow.

Vickers, J., and Yarrow, G. (1988). *Privatization: An Economic Analysis.* Cambridge: MIT Press.

Wilson, J. (1989). *Bureaucracy: What Government Agencies Do and Why They Do It.* Boston: Basic Books.

2

Special Interest Politics

President Reagan tripled the national debt in eight years. Half the
blame must reside in the excessive growth in defense spending. We
must also look to trim sacred cow entitlement programs like social security cost of living annual inflation adjustments.
> —Governor Mario Cuomo, 1992

Good budgeting is the uniform distribution of dissatisfaction. Not
enough of the federal agencies are dissatisfied.
> —Murray Weidenbaum, Former Chairman of the President's Council
> of Economic Advisers, 1989

Government is a burden, save when it finances the entitlement of
your special interest group. Our culture of contentment sets aside that
which, in the longer view, disturbs contentment . . . paying the fiscal
and social costs.
> —John Kenneth Galbraith, 1992

Special interest politics is the main cause of excessive spending and deficit
expansion. Can Congress reduce or eliminate unnecessary spending? For
two decades the American people have been asked to tune in after the next
election and find out. The budget crisis is the slowest developing crisis in
recent times. We can either raise taxes or reduce costs. But few people
volunteer their sacred cow programs for cost reduction, and few voters support higher taxes. With higher taxes the government becomes the other
team, the enemy, and the more you work, the more the enemy scores
your dollars. All of us have our special interests. The entire public pays for
additional spending, whereas only the special group members receive the
funds. To paraphrase Pogo, we have met the enemy which is ourselves,
and we must better balance the interplay between our fears and our aspira-

tions. Bureaucrats have been too efficient at feeding our special interests and pandering to the public. Ann Richards and Ross Perot are correct in stating that the public is sick and tired of bureaucrats with a handful of gimme and a mouthful of bull.

This chapter has four stanzas. First, we survey the self-interest theory of government. Second, we discuss ways to reorganize and cut the federal bureaucracy. Third, we suggest methods for trimming generosity in entitlement programs. In the fourth stanza we offer ways to manage future federal programs with improved efficiency and effectiveness.

SELF-INTEREST THEORY

The theory of legislation varies from the traditional public interest theory to the self-interest theory. Few analysts still believe that politicians and regulators always act as well-meaning conduits of the public interest. The antieconomic theory of the public interest claims there is no shortage of dollars and no shortage of problems, only a shortage of sympathy and national will. Contrary to this obsolete theory, the basic theoretical underpinning of this chapter is the self-interest theory of legislation. Under this theory government is not a bloodless exercise of computerized public policymaking. Instead, a serious weighing of competing programs includes a heavy dose of self-interest as politicians and regulators make decisions to enhance the political support they receive. Politics should be viewed as an exchange relationship just like any normal economic market. The currency can be information dollars (for reelection campaigns from lobbyists) or job security. Regulators are unlikely to risk job security by being too tough on the regulated industry.

According to the "capture theory of regulation" outlined by Truman (1951), the regulated industry gradually comes to dominate the decisions of the regulators until the "watchdog agency" is converted into an ally, or even a subsidiary of the private sector. Farm regulators lobby for farm spending, Defense Department regulators lobby for larger contracts with contractors. Truman argued that the public interest is too general and underfunded a concept to have sufficient power in the halls of government. The regulated have more cohesion and financial self-interest than the regulators: they keep closest track of the bureau (agency) and reveal any malfeasance or red tape by the agency at annual budget hearings. Bernstein (1955) carried the Truman argument further and suggested that most agencies pass through a life cycle that begins with zeal and then leads to a period of debility and decline in which the regulators become the captive of the regulated. The regulators receive job security, fewer hassles from Congress, and a higher paying job at retirement from government service (by working for the industry they regulated) if they do what is desired by industry.

Politicians, bureaucrats, and industry lobbyists make decisions based on self-interest. The public interest is still a minor concern in probate decision making (but a major concern for rhetoric in statements for public consumption). Lobbyists have a concentrated interest in the regulation that specifically impacts their clients. The dynamics of this activity was outlined by Ted Lowi's (1964) classic article concerning three basic types of legislation: producer regulation, spillover externality regulation, and redistributive regulation (e.g., welfare, Social Security).

Producer regulation, such as the 1989 bailout of the savings and loan industry at a cost of more than $600 billion over the next four decades, is a classic example of regulation to benefit the industry. The classic example of market failure spillover externalities, pollution, occurs when the polluting firm imposes costs on persons (victims) outside the market exchange process. The 1990 Bush administration legislation to sell pollution permits is an attempt to minimize the resource costs of achieving a given level of pollution reduction. The firms that are most cost-effective at pollution control have started to sell their permits to pollute to other firms, thus achieving a fixed amount of pollution reduction at minimum industry costs. Firms regularly trade in pollution permits. This market-oriented approach to pollution control, compared to the liberal approach of fixed standards or absolute bans on pollution, makes America unique in comparison to the nations that signed the Rio Earth Summit agreements.

For old-time believers in pure "good government," the special interest theory seemingly conflicts with the Jeffersonian notion that rationality will win out over irrationality. In fact, special interest politics is very rational for the players. The players, politicians and lobbyists, trade cash and information. The political process always has a hand outstretched, seeking cash and/or access to information. Politicians often receive political contributions from both sides on a given issue. Cash seldom directly buys votes, but it does buy access to the politicians to ask certain questions during a hearing or the mark up of a bill. Cynics are mistaken to think that outright bribes are a frequent occurrence. The process is subtler and more insidious. The lobbyist offers a series of favors and contributions, hopefully instilling a sense of personal obligation, until the politician has lost sight of the public interest and yields loyalty to the lobbyist's employer. The special interest group enjoys being the benefactor of this dance of legislation or regulation. Self-interest involves the exchange of subtle currency and subtle bias or shifts in the content of legislation. Subtle changes can mean the difference between bankruptcy and growth for a large number of firms (or households). Politicians will never admit they undertake actions for reasons of self-interest, but they will ask for contributions and votes from each organized group (industry, bank managers, the elderly). In the relentless pressure-cooker world of politics, it is not surprising that self-interest and special interest groups dominate the decision making process.

America is a representative democracy. However, we fall short of Edmund Burke's 1774 ideal which says that your representative owes you not only his industry, but also his judgment; he betrays you, instead of serves you, if he sacrifices them to your opinion. George Will (1992) is correct to suggest that members of Congress are insufficiently Burkean for the sake of deliberative democracy. The late Representative Silvio Conte (R–Mass.) eloquently summed up this failing with his poem at the end of the October 8, 1990, congressional budget debate:

> We shout and jeer and fuss and bark;
> We blame each other in the dark.
> We see no forest for the trees.
> We're frightened by the interest groups;
> We act like silly nincompoops.

DEFICITS: BY-PRODUCTS OF SILKY SPECIAL INTERESTS

All political stripes in American life, even the liberal economist Galbraith quoted in the introduction to this chapter, are disgusted with special interest politics. Each special interest group views its product as silk, even if the general public views its programs as entrails of a worm. Our federal budget is full of worm entrails. The worms of special interest must be brought under control if we are to slow the erosion of our infrastructure and our standard of living. Our 1992 Robespierre of revolution, Ross Perot, argued that a 99 percent cut in worm entrails would yield a one-third reduction in federal spending and a balanced budget. His estimated cost savings may have been high, but his spirit of change versus "worm politics as usual" certainly caught the public's attention.

Following the metaphor to the extreme, each collection of worms represents a special interest that claims it is worthy of federal funding. To be fair to the worms, they do produce nice silk—which in a fair market would be too expensive to sell. The most educated of the worm groups, public television, may not be worth a $1.4 billion federal subsidy. Public television's funding would be cut or eliminated if we enacted a balanced budget amendment that worked, but it could raise the additional funds by appealing for private donations. Instead, each worm group profits by feeding at the public trough, thereby producing an estimated $255 billion federal deficit in 1993 and an estimated $340 billion in 1998. The worms are correct in stating that they produce fine silk, but the silk is too costly and worn only by the influential.

The worms are not the only problem with our debt-soaked national balance sheet. All the worms need trimming (or eliminating), and our biggest budget item is income security (including Social Security and federal pensions). If Uncle Sam sent each American family a prospective statement of how funds are spent starting in FY1994, we would spend the following under current law: $5,800 per family on income security; $3,240 to $3,400 on net interest; $3,220 on defense; $3,140 on health care; $710 on commerce and housing credit; $570 on education; $390 on transportation; $400 on veterans' benefits; and $229 on the environment. At the end of December 1993 our national debt will exceed $4.4 trillion, or $17,200 per American. If each American family of four were to receive a debt bill/bomb of $69,000 in the mail on Christmas Eve 1993, this would provide stark evidence of our budgetary crisis.

Half of the public is generally quiet about the deficit issue because they either do not understand the long-run risks or they enjoy the short-run benefits. Almost 49 percent of the public received at least one form of federal aid in 1992; of the 49 percent, 28.4 percent received Medicare, 9.9 percent received Medicaid, 4.4 percent received welfare, 3.4 percent received unemployment compensation, and 2.9 percent received benefits from other programs. Interest on the national debt is 261 percent of what we will spend on the poor in FY1993. We could afford to spend more on the poor or more on education if we could only control our national debt. To paraphrase President John F. Kennedy: our problems are manmade, and they can be solved by men of goodwill. The search is on for men and women of goodwill to cut special interest spending and balance the budget, as projected in Table 2.1.

SPECIAL INTEREST GROUPS

Special interest groups display a basic law of political behavior: they are easily established in the public budget and difficult to displace even when their rationale for existing disappears. For example, the federal price support program for wool and mohair was initiated in 1954 to ensure that American troops had a sufficient supply of warm uniforms. Since 1989 the federal government has spent as much as $3.87 for each dollar of mohair at market price. The rationale for this program of price supports has disappeared since the 1970s with the introduction of warm synthetic materials. Yet in 1994 the federal government will spend $180 million to subsidize 9,900 goat ranchers and 99,000 sheep ranchers. The richest 2 percent of these

Table 2.1
CBO Baseline Projections for Mandatory Federal Spending (by fiscal year, in billions of dollars)

	1993	1994	1995	1996	1997	1998
Means-Tested Programs						
Medicaid	80	92	105	118	131	146
Food Stamps	24	24	24	24	25	26
Supplemental Security Income	20	24	24	24	28	30
Family Support	17	18	18	19	19	20
Veterans' Pensions	3	3	3	2	2	3
Child Nutrition	6	7	7	8	8	9
Earned Income Tax Credit	9	10	13	13	14	14
Stafford Loans	2	3	3	3	3	3
Other	3	3	3	4	4	4
Total, Means-Tested Programs	165	183	200	214	234	255
Non-Means-Tested Programs						
Social Security	302	319	335	351	368	385
Medicare	146	167	188	211	234	259
Subtotal	449	486	523	562	602	644
Other Retirement and Disability						
Federal civilian	39	41	44	48	51	54
Military	26	27	28	29	31	32
Other	5	5	5	5	5	5
Subtotal	70	73	77	82	86	91
Unemployment Compensation	33	26	25	25	25	25
Other Programs						
Veterans' benefits	16	18	17	16	18	18
Farm price supports	16	10	9	9	9	9
Social services	5	6	5	5	5	5
Credit reform liquidating accounts	3	1	-2	-9	-6	-6
Other	13	14	11	9	9	9
Subtotal	54	48	40	30	36	36
Total, Non-Means-Tested Programs	605	633	666	699	749	796
Total						
All Mandatory Spending Deposit Insurance	770	816	866	913	984	1,051

Source: Congressional Budget Office (1993).

ranchers receive 56 percent of the unnecessary subsidy. Texas, a state that receives 27 percent of wool payments and 86 percent of mohair/goat payments, is full of fatuous talk about efficiency in government. Efficiency is a program best attempted in the other guy's congressional district, so the pork spending subsidies are difficult to cut.

Special interest groups are expert at what economists call "rent seeking," searching for financial suppport from government action (regulation or deregulation) without earning it through normal productive activity.

Rent seekers look for an edge against the competition (e.g., steel quotas) or direct subsidy (e.g., farm price supports). All this activity can be described as if it were in the public interest, as if our special group needs this special help in the interest of "fairness." The unfortunate scaffolding of special interest politics is that every group's right to everything results in everybody's long-run victimization under the weight of a national debt.

The $11.3 billion Superconducting Supercollider in Texas is a classic example of pork spending. Subcontracts for this project come from the home states of 96 senators and 392 congressional districts. The project could have cost $2.1 billion less, but Congress stretched the completion date from 1999 to 2003. Some pork projects are larger in scope (the $31 billion space station), other programs are smaller in scale. For example, the Economic Development Administration (EDA) was supposed to target grants to the poorest 15 percent of counties. Instead, the idealistic EDA spends $225 million on a congressmen's building back home or glass sidewalk in the business district.

One of the largest special interest groups is the defense industry. Stanford University professor Alain Enthoven claims the ideal weapon system is built in 435 congressional districts, and it does not matter whether it works or not. The Defense Department begged Congress to cancel the V-22 helicopter, but Congress voted $625 million for the project in fiscal year 1992 to save 8,000 jobs at Textron/Boeing. In May 1992, 45 Democratic senators (and only seven Republican senators) voted to build two Seawolf Submarines. In the 1992 budget Congress voted $3.4 billion to build parts for 200 B-2 Stealth Bombers, but the parts will be placed in storage and only 15 planes will be assembled. One senator called this strategy "maintaining the vendor base, to gain no product or productivity but to gain local reelection." The Clinton administration "cut spending" in May 1993 by cancelling the republican Strategic Defense Initiative (SDI), "Star Wars." No real money was saved because the old SDI was simply renamed the new Ballistic Missile Defense Organization (BMDO). BMDO has the strategic advantage that it is ground-based, but BMDO has the same budget as SDI through fiscal 1997.

Defense Secretary Richard Cheney stated on May 8, 1992, that "nobody cuts programs out from under me, rather the Congress will not let me cut anything." The military sector does not desire a substantial peace dividend to result from declining political tensions with the Soviet Union and Eastern Europe. Rather than saving a projected $180 billion, the defense secretary experienced difficulty trimming 30,000 jobs and saving $35 billion real dollars over the first three fiscal years in the 1990s (Markusen and Yudkin, 1993). Without a substantial peace dividend to channel into education and some cost-beneficial social programs, the reduced Soviet threat has yet to translate into a higher standard of living for Americans. In 1993 dollars, America has spent $11.6 trillion on defense for 40 years to make sure the Russians will not bomb us, but we must spend more money over the coming 40 years on domestic/economic defense. Defense against the Russians was a relatively easy task by comparison.

The Clinton administration is trying to promote targeted Pentagon investment as a vital, "defense conversion" need to develop "dial-use" technologies for domestic use. Congress and the Pentagon are slow to adapt. They resist any intelligent plans to reduce unnecessary ships, expand cheaper land-based air force bases, and make the army lighter and more transportable. Military officials are not in a hurry to "system-reform themselves" out of a job or out of a well-paid graduation to private-sector work with a big defense contractor. Except for a shrinkage in civilian payroll from 13.2 to 12.4 percent of the defense budget, there are few changes at the Pentagon. Fiefdoms within the Pentagon and in defense industries own or rent certain politicians and so assist in the process of resisting change. Interservice rivalry makes it far harder for legislative leaders to achieve consensus on policy. The Center for Defense Information (CDI) holds that the budget can be cut to $196 billion in 1992 dollars by 1995. The CDI figure was developed by retired military personnel and was $14 billion less than Clinton's proposed target and $31 billion less than the Bush estimate.

The CDI estimate for the 1995 defense budget is not a radical or low estimate. We could still trim the budget an additional $90 to $95 billion in 1995 by trimming defense capacity to the levels actually used in the Gulf War. For example, the army could be downsized from 12 active-duty and 6 reserve divisions, to 5 active-duty and 3 reserve divisions. The Bush administration only wanted to cut back army divisions from 28 in 1990 to 18 in 1995. Instead of trimming fighter wings from 36 in 1990 to 26 in 1995, we could trim back to 10 fighter wings. Instead of having the 12 aircraft carriers planned for 1995, we could do with only 6 (and still fight Iran, Iraq, and an island in the Caribbean). The marines could cut 6 brigades, leaving 2 active-duty and 2 reserve. All of these cuts would trim the defense budget by less than 60 percent because the military has a generous early retirement program to ease the transition to civilian life. Education in the defense field should also be merged, thus saving money and improving effectiveness. The intraservice rivalry among the navy, air force, army, and marines has poorly served the nation by creating and encouraging poor communications and duplicative equipment and education programs. Finally, each service in the new unified defense programs should speed the rate at which it trims 165,000 civilian jobs from 1993 to 1998. The 1998 goal could be achieved by 1995.

Defense spending can be reduced through a reduction in force (lower labor costs) or reduction in capital spending (cancel or reduce budgets for weapons systems). Defending NATO will cost the American taxpayer $94 billion in 1993. It doesn't seem fair that Europeans receive $4,000 to $9,000 in free health care and college education while the average American taxpayer spends $800 per year to defend NATO. Labor costs could also be reduced by increased reliance on the reserves in place of active-duty military. Over 27 percent of the air force's planes are currently in the reserves, and they consume only 12 percent of the labor costs in the air force budget. We never needed the B-2 when existing cruise missiles could do the same job at only one-tenth the cost (and by using existing planes). A number of other programs could also be canceled, including the F-17 Stealth Fighter, F-16 Fighter, M-1 Tank, and SDI Missile Defense. Military down-staffing, or the so-called "personnel drawdown" planned through 1997, could be expanded to provide less than 1.3 million troops.

POLICY PROPOSAL No. 3: The military should be down-staffed from 1.3 million active-duty personnel in 1997 to a target of 700,000 (saving $278 billion over the period 1995–1997). The new lean military would have 275 ships, 5 carrier battle groups, 4 marine corps brigades, 5 army divisions, and 6 air force tactical fighter wings. This force would be sufficient to staff a second Operation Desert Storm and a Panama "Operation Just Cause" (27,000 troops utilized). The military could also save an additional $5 to $8 billion per annum over the next four years.

POLICY PROPOSAL No. 4: The military could eliminate the new warhead activities of the Department of Energy, cancel the Trident II (D5 missiles), terminate the Seawolf submarine program, and retire the B-1 Bomber. An additional $2.5 billion per annum could be saved if we canceled the air force's next premier fighter (the F-22), because the F-15 aircraft is sufficient to do the job. The F-22 is not worth the investment because the stealth technology is much less effective than has been promised. Any effort to economize should also include national guard and reserve troops, such that they constitute only 35 percent of the total force structure. *POLICY PROPOSAL No. 5:* Trim reserves from 1.04 million troops to 360,000 and reduce funds for reserve equipment by 70 percent (saving $32 billion over the four years 1994–1997). Following suggestions from the Congressional Budget Office, the part-time reservists, the Individual Mobilization Augmentee program, should be eliminated.

TRIMMING SOME PORK

Politicians plumb for more federal help for defense programs (including items like the $421,000 fax machine from Litton Industries) that are grossly overpriced. Other items are outdated but reinserted into the defense budget against the advice of the military (e.g., the F-14D training plane built on Long Island). Politicians also plumb for more government help in defense plants that are outmoded, unnecessary, and often dropped from the defense budget by military professionals (but reinserted into the budget by Congress; e.g., so what if the navy refuses to use that training plane, it creates jobs in my district, so buy it). No politician seems immune to the influence of special interest groups. Consider the case of Rep. Les Aspen (D–Wis.), chairman of the House Armed Services Committee, a major moral voice in the fight against a number of defense procurement scandals. In 1988 this same man forced the army to buy a large number of trucks made in his home state that the army did not want and did not need. President Clinton must take a lesson from President Truman. In the three years after 1946 Truman cut the defense budget 89 percent. These cost cuts gave him the funds for his two big programs (the GI Bill and the Marshall Plan). Without at least a 35 to 40 percent additional cut in defense, President Clinton will lack the funds for his two big programs (health care and education and job training).

Waste is not confined to the defense sector. To save scarce resources, the federal government should consider *POLICY PROPOSAL No. 6:* Eliminate airport grants-in-aid, thus saving $8.6 billion over the period 1994–1997. Airports do not have trouble financing improvements from fees collected, so they no longer need federal funds. Four additional cost saving ideas should be considered in rural and urban areas. The federal government should reduce deficiency payments to farmers by *POLICY PROPOSAL No. 7:* Reduce target prices by 4 percent a year starting with 1994 crops (thus saving $17.1 billion over the period 1994–1997). In urban areas, the federal government should consider *POLICY PROPOSAL No. 8:* Scale down the bureaucratic low-income home energy assistance program by $6.7 billion over the years 1994–1997. *POLICY PROPOSAL No. 9:* Scale down Community Development Block Grants (CDBG) eligibility for nonentitlement areas (saving $12.1 billion over four years) and spend federal funds only on programs with national benefit. *POLICY PROPOSAL No. 10:* Reallocate one-fourth of the block grant savings, or $3 billion, to rebuild Los Angeles and New York City.

SHIFTING THE POWER OF SPECIAL INTERESTS

Are members of Congress indecisive concerning cost control? Yes, in most cases their economic compass spins to the pressure pull of special interest groups. In the southwestern states, special interest politics centers around defense contracts, new highways, water projects, and coastal oil drilling. In Chicago, New York, Boston, and Washington, D.C., the major special interest groups are government employees and ethnic organizations. Moreover, Boston and New York have substantial defense contracts, and

California cities have increasingly powerful ethnic organizations. The American Political Science Association may be the last academic group to admit the obvious: the sum total of special interest group pressures does not advance the national interest. America will become a stagnant society unless we downplay the hold that special interest groups have on resource allocation. Special interest pressures have eroded the social cement of the nation. The solidarity concept of a "shining city on the hill," where every person is his brother's keeper, has been replaced by greedy "cause people," fighting tooth and nail for their share of the public pie. Just as monetary greed has tarnished some conservatives, so has cause greed tarnished the liberal/progressives. Both types of greed kill the common culture of the helping hand.

The political novice might ask why politicians fight to maximize employment or spending programs in their districts. After all, the American economy is vibrant and mobile. A civilian fired from a military base in Texas or Maine could easily find employment in another sector of the American economy. The short-run focus of most politicians was neatly summarized by Senator Phil Gramm (R–Tex.) in the fall 1990 issue of *Policy Review:*

If we should vote next week on whether to begin producing cheese in a factory on the moon, I almost certainly would oppose it. On the other hand, if the government decides to institute the policy, it would be my objective to see that a Texas contractor builds this celestial cheese plant, that the milk comes from Texas cows, and that the earth distribution center is located in Texas. (no. 52, 20)

Tax reform is an example of temporary reduction in the power of special interest groups from 1986 to 1989. As is outlined in detail in chapter 3, the tax reform act of 1986 defeated the special interest groups and their paper tax shelters which threw off passive losses in the form of deductions for depreciation and other expenses. The insurance industry was the only special interest group to survive the tax reform act cleanly in 1986. Unfortunately, the capital gains reduction act of 1989 (reducing the rate to 19.6 percent) repealed the 1986 reform for the timber industry. To acquire the support of 70 members of Congress in tree-growing states and achieve the one explicit promise made by George Bush in the 1988 campaign (to cut capital gains), this $2 billion tax set a precedent for the 1990s for all special interest lobbyists to get organized and attach their own special bills, lamprey-like, to the tax code.

Congress is good at shifting the blame. Members of Congress blame the 600 percent proliferation in congressional staff since 1950 on excessive legislative activity and micromanagement of various federal departments. Some staff members do promote their own legislative agenda, in addition to the legislative agenda of the various special interest groups. However, the large staffs may be the symptom and not the cause. Since 1980 an average of 7,000 bills have been introduced during each Congress, and fewer than 2.8 percent have been enacted. Committees spend lots of time debating impractical bills. Since there are over 300 committee and subcommittee chairs, most members of Congress feel compelled to produce some paper legislation. It need not be in the national interest, but something must be proposed to justify the continued existence of a large number of unnecessary committees. The proliferation of subcommittees makes the work of special interest groups more effective and economical; they can focus their lobbying efforts on a small number of politicians and staffers.

Congress and its large staffs best serve the largest special interest group in America, the middle class. The special interest group that helps to establish, finance (at public expense), and maintain a bureau or department also fights any attempt to reduce the size and scope of federal involvement. If federal civil servants are cooperative, or coopted by the various special interest groups, the special interest groups return the favor by fighting any reduction in the size of "their bureaucrats." For example, if the Veterans Administration (VA) suggests any reduction in VA employees, the various veterans' groups protest such attempts to improve productivity. Cost cutting is not easy when it comes to federal employees or local programs. Ehrenhalt (1991) suggests Congress has become an independent class of "political entrepreneurs" obsessed with reelection. Strong political parties no longer exist to protect members of Congress that ignore local interests to benefit the national interest.

CUTTING FEDERAL EMPLOYEES

There is ample room to improve productivity, the ratio of output-to-input, by cutting the federal government without dismembering the public purpose that led to the creation of each bureaucratic fiefdom. President Reagan's emphasis on budget cutting received a notable amount of continuing public sympathy, but one should note that the number of federal employees increased 7.2 percent during his tenure. Without resorting to the self-indulgent language of the typical conservative bureaucrat basher, one can easily observe that the federal government needs cost reduction and better incentives for efficiency. The American taxpayer often appears as a prisoner of Zenda, Zenda being that pork barrel bureaucracy famous for inefficiency and survival. Each member of Congress acts as a ward of certain branches of government, threatening battle when his or her pet projects or bureaucrats are threatened by talk of efficiency.

Consequently, in 1992 the ratio of government workers to employed citizens is higher in America (59 per 1,000) than in the former Soviet Union (58 per 1,000). Congress is the most heavily staffed legislative body in the world, with over 33,000 employees. The three million federal workers comprise what is called the "administrative economy." As with any bureaucracy, its number one goal is to survive and expand. Traditional bureaucrats are not interested in administering themselves out of a job (the pay hikes are not good, but where else could they work?). The Clinton administration is attempting a downsizing of the bureaucracy, trimming 70,000 positions (not in the Department of Defense) by 1996. Some bureaucrats leave federal employment for the other half of the administrative economy, the 3.6 million nonfederal government workers.

Popularists have uncovered a number of astounding lessons from working within the federal bureaucracy. Rule number one: good government managers in the field know how to work around central office control, but mediocre managers need a central office. Rule number two: central office employees may be inefficient and overstaffed, but everyone has a right to a job. Rule number three: a memorandum to a bureaucrat is like sex—it helps to perpetuate the species (of bureaucrats). Rule number four: to paraphrase Grand Gilmore at Yale Law School, in hell there will be nothing but administrative rulings, and due process will be meticulously observed. We need to reduce the layers of bureaucracy. The federal government can do better with fewer employees if we reform civil service, drop unproductive workers, and offer greater monetary reward for exemplary public service. As things stand, we have a sort of Gresham's Law where the worst push out the best. This is in stark contrast to civil service in Japan or Europe. Japanese civil servants are considered to have a higher status than private-sector executives, and if an individual leaves the public sector, this is labeled an "unfortunate descent from heaven."

PRIVATIZATION GAINS A FOOTHOLD

A major reform movement captured by the buzzword "privatization" has taken hold in America. It is irrelevant to study whether the private sector is always more efficient and effective than the public sector. What is important is that competition between the private and public sectors makes government workers improve performance and saves money in the long run. Supporters of the status quo claim that private contracting and open competition will demoralize federal workers. But, does the federal bureaucracy exist to serve the public or to serve the federal workforce? For example, no harm would be done if we were to subject the postal service monopoly to open competition. Doomsdayers predicted that open competition would cause AT&T to disappear in the late 1980s. But AT&T seems to have done better by the public in a more competitive telecommunications marketplace; likewise, the postal service would serve more efficiently and effectively under competitive pressures. Everything from military commissaries to federal prisons function better when turned over to private operators. Private-sector contractors have a better business sense; they know that what you save on capital costs (e.g., drastically cutting cell space per inmate) may be washed out by additional labor costs (hiring more guards to deal with increased violence from overcrowding). Public-sector workers would learn to innovate and operate higher quality service organizations. It does not matter whether private contractors expand to 40 percent of the market; we need their performance as a benchmark to keep public workers from growing complacent.

Privatization may reduce political pressure for inefficient programs. Federal programs rarely dismiss employees with poor performance records or cancel uneconomical services. Privatization can highlight the good deal federal workers have in contrast to the private sector. Federal employee unions are always coming up with studies claiming that they are 10 to 19 percent underpaid. If federal work is so underpaid, why was the voluntary quit rate only 4.1 percent per year from 1991 to 1993, almost 80 percent below the rate in the private sector? A cruel economist would suggest a pay freeze until the quit rate among federal workers in a given employment category reached parity with the private sector. For those with computer skills the wage freeze might last only one year, but other workers would see their wages frozen for many years.

A March 1988 Presidential Commission on Privatization chaired by David Linowes outlined a number of areas for better quality government service at a lower cost. The Democratic Congress has shown no appetite to support federal reform efforts that save money or threaten jobs. Government unions will always fight contract workers. Privatization as a cure to the budget deficit crisis, however, has been oversold. The Grace Commission identified 784 areas for saving (or collecting revenues of) $425 billion over the period 1985–1988. Harvard professor Steven Kelman offers an excellent critique of the 1984 Grace Commission savings estimates in the Winter 1987 issue of *The Public Interest*. For example, he questions the assertion that the federal Government Services Administration (GSA) employs 17 times as many people and spends almost 14 times as much on total management costs compared to private industry. Actual cost savings are probably closer to 10 percent. The Linowes Commission in 1988 managed to reduce the estimates of possible savings. Many skeptics feel these estimates are still high. But every little savings of a few billion dollars will help reduce our deficit problem. For example, our Defense Department spends billions on oversight but few dollars for efficiency. We pay 23,000 auditors in the procurement system to watch the 140,000 government acquisition personnel who issue 30,000 pages of regulation from 76 different government offices. All this to protect us from what?

REPEATED REORGANIZATIONS

One smart decision on the part of the Clinton administration was to avoid the urge to reorganize the federal government. It had been reorganized every four to six years, but the reform always leaves the dead wood untouched. President Johnson's reformation involved adoption of the McNamara concept of Program Planning and Budgeting Systems. President Nixon promoted Management by Objectives, while President Carter introduced the idea of Zero-Based Budgeting for ranking an agency's functions by priority. President Reagan supported privatization and modernization of outdated agency procedures through his Grace Commission (1982–1984) and Linowes Commission (1987–1988). Few innovations are implemented though, because cost reduction and bureaucracy are natural enemies. We may have to pursue radical reform of payment incentives (merit pay), budgetary incentives (dollars saved are not dollars lost for the next year's budget under public enterprise accounting), and the structure of departments. Structural changes may be most disruptive in the Department of Defense, where various groups often seem to place the defense of the nation second, as less important than the budget. When we invaded Grenada the four services communicated ineffectively in 150 different codes. In order to save lives, promote standardization, and budget better in times of limited resources, service distinctions may have to dissolve in the 1990s. We may have to give up some traditions to save our performance capacity. This is certainly better than doing what the British had to do in 1956. A conservative government under Sir Anthony Eden had to cut defense spending and scrap the Suez operation in disgrace because of the precarious indebtedness of the nation. A wasteful government leads to a weak economy, a weaker defense program, and a weak currency.

President Carter promised a reduction in the size of government, then constructed two new departments (energy and education). President Reagan promised to reduce the reach of the federal government, reduce the federal workforce, and abolish Carter's two new departments. Neither department is closed, federal employment increased by 7 percent, and Reagan constructed the 14th cabinet-level department (the Veterans Administration [VA]). Granted, the nation has a duty to veterans and their families, but should we organize our government by special interest constituency and soon have 15 to 20 cabinet-level bureaucratic enclaves? Government should be organized by function, such as health care. The health care needs of aging veterans are not separate from the health care needs of other gray Americans. If we consolidated the federal government by function, we could reduce the number of departments by 40 percent. For example, the Commerce Department could be merged back into the Labor Department (as it was from February 1903 to March 1913). Housing and Urban Development could become part of an expanded Human Services Department. As we trim the Agriculture Department down from its $53 billion peak in 1988, it may not be necessary to have such a department in the 1990s. That department was created in May 1862 when 40 percent of the population was involved in farming. But the department largely serves the rich mega-farms, and it has allowed 350 family farms per day to go out of business during the years 1984–1987. The subsidies are often less than cost-beneficial. In 1987 James Nichols, Commissioner of Agriculture in Minnesota, summarized the irrational nature of federal policymaking: "It is insane to spend $12 billion on corn to subsidize less than $3.6 billion in exports. It would be cheaper to dump the corn in the ocean."

In 1993 some $10 billion of annual farm supports will still be too costly, given that so much of the funding goes to big corporate producers. Farming should be a business, and the price supports should be minimal to help the small farmer weather the extremes of low prices and high supply. Too often Congress creates the problem it is trying to solve; perpetual surpluses are caused by federal price supports that reward farmers for overproducing. In addition to policy proposal no. 7, the farm support system could be scaled down in one additional area. *POLICY PROPOSAL No. 11:* Increase the proportion of each farmer's base acreage ineligible for farm deficiency payments from 15 percent under current law to 35 percent in 1994 (saving $7.2 billion over the years 1994–1997). The average full-time farmer in 1992 was a millionaire with a net worth of $1.3 million. The Department of Agriculture employs 101,000 bureaucrats to study 390,000 farmers and perform other duties. Some 24,000 of these bureaucrats might do good things like study trees for our Forest Service. But it would be difficult to argue that a cost reduction of 10 percent per year over four years in bureaucratic overhead would harm the national interest or hurt a single family farmer.

CAN A BUREAUCRACY HAVE PRIDE AND EFFICIENCY?

In Great Britain the slogan is, "The best shall serve the state." However, in America young people avoid a civil service that rewards longevity, incompetence, and size. Merit pay should not be limited to an executive corps of 2,200 senior civil servants. Automatic longevity raises should be replaced by an incentive pay system that rewards cost reduction and allows middle managers the leeway to manage. Federal managers and all employees should be stimulated to act as entrepreneurs and bring forth suggestions that change the standard operating procedure for the better. Major reductions should be made in the huge quantity of useless regulations that seek to guarantee "accountability" by substituting decree for thoughtfulness. Each decree is typically evaded at will, but the paperwork may waste 30 to 40 percent of the work week and hurt employee morale. For example, a biomedical researcher at the National Institutes of Health (NIH) should not have to spend 12 hours writing a justification for why an AIDS researcher should want to attend an AIDS conference. Such nonsense does not exist in the private sector. Yet the dead-wood, ossified thinkers with the longest tenure frustrate the reform movement. One health worker's bumper sticker sums up the issue: "Age and Treachery Will Always Overcome Youth and Skill."

In 1989 Paul Volcker, former Federal Reserve chairman, chaired a blue ribbon committee that suggested ways to improve the civil service and reform the petrified procedures of government. The report argues that to settle for mediocrity in our public services will, in time, become an invitation to mediocrity in all sectors of the economy. A climate of mistrust leads to many problems within the bureaucracy. Conflict often exists between political appointees and career civil servants. The conflict becomes dysfunctional when the political appointees subscribe to the sneak approach: never allowing the career types to have enough of the pieces to learn the entire picture of the policy being developed. This jigsaw puzzle philosophy of bureaucratic management treats people like mushrooms: keep them in the dark, feed them manure, and when they stick their heads up, slice them off. Poor morale, anonymity, and useless procedural red tape are not the only problems with the federal bureaucracy. If a branch of government appears tangled and inefficient, blame may often reside with Congress. For example, Congress passed the Sustained-Yield Act and the Multiple-Use Act for the Forest Service without fully superseding earlier laws, leaving the bureaucracy to implement conflicting objectives. Consider the newest cabinet bureaucracy, the Veterans Administration. The VA is micromanaged by members of Congress. The VA must go to congressional VA committees for many routine decisions. In a rational world we would consolidate and close many of the 120 smallest VA hospitals, the 130 military hospitals, and 350 military outpatient facilities. We cannot afford to deploy federal health resources irrespective of financial concerns. In February 1989, the Disabled American Veterans called for a fundamental sharing of facilities that would offer good economics and good medicine. The entrenched bureaucracy needs to follow such market signals and gear up for an era of limited resources. In 1992, however, veterans groups successfully lobbied the president to stop the opening of two VA hospitals to nonveteran patients. *POLICY PROPOSAL No. 12:* To promote efficient management, require that the VA system utilize the same hospital payment system and same fee schedule as Medicare, saving a minimum of $2.2 billion over the period 1994–1997. The savings would be higher if the VA can cut down on the $2 billion of unnecessary VA inpatient days (U.S. Congressional Budget Office 1993).

DECREASE SPENDING AND ENTITLEMENT PROGRAMS

In 1984 R. J. Grace, head of the Grace Commission, spent his own money to advertise the deficit crisis with a television commercial of a baby crying. The baby had just been informed that a $50,000 mortgage had already been entered on his balance sheet because the federal deficit must be paid. No American likes the idea of a deadbeat federal government presenting our children with such a bill. A corollary to this credit card ethic is to assist the nonpoor and claim it is for the good of the poor. Consider a case example for a service most Americans support, day care. The Child Care Tax Credit gives $1 to the poor for every $10 we give to the rich and the middle class. In 1992, less than 10.4 percent of tax benefits went to families with adjusted gross incomes below $18,000. The nation needs to better target taxing and spending policies. We could place an income cap on the credit and cut out 89 percent of the expenditures. We could use that savings to double expenditures on day care, child care, and health care for the poor. The Medicaid transition benefit could be made more generous so that welfare mothers would not be discouraged from working.

Government functions best for the benefit of the middle class. We let the Federal Electrification Administration subsidize telephone and electric services to such "ghetto" areas as Hawaii and Hilton Head Island. Our politicians are two-faced and want to slide home some social spending and tax relief to the nonpoor (a large proportion of which return the quid pro quo with campaign contributions).

Americans have always been willing to use government as a means to their own personal ends. The 1986 Nobel Prize winner in economics, James Buchanan, argues in his theory of public choice that the difference between politics and commerce does not lie in the values that individuals pursue, but in the conditions of exchange. Politics is simply a structure of more complex trades. Economists can assist special interests in lobbying for their particular pork programs, or help in the continuing search for rules of the political game that will best serve the national interest. A pessimist would conclude that this second task may prove impossible. As some politicians have matured (e.g., Goldwater, Kennedy, Long), they hold out hope that the public conception of the federal role can prove superior in wisdom to a collection of selfish special interest groups. Mature politicians learn to turn a deaf ear to self-serving special interests.

SELECTIVE COSTS OR SPENDING FREEZE?

Over 82 percent of the public may favor the idea of a balanced federal budget (through saving their own programs and cutting the other guy's funding), but a balanced-budget constitutional amendment stands little chance of passage in the 1990s. Perhaps the political will does not exist to cut various government programs by varying amounts, in which case a two-year freeze on spending and a national spirit of sacrifice in times of crisis might be our only hope to get the federal deficit down to under $60 billion, or one percent of the GNP. We could call this goal of a deficit equal to one percent of the GNP a near-balanced budget (NBB). We might achieve this goal by an across-the-board spending freeze or a flexible freeze on certain programs.

The more programs exempt from the freeze, the longer the duration of the freeze to achieve an NBB. This poses problems. Should we exempt housing or education from the freeze? Each special interest will lobby to remain exempt, often citing the special interest credo of the late Congressman Claude Pepper (D–Fla.): "No American will go bankrupt financing our program, but most Americans will continue to face moral or economic bankruptcy without ——. For those of us who are moral, do expand government and raise taxes" (U.S. House speech, July 24, 1987).

Even after passing an NBB, we would still be left with a $4.4 trillion total federal debt. There are only three things we can leave our children: roots, vision, and monetary endowment. In the current situation, our endowment may be credit card bills totalling more than $50,000 per American by the year 2000. One obvious first step seems to involve taking away Uncle Sam's credit limit. The credit card analogy may help to explain the federal deficit problem as well as it helped explain the New York City financial crunch of the mid-1970s. The public has a commonsense understanding that there is a cliff out there, and if total debt grows beyond 60 to 70 percent of annual income, even if annual debt service is only 20 percent of annual spending, insolvency threatens. We must retire the expensive Claude Pepper school of political spending, appeal to our better instincts, and participate equally in shared sacrifice.

THE COLA WARS—TRIMMING GENEROSITY TO
THE RICH

The federal government is now hostage to special interest groups. Because of our high deficits, national economic growth has been needlessly slow. Taxes need not be raised as much as they should be redistributed. Taxes should be higher on alcohol and tobacco and $1 higher in income tax for every $1 tax reduction in Social Security. Economists have done a poor job of explaining the rationale for this last policy prescription in the context of general equilibrium models. The essential point of such models, as advanced by Boston University economist Larry Kotlikoff (1989) and others, is that the excessive building up of Social Security trust funds and program benefits robs a younger generation to benefit the current older generation. Our government has expanded the consumption opportunities of a generation born in the 1920s and 1930s so that we can undereducate, underfeed, and poorly house the generations born in the 1970s, 1980s, and 1990s.

The American economy is strong enough to devote some of its wealth to cushioning the fall of the frail, the sick, and the elderly. The question is not whether compassion and generosity will die; the question is how much generosity is needed. Many young people attack Social Security with a rhetoric that suggests the elderly have the "audacity" to live above the poverty level. Many elderly work and draw income from investments. The inflation adjustments for pensions are too generous (unneeded) for the rich elderly. If we trim the inflation adjustment by 2 percentage points for an elderly woman living $700 above the poverty line, compounded over five years (1993–1997), we will have clipped 15.3 percent of her income. But if we pursue the same policy for an elderly woman earning $50,000 per year, we will clip but 1.9 percent of her income. Cost of living adjustments (COLA) should be higher for those with total annual incomes under $10,000. There is a disproportionate number of near-poor elderly: 8.3 percent of the elderly have incomes less than 25 percent above the federal poverty threshold, in contrast to 5.1 percent of the nonelderly. Resources can be conserved without scalping the frail elderly or the truly needy. We should not set the COLA equal to zero percent. To freeze the budget by a total withholding of the COLA would push 340,000 elderly below the poverty line in 1993.

This section will review the current struggle to restrain COLAs as a case example of how difficult it is to fight off a politically powerful special interest. The elderly represent the colossus of special interest. The issue is not pork spending; the issue is excessive generosity. Even after the buildup in education and medical services to children, we still spend tenfold as much federal resources on the elderly per capita (with insufficient help for the frail elderly). Old-line members of Congress are biased against children. Education and health care for children are not properly called "investments"; instead they are labeled "discretionary spending." All programs for the elderly are called "entitlements." The generosity bias in favor of the elderly crept up on social policymakers through the mechanism by which we annually inflate pensions. Congress started automatic COLAs for Social Security in 1972 and federal pensions in 1962. The problem with COLAs is not that they insulate the poor elderly from inflation, but that they overpay the rich elderly and add up (through the miracle of compound interest) to a huge sum of money. Limiting the COLA for the nonpoor elderly to 70 percent of the inflation rate (label it a diet COLA), and raising the COLA for the poor elderly to 120 percent of the price index (cost: $3 billion) would save $33 billion over the period 1993–2008. It is surprising that democratic politicians do not support such a policy with a 1918 precedent. In 1918 the Shipbuilding Labor Adjustment Board awarded a decent COLA to workers on the condition that the full amount be given only to the lowest income individuals.

Can we have the rate of growth in pension benefits more than keep pace with our inflation rate (or the average standard of living), while the employed do not keep pace with inflation (because they are paying so much in taxes)? For example, the young may have to sacrifice the ability to buy a home. According to 1990 Census Bureau data, 36 percent of those aged 25 to 29 owned their home, and 65 percent of those aged 35 to 49 owned their home. Such figures may be cut in half over the next 15 years as the Social Security tax rates increase, the economy deteriorates, and more income must be dedicated to pay for the cost of food and education. Home ownership may become the dream deferred, or the dream eliminated, as Social Security tax rates rise into the 18 percent zone (9 percent from the employee and 9 percent from the employer).

A higher percentage of voters are elderly and rationalize their calls for higher inflation adjustments with the logic, "We paid for it, we deserve it." The federal bureaucracy offers sponge-like resistance against the development of a uniform social definition of "it." Should the elderly be informed of the fact that their tax payments were invested in overgenerous payments to past pensioners, so that the only way we can offer any COLA above a zero percent inflation adjustment is through overtaxing the young? Our children have neither the privilege not the political power to choose. Such unintended generational conflict is another classic example of what Representative Richard Armey (R–Tex.) calls the "invisible foot of government."

The conservative opportunity society of Republican presidential candidate Jack Kemp proclaims economic growth and lower taxes as a surefire solution to financing generous pensions for the elderly. This is in stark contrast to financial conservatives, who offer what voters reject as "root canal economics" or the "politics of pain." A better label might be "paying the bills," rather than shoplifting the future of our children. Behind this policy proposal is the ethic of sharing: we are all in the same boat. Why should the elderly live untouchable and risk-free, when the working class sees its standard of living erode 2 to 3 points per year?

TRICKLE-DOWN LIBERALISM: THE WORST FORM OF OPPORTUNISM

In the 1950s Eisenhower conservatives were roundly criticized for trickle-down economics, the idea that if we assist big business and rich corporations the wealth will trickle-down to the poor. Some wags such as John Kenneth Galbraith suggested that the trickle-down was a yellow liquid filtered through the kidneys of the rich, or the solid droppings left by the rich for the poor birds. However, the real danger was trickle-down liberalism. Start a program in the name of helping the poor, but focus most of the dollars on the middle class and the rich. For example, tax subsidies for child care do not go to the poor: 92 percent go to the rich and the middle class. Only 19 percent of Social Security and Medicare dollars go to benefit the poor. We must means-test more federal programs so all the expenditures are not trickled-up to the nonpoor. A number of federal programs are means-tested, where eligibility depends on income—Medicaid, food stamps, Supplemental Security Income, homeless aid, and aid to families with dependent children. These programs will add up to only $61 billion in 1993. Four programs adding up to $452 billion are not currently means tested: Social Security, civil service retirement, military retirement, and Medicare.

Some responsible Democrats may rally against a proposal to means-test the sacred entitlement programs. They will argue that society does not means-test public works, public forests, or public education. Their ethic is simple: resources are not scarce, everyone pays and everyone deserves to receive a pension check or Medicare card. Unfortunately, resources are scarce, and the federal government must remodel or flounder. Worthy programs for the nonelderly sick and hungry are seriously crimped so that non–means-tested programs can exhibit excessive generosity to those least in need. This is the essence of trickle-down liberalism: the money flows up to those not in need. We forego prenatal care for poor mothers to make the inflation adjustment 3 percent for all. The nonpoor should receive less in order to assist the poor, for instance, offer a 4.2 percent adjustment for the poor retiree and 2.8 percent for the nonpoor pensioner. To means-test the inflation adjustment is much less constrictive on the nonpoor elderly than actually eliminating total eligibility to the pension or Medicare program. It also incorporates some of the casino nature of the American economy into these social programs. For example, if two men start receiving a military pension at age 50, and one falls on economic hard times while the other has a thriving management consulting business, who should get the bigger COLA? Inflation adjustments could be more generous than the inflation rate (1.2 percent of the full COLA rate) for those who have fallen on hard times. If we do not restructure COLAs, the day will come when all COLAs are eliminated or severely restricted. We must act now or face a much more painful price in the future.

BEWARE OF BACKDOOR SPENDING

The federal deficit crisis makes new spending programs or subsidies more difficult to maneuver through Congress. Those interested in expanding the federal government off-budget have come up with two backdoor strategies. Strategy number one is to focus benefits on a selected constituency (e.g., textile workers) while spreading costs across the total population. Off-budget legislative schemes are a contraption for shrouding the source of "big brother" involvement in society. The costs are not collected by a tax man; they are collected in the higher prices we pay for goods and services. For example, placing import restrictions on textiles results in the general population paying more for clothing.

The second backdoor spending strategy involves earmarking specific new taxes for specific beneficiary groups. Earmarking a tax for home health care is dangerous in a number of ways. It may insulate a specific program from necessary cost-containment efforts. Defenders of the program will argue that Congress cannot cut this program because it has its own tax (e.g., a highway program with its own highway tax to finance it). Every interest group is fighting to get its own federal tax to expand service. The weak, lacking any lobby in Washington, will suffer under the competitive climate (e.g., housing for the homeless or prenatal care for the working poor).

Before outlining one case example of a backdoor tax for a new program (catastrophic health insurance passed in 1988), consider the public finance professor's rationale for passing a specific tax for specific programs. In theory it seems to make sense to link sources of funds and public expenditures. By linking the function to the resource tax, one can track the fund's flow. In the workday jargon of economics, one can observe how different constraints on resources can cause different shadow prices on income received from different sources (user fees, general revenues, specific target group taxes). This can lead to better allocation of resources and selection of appropriate user fees. In practice, the shadow price studies seldom lead to congressional action, and we see a tax system growing more complex. The 1988 catastrophic insurance bill imposed dozens of new tax brackets on the elderly, compared to two new brackets for the nonelderly. For the nonpoor, working pensioners in the middle class, the tax would have been raised from 15 percent to 21.8 percent (catastrophic tax assessed above $6,000, rising to a maximum additional tax in excess of $750 in 1990 for individuals and $1,500 for couples). A millionaire would pay the same tax as a single retiree with an income of $18,000; yet which individual views this new tax as a household catastrophe? Repeal of the program in 1989 was good for the elderly with above-average incomes but not for the 48,000 elderly impoverished annually by huge medical bills.

LESSONS ON NICE IMAGES FOR TAXATION

Would the public buy a large tax increase? The public seems much more willing to go along with a tax increase if the political leader totally dislikes the philosophy of "tax and spend." Mondale loved to tax and got beat in 1984. President Reagan accepted five tax increases after 1981 that in total erased 106 percent of the $1.57 trillion benefit of his 1981 tax cut. But Reagan hated to tax us, so the public loved him. Margaret Thatcher was smart enough to play this game even more effectively in Great Britain. She preserved her antitax image while hiking the 1979 tax burden (34 percent of the GNP) to 41 percent of the GNP in 1991. Indeed, the British government managed a $19 billion surplus in 1988. By producing a tough deficit elimination program Thatcher allowed the national bank to pursue an expansionary monetary policy. The British experience may not readily translate to a different time and place. Medicine and macroeconomics are two professions perpetually translating between the particular example and the global truth. Thatcher repealed the long-standing policy of punishing the productive and decreased the top tax rate from 98 to 40 percent. Britain now has a two-bracket income tax system of 25 and 40 percent.

Thatcher fondly refers to her housewife theory of economics by suggesting that nations should mirror the homemaker as an economic manager and never spend more than what is on hand. However, Thatcher also implemented substantial spending cuts. Thatcher's simple theory seems more honest than the liberal theory the author learned in a class in 1970 with Professor Paul A. Samuelson. Samuelson suggested that great nations need not come close to balancing the books except in the long run. Such a banal generality may have worked when deficits were low, such as when a nation was at war or when interest rates were 1 percent, as in 1946, but not today.

Liberal economists would profit from reading Alexander Hamilton's 1790 "Report on the Public Credit" to Congress. As secretary of the Treasury, Hamilton argued that in time of peace, when the economy is not in a depression, the federal budget should be experiencing a surplus. Americans should ask, what do we do when deficits are 15 percent of spending and the politicians feel free to spend on the national credit card and never pay the bill?

Congress has become so dependent on inaccuracy, through accounting gimmicks to meet budget targets, that we have lost perspective on this issue. In 1987, Representative Joseph DiGuardi (R–N.Y.) introduced legislation that would require the IRS to mail out a taxpayer credit card statement for the United States. What would the public say if they now realized their federal credit card bill grows $2,500 per year? The news is not good if our incomes grow $1,000 per taxpayer per year. If we raise taxes to recoup that $2,500 per taxpayer per year, economic growth will stall (or decline) and personal income will fall further behind. Deficit reduction might best be accomplished if 80 percent of the reduction is a spending freeze and only 20 percent is through a tax increase (including higher oil import fees and "sin" taxes on alcohol and tobacco). Taxes should not be directed at curtailing already insufficient rates of savings and investment; rather, taxes should be directed at consumption. Double negatives are usually in bad form, but Americans do not have an insufficient rate of consumption.

MANAGING FEDERAL PROGRAMS

Federal finances are neatly summarized by the old lyric: "another year older and deeper in debt." Professional pundits blame the unabated growth in federal deficits for the uncertain economic and social outlook of the public. In reality, the deficits are a symptom of our uncertainty, not the root cause. Not making choices when faced with limited resources is the etiology of our deficits. Americans are undecided about specific cuts in government, even if they in general think that government is very wasteful. In many areas we support substantial increases in spending: NASA, education, medical care. The idea that we can preserve a generous social contract with the aged and the poor, not raise taxes, fund new pork projects, and not raise taxes is hogwash.

The types of leaders we need are not those who promise quick-fix solutions through perseverance in special interest politics (the biggest special interest being the "we don't like to pay the bills" lobby for no new taxes and free lunches). We need the intelligence and courage to present the federal deficit's stern, but appropriate surrender terms: $10 to $30 billion of new consumption taxes, a totally "porkless" federal diet (which may save "only" $7 to $9 billion per year), a renegotiated social contract with the rich elderly (tax or reduce their Social Security benefits), a 10 percent cut in bureaucratic overhead in the greater Washington area ($8 billion potential savings), and an overhaul and trim of military retirement and civil service pensions by 6 to 8 percent (to save $3 to $4 billion and assure that the income of the retired does not outstrip the earnings of the employed). Congress favors doing economic damage to the worker and making the pensioner richer. A $10,000 salary earned in 1967 by a GS-9 employee had deteriorated by 1992 to $8,084 adjusted for inflation, but a $10,000 pension in 1967 had grown to $11,185 by 1992.

A very large problem like the deficit will require a series of major changes in federal taxing and spending. The 1990s should eschew the puritan rhetoric of binge-and-punishment and trim the annual deficit to below 1 percent of the GNP. This goal may be as critical to the economy in the 1990s as our primary achievement of the 1980s, the abolition of the Phillips curve. Prior to 1981, many economists postulated an inexorable link between the inflation rate and the employment rate, the Phillips curve (1959). Presidents Johnson, Nixon, Ford, and Carter suggested that you could not help one number without hurting the other. While the sum of the two rates (the misery index) equaled 20 percent in the Carter years, President Reagan was able to improve both numbers at once (and get the total down to the 7 to 9 percent range), thus eliminating that principle.

SPECIAL INTEREST GROUP NO. 1:
THE AVERAGE FAMILY

One of the biggest special interest groups is the middle class. The middle class is composed of individuals with two conflicting value systems. They value individualistic capitalism when their tax rates are reduced and their employer stays in business. However, as Olson (1971) indicates, the middle class likes collective action as long as the government keeps collective welfare as the paramount concern. It is easier to get $20 billion of tax subsidy for the middle class than $200 million of aid for the homeless. Self-interest dominates American politics. The middle class has the education and experience to fight for home ownership deductions or day-care tax benefits. Day-care subsidy for all is a laudable goal. However, in a world of limited resources, advocates for the poor and disabled have to take a backseat to laudable, discretionary subsidies (with an inferior cost-benefit ratio). It does not seem fair that necessities are underfinanced so that middle class claimants can be overfinanced. But the middle class is better organized and always willing to find a program that in the name of helping the poor allows the average family to help itself. One reviewer of this book suggested that

that gives the middle class pride to say that it finally got something out of its taxes, "rather than wasting my tax dollar on the poor and needy." Some Democrats emphasize "investing in human capital," a less uplifting version of the "putting people first" slogan Bill Clinton used in the 1992 election.

American public opinion concerning the poor operates in two different directions: offer reasonable assistance for the needy, but hold deep resentment toward those "other people" ("welfare cheats," "welfare queens"). We have two basic forms of assistance: teach the poor to earn (through education and on the job training) or give them other people's money. Over 14 million mothers and children are enrolled in the Aid to Families with Dependent Children (AFDC) program, at an annual expense of $30 billion for federal and state governments. Welfare spending (AFDC) will represent only 3.5 percent of total state spending in 1993 (up from 3.3 percent in 1990). Many citizens have a vindictive spirit against that Great Society program for "welfare queens." Actually, AFDC is not a Great Society program (it was started in 1935 to assist widows in the Depression). To improve welfare incentives in the 1990s, Isabel Sawhill of the Urban Institute suggested the Do-The-Right-Thing Voucher program to provide an individual training account of $10,000 that low-income youths could draw on, once they complete high school, for additional education, training, or relocation to accept employment. Such vouchers may make workfare a trampoline rather than a soft sofa and may help prevent poverty in the long run. In the short term, we should trim paperwork complexity and waste by *POLICY PROPOSAL No. 13:* Combine funding to states for welfare (AFDC), Medicaid, and food stamps into a single indexed grant, saving $5.7 billion over the period 1994–1997, according to the Congressional Budget Office.

RECASTING GOVERNMENT: WITH SOUL AND COMMON SENSE

Behind closed doors, congressional conferees make no accommodations for foreign concepts, like the national interest not to waste money. Unfortunately, the "good old boy" tendency to trivialize the damage of deficit spending or alcoholism (or nuclear power plant leaks or termites on the front porch) becomes pathological over time.

How could we change our system of electing members of Congress so as to minimize the link between pork barrel local spending and reelection? *POLICY PROPOSAL No. 14:* Break the link between waste promotion (burning taxpayer funds) and getting reelected through public financing of elections. For example, if an elected member of Congress promoted programs that failed a basic cost-benefit criteria (wasted funds), he or she would be ineligible to be funded for reelection. However, the drastic alternative, to move Congress to the tight parliamentary system, with less possibility for local pork spending (consider the English and Israeli parliaments' heightened concern for the nation interest), offers a big solution to an equally big problem. One member of Congress put the perverse incentives of a locally elected Congress in perspective:

If I am concerned, and spend my time on the ozone, or public health, or debt relief, I will not get reelected. But if I help the local jobs with this $39 million contract, and this big unnecessary water project, my people will reelect me. I wish I could spend fivefold more time on serving the American people. Problems of deficits and foreign competition are real, but I am stuck always raising money for my next election, or my party members' next election. (1991)

Tactical short-term issues of the next election dominate congressional thinking, while strategic future decisions of national importance often seem in a state of paralysis. Special interest groups are expert at presenting future-averting spending options: spend more, make more friends, and do it all with borrowed money. Ignore federal debt levels (and corporate debt levels). Now our problems cannot be ignored. The solution will require neither ruthlessness nor magic to reduce the budget deficit problem to below 1 percent of the GNP. The one element that is necessary, however, is political courage. A new generation of politicians must do the tough job of telling voters that they cannot have everything they want and that they must pay for everything they previously received. Social and defense commitments must be brought in line with capabilities, and collective goals must be in proportion to collective resources.

Our national politicians do not like to trim revenues earmarked for special interest groups. Special interest as a national vice is deplored in speech after speech but rewarded in the backroom and through the process of continuous reelection. President Clinton promotes the notion that the government's duty is to provide opportunity and that individuals must in return take responsibility through workfare. The "overclass" also need a lesson in frugal responsibility each time they ask for a new benefit or adjustment. Ross Perot did little to erode the power of rich special interest. He never did have success utilizing the power of cash (his) to reduce the power of cash (special interest "gifts").

Government can help the poor in three basic ways: (1) through investment in "human capital"—education, Head Start, and nutrition programs; (2) through cash payments like AFDC; and (3) through the tax system. The importance of the second method is often overstated, while the third method is frequently overlooked. AFDC payments ballooned to a peak of

$168 per recipient per month in constant (inflation-adjusted 1964) dollars in fiscal year 1969. AFDC payments in constant dollars declined to $159 under President Carter in 1980. AFDC monthly payments per recipient continued to decline to $148 under President Reagan in 1985 and $130 under President Clinton in 1993. Is this cruel rollback in AFDC funding orchestrated by both Democrats and Republicans? No. The declines in AFDC payments are largely a statistical artifact of the increased eligibility of children in larger families. The proportion of children under 18 receiving AFDC benefits increased 55 percent from 1965 to 1970 and increased an additional 34 percent from 1970 to 1992.

It must be difficult for liberals to come to the realization that growth in the general economy does more to reduce children living in poverty than AFDC payments. In the five years prior to initiating the Great Society programs that supplement AFDC, the child poverty rate declined from 26.6 percent in 1960 to 20.7 percent in 1965. The black child poverty rate was reduced by one-third, as the GNP grew 4.6 per annum over the 1960–1965 period. How much has the child poverty rate declined from 1966 to 1992? The percentage of children living below the federal poverty rate declined from 20.5 percent to 18.7 percent in those 26 years. What public policy investment might have been more effective in helping children, holding families together (so they don't break up to attain AFDC eligibility)? The 1991 Rockefeller Commission on Children indicated that dependent exemption sheltered 26.5 percent of a median family's income in 1960. In 1993 the comparable figure is only 10.8 percent. *POLICY PROPOSAL No. 15:* Change the tax laws so the full value of the child tax exemption can be restored to inflation-adjusted 1960 levels. This tax subsidy of $920 per child in 1995 would be administratively simple, it would be pro-family, and it would reduce the reliance on greedy welfare rights bureaucrats. Such bureaucrats care about defending their jobs and defending the "right" of the poor to stay poor. The time has come for Congress to help the poor by re-creating a fair child tax exemption and by investing more in education and nutritional programs. The 1993 budget deal, with the earned income credit, makes strides in this direction. More changes in tax policy will be suggested in chapter 3.

REFERENCES

Berstein, M. (1955). *Regulating Business by Independent Commissions*. Princeton, NJ: Princeton University Press.

Besley, T., and Coate, S. (1992). "Workfare versus Welfare: Incentive Arguments for Work Requirements in Poverty-Alleviation Programs," *American Economic Review* 82:1, March, 249–61.

Boardman, A., Vining, A., and Waters, W. (1993). "Cost and Benefits through Bureaucratic Lenses: Case of Highway Projects," *Journal of Policy Analysis & Management* 14:3, Summer, 532–54.

Carson, R., and Thomas, W. (1993). *The American Economy*. New York: Macmillan.

Carter, J., and Schap, D. (1990). "Line-Item Veto: Where Is Thy Sting?" *Journal of Economic Perspectives* 4:2, Spring, 103–18.

Eastaugh, S. (1992). *Health Economics: Efficiency, Quality, and Equity*. Westport, CT: Auburn House.

Ehrenhalt, A. (1991). *The United States of Ambition*. New York: Random House.

Fitzgerald, E. (1989). *The Pentagonists*. Boston: Houghton Mifflin.

Funiciello, T. (1993). *Tyranny of Kindness: Dismantling the Welfare System to End Poverty in America*. New York: Atlantic Monthly Press.

Galbraith, J. (1992). *The Culture of Contentment*. Boston: Houghton Mifflin.

Gross, M. (1992). *The Government Racket: Washington Waste from A to Z*. New York: Bantam Books.

Gueron, J. (1993). "Report of the Manpower Demonstration Research Corporation [MDRC] of New York." New York: MDRC.

Hahn, F. (1993). *Economic Analysis of Markets and Games*. Cambridge: MIT Press.

Hardin, G. (1968). "Tragedy of the Commons," *Science* 162:13, December, 1243–48.

Heilbroner, R., and Bernstein, P. (1989). *The Debt and the Deficit: False Alarms/Real Possibilities*. New York: Norton.

Jackson, B. (1988). *Honest Graft*. New York: Knopf.

Kotlikoff, L. (1989). *Dynamic Fiscal Policy*. New York: Cambridge University Press.

Kotz, N. (1988). *Wild Blue Yonder: Money, Politics and the B-1 Bomber*. New York: Pantheon.

Lowi, T. (1964). "American Business, Public Policy, Case Studies and Political Theory," *World Politics* 16:4, July, 677–715.

Markusen, A., and Yudken, J. (1992). *Dismantling the Cold War Economy*. New York: Basic Books.

National Research Council (U.S.). (1977). *Health Care for American Veterans*. Washington, DC: National Academy of Sciences Press.

Olson, M. (1971). *The Logic of Collective Action*. Cambridge: Harvard University Press.

Payne, J. (1993). *Costly Returns: Burdens of the U.S. Tax System*. San Francisco: ICS Press.

Phillips, A. (1959). "The Relation between Unemployment and the Rate of Change of Money Wage Rates in the United Kingdom, 1861–1957," *Economica* 25:11, November, 283–99.

Rivlin, A. (1992). *Reviving the American Dream*. Washington, DC: Brookings.

Schultze, C. (1992). *Memos to the President: A Guide through Macroeconomics for the Busy Policymaker*. Washington, DC: Brookings.

Spiller, P. (1988). "Politicians, Interest Groups, and Regulators: A Multiple-Principals Agency Theory of Regulation (Let Them Be Bribed)," Hoover Institution, Stanford University, June, working paper E-88-12/3.

Stern, P. (1988). *The Best Congress Money Can Buy*. New York: Pantheon.

Summers, L. (1990). *Understanding Unemployment*. Cambridge: MIT Press.

Truman, D. (1951). *The Governmental Process: Political Interest and Public Opinion.* New York: Knopf.

Tyler, P. (1986). *Running Critical.* New York: Harper and Row.

U.S. Congressional Budget Office. (1993). *Reducing the Deficit: Spending and Revenue Options.* Washington, DC: U.S. Government Printing Office.

U.S. Department of Commerce, Bureau of Economic Analysis. (1993). *Handbook of Cyclical Indicators.* Washington, DC: U.S. Government Printing Office.

Will, G. (1992). *Restoration: Congress, Term Limits and the Recovery of Deliberative Democracy.* New York: Free Press.

3

Tax Policy and Sharing the Burden: Incentives and Alternatives for the Future

The federal tax code is now longer than the Bible, and more people are paid to cope with its intricacies than to teach high school English. The code needs simplification and less inequity and inefficiency.
—Senator Bill Bradley (D–N.J.), 1990

We must change from a tax and spend party, and go for investment and growth.
—Barbara Jordan, 1992

All important economic decisions are based on expectations. What matters for current actions—investment, saving, the choice of jobs—is not the current tax rates but the rates that are expected.
—Martin Feldstein, 1988

Laws are like sausages. It is better not to see them being made.
—Otto Von Bismarck, 1888

The rejected Clinton reform plan for capital gains taxation suffered from one obvious weakness. Lower taxes on gains for new investments would stimulate less real economic growth and more lawyers and paperwork subdividing existing companies into new businesses with "new investments." If achieving the Clinton goal of targeting new investment only is impossible to achieve, the Bush goal of one-third capital gains exclusion is a two-edged sword at best. One can achieve the Bush goal of excluding one-third of capital gains by either trimming capital gains tax rates to 17 percent or, following the democratic plan, raise income tax rates to 36 percent and 39.5 percent for the superrich. The unforeseen effect of taking this second option in fiscal year 1994 is that it has produced the rebirth of 1985-style tax shelters, where American society wastes time and resources on paperwork

Table 3.1
Trends in Real Interest Rates, Business Investment, and Savings among Four Nations, 1988–1992

	USA	FRANCE	GERMANY	JAPAN
1. **Real long-term interest rate (1988-1992)**	2.8%	4.7%	5.1%	0.4%
2. **Net business fixed investment as a percentage of business sector value-added (OECD, 1988-1992)**	6.4%	6.5%	7.9%	13.6%
3. **Net national savings ratio (Net savings as a percentage of GNP, 1988-1992)**	3.6%	8.4%	10.8%	15.4%

Source: OECD, Organization for Economic Cooperation and Development, Economic Studies, Paris.

so that investment capital will chase the best tax loopholes. Loophole-itis is a disease that was stamped out by tax reform in 1986, largely reborn by Congress in 1993, and in need of eradication by reinvention of the fairness and equal tax rate doctrine in the near future. If our federal government were a public corporation the voters might retire Congress for reinventing the tax avoidance schemes of unnecessary lawyers and accountants. Each profession often argues that theirs is the oldest. The accountant argues that "the Good Book says that in the beginning, before chaos, was the word, the law. So tax accountants clearly came first to establish commerce." But the churlish tax lawyer responds: "And who do you think created the chaos?"

A number of former liberals have come to the realization that creating a better economy is more vital than creating entitlements. Conservatives like Massachusetts Governor William Weld are coming to the realization that reducing income polarization, the gap between the rich and survival-wage citizens, is vital to our standard of living. Fair taxation of individuals and corporations is not an easily defined concept. For example, while the number of corporations paying no taxes to the federal government has been substantially reduced since the 1986 Tax Reform Act, a number of corporations involved in leveraged buy-outs pay no taxes for years because interest expense on their inflated corporate debt is deductible. When the public reads of some billionaire paying minimal tax rates it does damage to the cherished ideal of equal sacrifice (Kaus, 1992). However, equal sacrifice need not equate with equal rates of taxation. Public policy may highly tax certain activities (e.g., pollution) and undertax certain nation-building activities (e.g., housing, education).

The tax code largely guides the allocation of capital in every nation. The incentives drive investment decisions, but the fund flows need not be controlled by government. The American tax code has onerous reporting requirements and minimum government control of private fund flows. The tax system helps stimulate the American spirit of giving. American private giving as a share of national income increased 58 percent from 1980 to 1992 in comparison to the 1955 to 1979 period. Contrary to the assertion of some liberal Democrats, a "gale of greed" was never the diagnosis appropriate for the American people. However, the American people do have two other problems: capital formation is at a rate less than in countries like Japan and Germany (see Table 3.1, line 2), and the savings rate has declined dramatically (line 3). The shortage of savings is created, in part, because the national budget deficit absorbs 80 percent of savings. We will analyze these problems and their etiology in the tax code in future sections of this chapter.

To give the reader a brief overview, consider that in 1992 federal revenue sources came: 39 percent from personal income taxes, 36 percent from social insurance (e.g., Social Security, military pensions), 11.7 percent from corporate income taxes, 5.1 percent from excise taxes and other user fees, and 8.4 percent from borrowing. Borrowing represented 8.4 percent of revenues but 15.9 percent of expenses (because we must pay the service on our $4.4 trillion national debt).

Before surveying recent history, the reader should reflect on two political propositions that were "dogma" from 1915 to 1976. Republicans favored tax hikes to combat unemployment, and Democrats were the party of big deficits. Republican President Hoover favored taxation over borrowing based on the conventional wisdom of the 1920s that borrowing would compete with private investments for scarce capital and hence be deflationary. Fears of deflation and unemployment are not major policy concerns today. Old-style (pre-Reagan) conservatives support deficits (if the president is Republican) because they reduce the public pain of taxes. Reagan conservatives like deficits only to the degree that fear of tax hikes restrains the growth of big government. Big government can get bigger if it is not constrained by fiscal limits. Thus, Republicans maintain that a fear of big deficits is an effective brake on government growth.

THE MYTH OF TAX CUTS AND REFORMATION

Reagan conservatives desire a tax code with less administrative burden and lower taxes. Their goal is a smaller, less intrusive federal government.

Liberals desire maximal accountability and ever-increasing engagement of government in the problems of society. Because builders (liberals) tend to dominate conservatives in Congress, taxes are a higher proportion of the American GNP in 1993 in contrast to 1980. There is a very basic tax creation cycle: tax, spend, borrow, and tax more. Since Congress started income taxation in 1914, the process of raising revenues has become the art of plucking the most amount of goose feathers with the least amount of squawking. When Louis XIV's finance minister, Colbert, coined this phrase, few citizens paid taxes. Only Americans earning 5 to 6 times the national average for white males paid any income taxes from 1914 to 1917. Now the majority of citizens have the "joy" of being plucked. The 1986 exercise in tax reform without raising federal revenue was all squawk and no feathers. The feathers could have been beneficial if allocated to deficit reduction, but the process was politically constructed to be revenue neutral. The 1986 reforms simply redistributed the burden by raising corporate taxes and eliminating income taxes for six million working poor Americans. The tax rates were reduced but so were the deductions for sales taxes and personal interest expenses paid to purchase consumer goods.

The reshuffling of tax incentives has a number of positive benefits. Eliminating income taxes for the poor reduces their financial incentive to stay on welfare. Maintaining the home mortgage deduction dissipates the American tendency toward self-indulgent consumption (leading to bankruptcy). Reducing individual tax rates nurtured the incentive to work but only raised the labor supply by 1.1 percent, or 2.5 days per worker per year. Low savings rates are but one symptom of the larger cultural problem of under-attention to the future. Public opinion polls since 1980 suggest that Americans regard money saved as money taken out of circulation and not used for growth and job creation, whereas in Japan, Germany, and South Korea there is a strong sense of the need for life, education, the importance of merit, and saving for the future generations.

Future tax reforms should create incentives to work and save and reduce incentives to overextend (exceed debt capacity) or remain idle (stay on welfare). Before suggesting future tax reform alternatives, four basic myths must be outlined.

Myth One: Reduced income taxes translate into reduced federal taxes. For example, a family of four making $30,000 in 1992 inflation-adjusted dollars contributed 19.86 percent of its income to federal taxes in 1992, compared to 18.98 percent in 1979. The reason for the increased tax burden was the marked increase in Social Security taxes (see Table 3.2, column 3).

Myth Two: The 1981 Reagan tax cut saved taxpayers $1.5 trillion in the 1980s. Fact: Congress recouped 103 percent of the Reagan tax cut from the public over the period 1982–1989. The following collection list was pursued:

- $648 billion, 1984 Deficit Reduction Act
- $293 billion, 1982 Social Security Tax Rate Hikes
- $318 billion, 1982 Tax Equity and Financial Responsibility Act
- $90 billion, 1983 Social Security Amendments
- $63 billion, Miscellaneous Tax Increases 1986–1988
- $28 billion, 1983 Gasoline Tax Increases

Liberals promised equal spending cuts to counterbalance tax increases, but the public received a full measure of the "revenue enhancements" and only a quarter of the spending cuts.

Myth Three: The 1986 tax reform act ended progressive income taxation (i.e., the rich paying a larger percentage of their earnings on income taxes). Fact: progressive taxation previously existed on paper only because the rich could reduce their burden through tax shelters, exemptions, and deductions. Moreover, the 1986 Alternative Minimum Tax prevented the super-rich from avoiding taxes. The 1986 tax reform bill reduced the effective tax rates to 25–26 percent, which coincidently equals the actual tax rate paid by rich Americans from 1968 to 1985 (peak effective rate, 29.4 percent in 1969, compared to only 24.2 percent in 1982). In fact, from 1988 to 1992 there had been more than three tax rates (31 and 28 percent for the non-poor, 15 percent for the poor). A bubble exists in the tax rate schedule which taxes personal income at the 31 percent rate. The tax rate declined back to 28 percent for all income above upper limits. For 1994 Congress enacted two new tax brackets: a 36 percent rate for the rich (the 96 to 99.5 percentile of income distribution, individuals making over $115,000, couples making more than $140,000), and a 39.6 percent tax rate for the super-rich (top half-percent, individuals making more than $250,000). Does charging the rich a higher tax rate collect more money? Not in the recent past. In 1990 the rate was raised for the rich, and for the two years 1991 and 1992 tax receipts from the superrich (850,000 Americans) declined by a cumulative total of 10 percent ($10 billion). As tax collections from the superrich declined 10 percent the taxes collected from the nonrich increased 1.1 percent.

The voting public since the 1960s has considered the redistributionist dogma as some alien philosophy of resentment: they do not resent the rich, they desire to be rich. Democrat George McGovern was lambasted in 1972 for proposing a big tax on all inheritances over $500,000. Lower tax rates as a stimulus to make the most productive individuals work harder became a worldwide movement for a wide variety of governments (Australia, Poland, China, and the Soviet Union). Socialist governments from France to

Table 3.2
Revenues by Major Source, Fiscal Years 1963–1993 (as a percentage of GDP)

	Individual Income Taxes	Corporate Income Taxes	Social Insurance Taxes	Excise Taxes	Estate and Gift Taxes	Customs Duties	Miscellaneous Receipts	Total Revenues
1963	8.1	3.7	3.4	2.3	0.4	0.2	0.2	18.2
1968	8.1	3.4	4.0	1.7	0.4	0.2	0.3	18.0
1973	8.1	2.8	4.9	1.3	0.4	0.2	0.3	18.1
1978	8.4	2.8	5.4	0.9	0.2	0.3	0.3	18.5
1983	8.7	1.1	6.3	1.1	0.2	0.3	0.5	18.1
1988	8.3	2.0	7.0	0.7	0.2	0.3	0.4	18.9
1993	8.3	1.7	7.1	0.8	0.2	0.3	0.4	19.8

New Zealand to Denmark voluntarily reduced their top tax rates by 18 to 30 points in the mid-1980s.

Myth Four: One of the basic goals of tax reform, tax simplification, and reduction of paperwork was achieved in the 1986 law. Fact: The tax "simplification" act spawned seven new tax forms for individuals, 42 new tax forms for corporations, and revisions and additions in 204 other forms. The road to tax simplicity could never be found through reductions in the number of tax brackets from 13 to 3 (15, 28, 31 percent), because most taxpayers utilize tax tables or accountants to compute their tax bill. Simplicity can be designed by redesigning the forms after lowering or eliminating the value of itemized deductions. The one itemized deduction that appears sacrosanct is the deduction for interest expense on a home mortgage ($42 billion in lost revenue in 1993). More expensive homes have a larger tax subsidy. With this tax deduction Uncle Sam gives the average taxpayer $28 back for every $100 invested as a homeowner. Why shouldn't this deduction be labeled sacrosanct if it offers citizens the best federal return on investment? In 1987 Congress capped the home mortgage deduction at $1 million for a first mortgage and $100,000 for home-equity loans. The deduction could be capped at one-fifth this level to reduce subsidization of expensive homes. *POLICY PROPOSAL No. 16:* The home interest deduction could be capped at $15,000 a year, thus raising an additional $21.8 billion in 1994–1997 tax collections from the rich. At 1992 interest rates, the $15,000-a-year cap represents the interest on a mortgage of $200,000. This cap would affect only 2.7 percent of the taxpayers nationally, but 5 to 10 percent of the homeowners in Boston, California, and Washington, D.C. Liberal social planners may lobby for a complex formula that equalizes the percentage of family income spent on mortgage payments across income groups. It seems unfair that 57 percent of mortgage interest deductions go to the top tenth of income earners. Currently, working poor homeowners spend 45 percent of their income on mortgage payments in contrast to 20 percent for the middle class and 11 percent for the rich. A more enlightened tax policy might target more of the tax benefits to the financially distressed soon-to-be-homeless and reduce any tax benefits of home ownership for the rich. Unfortunately, the real estate industry would fight for retaining present tax policy because its fees are dependent on upscale home sales.

If the rich can be expected to fight against any attempts to cut their mortgage deductions, they are equally emotional on the subject of high inheritance tax rates. Any tax relief for the rich could be tied to a "productivity enhancing trust fund for the idle rich." A tamper-proof, lifetime trust fund could be set up to provide the sons and daughters of the rich with one dollar of additional income for every two dollars of wages earned. It is an unanswered question as to how much idle wealth creates economic rot. A direct-wealth tax would be too complex and expensive to administrate within the Internal Revenue Service.

Not all tax reform ideals are destined for acceptance. For example, the tax reform initiatives outlined by Hall and Rabushka (1985) failed to excite the public with the idea of a single tax rate for all. The so-called flat-tax idea has been suggested by a wide array of political thinkers including Democrat Jerry Brown (1992), Robert Kennedy (1966), and Milton Friedman (1968).

ATTEMPTS AT A SINGLE FLAT-TAX FAIL

The current income tax structure of three tax brackets has been labeled reactionary by some. While the current top tax of 28 percent on highest income levels has been compared to the 25 percent top rate in 1929, predictions of a depression hardly seem warranted. On a historical note, the concept of flattening the number of tax brackets to two was originally a liberal idea promoted by Senator Robert Kennedy (D–N.Y.). Kennedy suggested a flat tax (single rate) of 20 percent for all. This liberal idea was reminiscent of the old-school conservative definition of liberalism: the central government should not tinker with the social fabric through the tax system. As the government has grown to consume 25 percent of the GNP, this Kennedy commandment to tax all sources of income at the same rate (20 percent) would create a surplus of $29 billion in 1993!

The income tax rate need not be as high as 20 percent if the tax code trims the deductions available. First, all revenues are not collected in income taxes. The federal government expects to collect $530 billion from individual income taxation, $100 billion from corporations, and $310 billion from employment taxes such as Social Security in 1993. Second, careful estimates have been made regarding the revenue neutral rate necessary for a flat tax. The Joint Economic Committee of Congress estimated in 1986 that a pure flat tax, with no exemptions or deductions, would generate the current amount of revenue that could be collected with a 19 percent flat tax.

The flat tax idea will surely be discussed if a second tax reform movement occurs in the mid-1990s. Unfortunately, powerful vested interests will attempt to preserve the existing deductions, and liberal Democrats have a preference for the 15 percent marginal tax rate for the poor. To compensate the poor for raising their tax rates above 15 percent, the tax credit for family size could be inflated. By restricting this family tax credit to minimum-wage workers nearly fully employed (over 28 hours work per week), this policy would de facto raise the minimum wage: (1) in a targeted way to help the truly needy and (2) not directly add to the cost of labor so as to reduce employment (in contrast to raising the minimum wage). The pressures for reform are strong, and the benefits are not simply in deficit reduction. For example, capping the interest deduction on a home mortgage could help reduce housing prices in many areas. By making the consumers bear the full burden of their housing costs among the households most able to pay, price competition would act to reduce the sale price of homes, partially commensurate with the decline in federal tax subsidization for home ownership. This cap on the mortgage deduction would help the first-time home buyer through reduced prices and would not harm the elderly (since most do not have a big mortgage on their homes).

Tax policy experts talk in terms of tax incidence. Who bears the burden most? Do we tax Social Security benefits, reduce the incentive to buy a house, create more or less incentives to save and invest? We shall survey the trade-offs in this chapter, but one knotty truth must be stated: we cannot understate public anger with a tax system that takes 28 hours of paperwork for the average American each April. Ross Perot tapped into public anger by stating that all tax filings should be computerized, through the employer, and not involve 28 hours of stolen family time to fill out forms. In the Perot world, the public hires politicians to figure out how to collect more without taxing them and spend less without cutting their favorite programs. The public demands complexity in the name of fairness, then complains if tax forms are less understandable. Some problems have simple solutions: if the marriage tax exists such that a married couple pays more than a couple living together out of wedlock, let the couple have the freedom of choice to file either as individuals or as a pair. Alternatively, Professor Feldstein (1989) has suggested that we reduce the second earner effective marginal tax rate to 25 percent. Under this scenario, the treasury would not have lost $3.2 billion after revenue loss from the rate reduction plus added work and tax collection from the increase in labor supply. Hours worked would increase because second earners are much more sensitive to marginal tax rates in the decision about whether to work and how much.

WHO CARRIES AN INCREASING SHARE OF THE TAX BURDEN?

Poverty activists like to focus on the fact that the rich are getting richer, neglecting the basic fact that wealth creation will diminish if society penalizes those who initiate the process. Republicans tend to focus on the fact that the top 10 percent of wage earners pay an increasing proportion of the total income taxes. The wealthiest 10 percent of families paid 51.3 percent of the income taxes in 1977, 51.8 percent in 1985, and an estimated 56 percent in 1993. The wealthy are reporting an even larger proportionate share of taxable income. The top 1 percent of earners (earning $340,000 or more in 1993) pays more in income taxes than the poorest two-thirds of Americans combined. The U.S. Congressional Budget Office (1993) report indicates that "effective federal income tax rates" (percent of total income paid out in taxes) declined from 1984 to 1993 for all income classes except the richest 10 percent (top tenth). In other words, the richest tenth are paying more so that the other 90 percent of Americans can pay less. For the richest 10 percent, the effective rates increased from 15.1 to 15.6 percent over the period 1984–1991. For citizens in the next four-tenths above the median (but not in the top tenth), effective federal rates declined from 9.6 to 9 percent by 1991. For the poor half of the population, rates declined from 4.1 to 3.5 percent in 1993. These effective rates are lower than the marginal 15-28-31 percent rates on the last dollar of income earned because: (1) taxpayers take full advantage of their deductions and credits and (2) the CBO inflates total income by including payroll taxes and health care benefits that the employer pays on behalf of the employee.

Tax policy decisions do more to apportion resources between consumption and investment than to distribute wealth among income groups. In a modern world in which capital knows no international boundaries, it would be impossible for any future Democratic president to force the rebirth of progressive income taxation circa 1964. The financial world today moves billions in minutes. If the American economy ever did go sour, and capital flight became a problem, it would be impossible for a U.S. president to be as effective in instituting capital controls against moving funds out of America as was President Johnson in 1966. The next four sections will outline options to improve consumer savings, capital gains, corporate taxes, and consumption taxes.

SAVINGS AND ECONOMIC GROWTH

Net private savings, defined as net income saved by private households and firms, declined from 8.1 percent of the GNP in the 1970s to 5.6 percent in the 1980s. Viewed from another statistic, net national savings declined to below 2 percent of the GNP for three years in the mid-1980s. Net national savings, defined as private savings minus public sector deficits declined from 7.1 percent of the GNP in the 1970s to 3.2 percent in the 1980s. Americans are the industrial world's worst savers, saving about 5 percent of their disposable income, in contrast to 15 to 17 percent for the Japanese and 9 to 11 percent for the Germans during the 1990s. Some of this differential savings rate is explained by accounting conventions, but

Americans could achieve a target savings rate of 8 to 9 percent if they were able to change behavior through incentives and disincentives.

In the 1990s, net private savings has declined to 4.7 percent. Disincentives to spend, such as consumption taxes, could channel more funds into savings. Incentives to save for the future, including future educational expenses, could increase the national rate of savings. Why care about savings? Many naive journalists report the good side of increased consumption and decreased savings namely, higher levels of short-run business activity. The bias to downweight long-run concerns seems to permeate American culture. Savings is crucial because savings leads to investment. Investment leads to research and development, improved products and services, and improved productivity and technology. A number of policies to reduce the federal deficit, such as raising income taxes, would only harm the savings rate (i.e., disposable income minus consumption divided by disposable income) by soaking up the limited family income available to be saved.

Comparisons concerning the national savings rate can either be made on normative terms (relative to other nations) or on a time trend basis. On a time trend basis our rate of savings has eroded to where the 1988–1993 savings rate is one-forth the postwar 1948–1963 rate. Part of the change is reflected by demographic factors and cost factors: the postwar boom was atypically ripe for growth, and the environment is less conducive to savings in 1990s America. The high costs of education and student loans plus the high cost of housing make savings more difficult in the 1990s compared to the 1950s. What of the normative comparisons between the unstandardized (i.e., uncorrected for age and other demographic factors) American rate of savings and rates of savings in Germany (11.8 percent) or Japan (19.2 percent)? Two basic myths exist concerning savings:

Myth One: The higher the rate of savings, the better the economy is in the long run. By this logic the best economic engines must be the three countries with the highest savings rates: Turkey (20.7 percent), Portugal (21.5 percent), and Switzerland (22.5 percent). No citizen that this author has ever met from Turkey, Portugal, or even Japan would argue that his or her standard of living is as good as the American level.

Myth Two: The aggregate level of savings is more critical than the structure of savings and investment. The biggest problem with American savings is that most of it is poorly handled by pension fund managers and other fiduciaries. In basic parlance, its not how much money you have, its where you put it that counts. In 1953 only 0.8 percent of total equity investments were in pension funds, but by 1993 such funds managed 29 percent of the equity. Herb Whitehouse (1992), formerly a manager of $2.2 billion in trust funds, argues that pension fund managers and other fiduciaries play with too many investments of poor quality. Pension funds act too often like the unethical dealer Old Man Potter in the Jimmy Stewart movie *It's a Wonderful Life.* Our problem is not the size of the savings rate (3.6 percent, Table 3.1), but how we manage those savings. Pension funds all too often eschew long-run concerns because the MBA/fiduciary is looking for the quick buck return. This investment policy totally ignores economic development and community restoration. These last two factors are of prime concern to the Jimmy Stewart types who direct Japanese savings toward good investments. To drive the Old Man Potter crooks out of pension fund management Congress must pass a law to bring the Jimmy Stewarts back to the forefront. How? *POLICY PROPOSAL No. 17:* Enact a pension fund investment law based only on the 1977 Bank Community Reinvestment Act. Pension funds should act like banks and be regulated to ensure that the funds adequately supply the needs of their communities. The pension funds will lobby Congress with cash to blame the whole problem on the victim, the American worker. But, the facts suggest no intrinsic problem with individual Americans. Personal savings rate by individuals is down a negligible three points, from 7 percent in 1977–1984 to 3.9 percent of disposable income in 1988–1992. Individuals and community groups do a better job of savings allocation and investment than their fat pension funds. Making pension funds subject to the bank laws against "red-lining" will bring savings forth to invest in the job creation machine of the American economy, small businesses.

America faces the twin problems of poor savings management and poor tax policy. The Japanese, blessed with great social investment philosophy among their fiduciaries, can afford even to dampen their savings rate by raising taxes. Why study Japanese economic policy? Since the Japanese represent our principal economic competition, normative comparisons of their rate of savings are useful. The Japanese savings rate in 1990–1991 dipped to 15.4 percent because in April 1988 the government lifted the tax exemption on savings below three million yen ($25,000) and began to tax savings 20 percent. The tax exemption on savings still exists for the 18.6 percent of Japanese who are single mothers, handicapped, or over the age of 65. In contrast to the Japanese, the American elderly already have a substantial rate of savings, but single parent families find savings for education a luxury they can hardly afford.

POLICY PROPOSAL No. 18: Exempt half the interest earned on savings up to $4,000 for single parents and up to $3,000 for other households from taxation. Individual retirement accounts (IRAs) did little to stimulate savings (only $343 billion) because: (1) $2,000 was an insufficient (low) cap and (2) the consumer had to open a specific account and incur an administrative expense. The 1981 IRA law simply allowed consumers to cycle funds out of their banks' borrowing door and cycle it into their banks' deposit door. The results: no substantial impact on economic activity but substantial growth in needless paperwork. Another variant of the IRA concept suggested in the 1988 presidential race involved the establishment of 100 percent tax-exempt educational IRAs. A typical single parent investing $4,000 in an account at one time would after ten years have avoided $580 in taxes. Cynics might argue that this is not enough of a stimulus to save, in which case tax policy could be rewritten to bring forth enough additional savings to make the revenue loss worthwhile. Congress is considering a number of expanded versions of tax-deferred individual retirement or investment (educational) accounts.

If interest on bank savings accounts deserves a 50 percent exemption from taxation, then dividends incurred from direct investment in business are perhaps deserving of a full 100 percent tax exemption. Conservatives have often complained about double taxation, whereby a business pays corporate taxes on earnings that are passed on to shareholders who then pay taxes on dividends. They take this obvious inequity and all too often argue for the abolition of corporate taxes, with no forthcoming popular support. Helping corporations is not exactly a popularist slogan. Instead, conservatives should argue for less taxation of dividends so that we might improve the national savings rate. A preferential tax treatment of dividends is one major step necessary to bring Middle America back into the marketplace, offering patient money as a stable source of equity capital. Patient money is concerned with economic fundamentals, rather than a fast-buck, short-run investment.

POLICY PROPOSAL No. 19: Exempt half of dividends earned from taxation up to a maximum of $4,000 for single parents and up to a maximum of $3,000 for other families for investments held for over two years. The dollar limits should be indexed for inflation. Many economists have observed that the double taxation of dividends (corporate and personal taxation) offers a main reason why corporations prefer debt to equity. Interest paid on debt is tax deductible, so corporations increasingly rely on debt. The two-year holding limitation proposed for preferential treatment of dividend income is designed to encourage "patient money," that is, investors interested in economic fundamentals and not a fast-buck investment. A more detailed discussion of the economic rationale for preferential taxation for "money with patience" will be included in the capital gains section of this chapter. Perhaps if dividends could be made half deductible for individual taxpayers, they could also be made half deductible for the business paying them. This reduction in corporate taxation would reduce the reliance on corporate debt, slightly rebuild balance sheets, and finance higher rates of capital investment.

These last two policy prescriptions might facilitate the rebirth of a healthy level of net private domestic investment. Such investment declined from 6.94 percent of the GNP in the 1970s to 4.66 percent in the 1980s. The rich may complain that these changes in tax policy do not do enough to assist those with the most money to save: the wealthy. Wealthier Americans may resent the existence of any caps on tax exemption, but the middle class is the principal group that undersaves, and it has the most political support in the Congress. This preferential treatment for savings and dividends could be presented to the rich as the quid pro quo they receive after Congress also caps their mortgage interest deduction.

Noneconomists need to understand our financial situation in global macroeconomic terms. We require a two-sided strategy for reducing the deficit and increasing the rate of savings such that the central government eats up only less than one-third of savings. Savings creates the investments that offer workers and firms better designed equipment (inputs) and products (outputs) to remain competitive. A higher rate of savings can create the technology, new products, and new plants to enhance (and not replace) human skills. Higher savings provides the financing for more jobs and a more autonomous and engaging work environment. Contrary to the conventional wisdom in the 1960s and 1970s, increased consumption is not the only way to create jobs. Savings creates more and better jobs. A society that does not save for a rainy day and a better workplace will experience a lifetime of rainy days.

PAYING THE PIPER

To improve the IRA investment portfolio, consider *POLICY PROPOSAL No. 20:* The federal government should impose a 4 percent tax on investments in pension plans and IRA accounts. The federal government would collect $29 billion over the years 1994–1997, and the retirement accounts would shift their portfolio from bonds and short-term investments to long-term investments in growth stocks. The entire economy would benefit from the focus to long-term strategies to modernize, and the government could collect the revenues necessary to finance Proposals 18 and 19.

If Congress does not act to stimulate increased consumer savings and investment, fear may one day motivate Americans to save. If the Social Security Trust Fund becomes a poor performer in the era 2010–2030, America may replay the Italian experience of 1960–1990. Italians have the third highest saving rate in Europe (12.8 percent) in large part because they totally mistrust government pension plans. Because Italy has triple the American rate of savings they can afford to self-finance a deficit that is 150 percent larger than the American deficit. Those who dislike poor economic performance or declining respect for government should find cold comfort in suggesting an Italian solution to the problem of low American savings rate.

The Japanese government debt as a percentage of the economy is almost equal to that of the United States, but they service this debt at below half the American interest rates. Some dogmatic supply siders have used the Japanese example to suggest no correlation between government debt and interest rates, often blaming most macroeconomic problems on the Federal Reserve Bank's restrictive monetary policies. One needs to better understand the strength of Japan, and the weakness of the supply side argument that the evil Federal Reserve makes Americans pay more for their government bonds compared to countries with even higher government debt.

The lowering of tax rates in any nation would be good if it produced a dosage of *both* economic growth and booming private investment. America has experienced only record economic growth and has opted for a double dose of an old drug, consumption. Japan has had a balance of growth, investment, and consumption, while America has experienced mainly growth and consumption (Hayashi, 1993). The American imbalance was good in the short-run (the 1980s, before the big recession in the early 1990s), but it will yield an eventual hangover and diminished long-run capacity.

Finally, the Federal Reserve had to maintain high interest rates to attract $540 billion worth of foreign buyers of federal paper in the last four years of the 1980s. If the interest rates had been lower, the foreigners would not have underwritten our consumption boom. When one accounts for savings rate statistical conventions among nations, the Japanese and Italians save at only 1.7–fold the American rate of savings, but they have less to pay for (fewer home mortgages, less national defense, less consumption). Government debt in Japan eats up 22 percent of net savings, compared to 45 percent in Italy and 80 percent in America.

HISTORIC INTEREST RATES

Real interest rates in the United States are nearly double those of the 1950–1979 era. A federal bond interest rate of 7.9 percent, and an expected interest rate of 4.2 percent over the life of the bond, translates into a real interest rate of 3.7 percent. In contrast, during the 1950–1979 period real interest rates averaged 1.87 percent. High future federal deficits lead investors to demand high real interest rates. The rates must remain high to attract sufficient funds from investors and effectively limit the demand for money by American corporations and consumers. The nation's debt is soaking up too high a fraction of national savings to let the interest rates decline or stabilize. The Federal Reserve cannot afford to be so generous in lowering interest rates that excessive double-digit inflation returns to the economy, but the Fed should not be so restrictive in holding interest rates high that excessive damage is done to business formation or the housing industry.

The foregoing analysis has considered Fisher's classic inflation-adjusted real rate of interest. Another classic economist named Wicksell had an alternative second measure of the real rate of interest (Mishkin, 1986). Knut Wicksell preferred to discuss a measure based on the marginal productivity of capital, labeled the natural (or "in-kind") real rate of interest. The 1980s boom was driven by a strong natural rate of interest, which: (1) produced declining marginal costs and (2) controlled inflation, even while capacity utilization in business stood at a mere 80 to 86 percent (the older capital lay idle, the unions became less powerful, and the new capital cut costs).

At the most basic level, the Federal Reserve deals in exchanges across time. Consumers may complain when the Fed raises interest rates. These hikes act in the short run like tax increases on the consumer sector; the effect of the changing interest rates are not hard and fast, but spongy. For example, the time lags vary such that depositors enjoy higher interest rates immediately (since bank deregulation uncapped rates in 1981), but adjustable debt may not be repegged for 2 to 24 months, thus fueling consumer spending in the short run where 80 percent of loans are pegged to the prime rate of interest and 60 percent of home mortgages have adjustable rates. Supply siders, however, do not point out that this tax increase evaporates if the Fed proves successful in the long-run fight against inflation. To paraphrase an analogy borrowed from Winston Churchill, this author would rather fight the fire (inflation) and trust the fire fighter (the Federal Reserve). Avoiding the long-term inflationary fire hazard involves temporary hardships of recessions to the economy, or temporary increases in interest rates to retard business activity (slower growth, but not negative growth or stagnation). The Fed attempts to increase the money supply fast enough to heat the home economy, but not so fast as to tip over the oven and ignite an inflationary fire.

Hopefully, Americans will only have to experience a little higher inflation and interest expense during the 1990s. Each 1 point rise in interest rates adds $29.3 billion in interest expense to our 1993 $4.4 trillion national debt. Economics became the dismal science for many because questions are often posed in the negative: how would you like your pain distributed—hyperinflation, deflation, and unemployment, or a dose of slow, painful disinflation for the economy?

CONSUMPTION AS SAVINGS: WHETHER PIGS GROW WINGS

Except for the United States, most nations use accounting conventions adopted by the United Nations. If the 1992 American Commerce Department savings rate of 2.9 percent is converted to the comparable UN measure, our savings rate becomes 5.6 percent. The major differences between nations involve consumer attitudes about consumption. Moreover, one of the reasons why the savings rate in Japan has declined to under 15 percent in 1992 is because more of Japan's young people are catching the "American disease."

The 1970s and 1980s made America a land of dice players in the way that much of the consumption became a savings account with resale value if times get tough (luxury car, expensive watch, or vacation palace). That Rolex watch became the upscale analog to stuffing the mattress during the depression. As Kenichi Ohmae pointed out in a recent issue of the *Japan Economic Journal*, Japanese save in the bank, but Americans save in their home or car. The Japanese borrow 60 percent of the purchase price for their homes, in contrast to 80 to 90 percent in America. Of the net Japanese savings rate, almost two-thirds represents real estate down payments. If we factor out home ownership differentials between nations, the Japanese in 1993 save only 3 percentage points more than Americans.

But those three points are not trivial, and we must follow their example. Think of what America could do with an additional $110 billion of nation-building investment, including an extra $20 billion for education. The doomsayers claim that fiscal imprudence by citizens and the federal government explains our economic problems. But the problems are not insoluble, the Japanese do not save fourfold better than Americans, only 3 points better. In the language of global competition, a 3 point game is winnable. Spend 3 more points of the GNP on savings and 2 more points on research and development, and America will be reborn as the world capital for capitalism.

As recently as 1941, America had a whopping 18.8 percent savings rate. Unfortunately, the post–Vietnam War decades taught Americans that saving was a mistake, and spending was better than passively letting your money get eaten up by inflation. How do we enhance savings, decrease consumption, and invest less through the insurance sector? Let society:

1. encourage risk-taking and pursuit of capital gains.
2. restructure corporate tax policy to stimulate investment, research, and development.
3. remove preferential tax treatment for insurance firms.

4. initiate high consumption taxes to discourage excess spending, and encourage better health and conservation.

CAPITAL GAINS TAX POLICY

Capital gains tax rates declined from 50 percent to 20 percent in 1978–1985. Capital gains occur only following a voluntary action: when the taxpayer decides to sell an asset. Not surprisingly, sales of assets are highest following a lowering in the capital gains tax rates. In 1969 when Congress doubled capital gains tax rates (to 49 percent), revenue declined from $171 million to $97 million (1970), then to a low of $10 million in 1975. Revenue increased following the reduction in capital gains to 28 percent in 1978 (up from $39 million to $599 million) and the reduction to 20 percent in 1981 (up $4 billion in 24 months). Federal revenue from capital gains was 112 percent higher even after factoring in inflation (and GNP growth) in 1985 compared to 1978.

Then Congress raised the cost of capital, and thus reduced the incentive to invest by raising the capital gains rate to 28 percent. This not only reduced federal tax collections, but state revenues from capital gains declined by $3.1 billion over 1987–1992. In sharp contrast to when American policy on income tax rates stimulated a worldwide trend to reduce tax rates, the congressional Democrats' promotion of higher capital gains tax rates ran sharply against the tide in other nations. Japan, Germany, Korea, and 9 other industrial nations imposed no tax on capital gains, and 50 other industrial competitors had rates lower than 28 percent.

Democrats successfully proposed increased taxation of capital gains based on a principle and a hope. The hope was higher tax rates would yield increased revenue, but in fact annual revenue from capital gains sharply declined by one-third from 1987–1992. The principle that Democrats espoused was that all forms of income, whether from wages or capital gains, should be taxed at the same marginal rate (28 percent). (In point of fact the 1986 law retained limitations on the deduction of losses, so capital gains are taxed slightly higher than ordinary income). While such an equal rate principle is fine in theory, it suffers in practice because the tax law refuses to account for inflation. Wages are earned over a period of months, but capital gains are frequently earned over a period of years. Congress would rather tax individuals for invisible capital gains, that share of the gain representing general inflation, rather than the real economic gain of holding a capital asset (adjusted for inflation). The principle of taxing all forms of income at the same marginal rate would make sense if adjusted for inflationary impact beyond one year's duration. Thanks to inflation, many taxes paid on capital gains are in fact capital losses. The lack of any inflation adjustment is especially acute in real estate, even for the homeowner who takes the once-in-a-lifetime $125,000 exclusion on the sale of a residence. Alas, Congress cannot drop its collective dislike for indexing capital gains to inflation any more than Galileo could drop the Ptolemaic world view. Two major exceptions to this generalization are Senator William Armstrong (R–Colo.) and Representative William Archer (R–Tex.) as strong advocates of an inflation adjustment to tax only real gains, not gains attributable to the general inflation rate.

Congress is not the only "villain" in the face of legislation that raised capital gains tax rates. Carrying the analogy to the extreme, if Congress is a rigid Galileo, then the Capital Formation Lobby, which pushed for a 15 percent rate, plays the part of the Spanish Inquisition. Capital Formation lobbyists primarily represent the rich and those interested in making a fast buck by turning over stocks, bonds, and expensive artwork. If Congress is to be responsive to the "little guy," the most formidable advocate for lower capital gains must come from small business concerns. The man in the street cannot sell those parcels, the software package, or the truck because tax levels do not make it worthwhile. Capital markets are less efficient as investors are locked in and refuse to forego selling inflation-generated "fake" gains.

POLICY PROPOSAL No. 21: Tax the initial $40,000 of capital gains for job-creating assets held over six years at a 15 percent rate, and implement in 1994 a graduated capital gains tax of 18 percent for additional gains earned over five years, gradually increasing to 33 percent on gains earned in less than a year. Pure wealth-creating assets that do little for job creation, like coins, paintings, classic cars, and other collectibles, and investments that are easily depreciated (e.g., apartment buildings) would continue to be taxed at a higher rate (e.g., 33 and 28 percent, respectively). This formula is imperfect, but it takes partial account for expected inflation and limits tax relief accrued by the rich, while offering enough incentive to benefit the small investor. At minimum, capital gains tax relief should focus on corporate stock for small and large business concerns, representing only 38 percent of the capital gains reported in 1987–1991. By 1998 this proposal would increase capital formation by $530 billion, increase jobs by 150,000, and add $132 billion to the gross domestic product (GDP). Investors would be secure in the knowledge that inflation had not gobbled up the majority share of their profit.

Many analysts have suggested that the American investment community suffers from an overemphasis on fast-buck deals and quick returns. Corporations blame their large shareholders (e.g., pension fund managers whose job security depends on 90-day portfolio returns). These proposed graduated capital gains formulas offer preferential treatment to money with patience and are sympathetic to the classic long-run stakeholder philosophy that returns can result over a multiyear time frame. This allows the corporation the luxury of making smart, long-run investments (new technology, job skill development, research). The Ross Perots of our society will continue to turn a profit on short-run deals even when capital gains are taxed at 28 or 31 percent. However, the American problem of a paucity of small investors can be solved if we tax money with the patience of a stakeholder at 14 percent.

Supply side economics may be a failure for involuntary taxes (e.g., income taxes), but a cut in rates for a tax collected after a voluntary action (selling an asset) has traditionally increased federal revenues. The suggested gradual scale for capital gains may elicit $4 billion in additional revenue in FY1994, $5 billion in FY1995, and $6 billion in FY1996. These estimates ignore the secondary long-run benefits of reducing the capital gains rate: more investment will create additional wealth, enhancing tax revenues generally. The proportion of capital gains reported from small start-up companies could double under this proposal.

Congressional liberals in search of tax revenue have suggested taxing capital gains at death. Under current law capital gains can be passed to heirs free of capital gains tax but subject to an estate tax. Such a policy would punish the family farm and family small business, unless the capital gains were subjected to exclusions. Wealth would be better taxed at death under *POLICY PROPOSAL No. 22:* Tax capital gains held at death on the final tax return of the deceased, thus raising $16.8 billion in 1994–1997. Gains on assets given to charity or inherited by the spouse would not be taxed. In order that only the wealthy, lucky, top 4 percent of taxpayers would be taxed, three exclusions would be allowed: (1) the existing $125,000 exclusion on the gain from sale of the principal residence could be claimed; (2) to reduce paperwork, an alternative basis of one-half of an asset's current value could be utilized; and (3) a $75,000 exclusion would be allowed to any remaining capital gains. Before the rich pensioner escapes the IRS, we might better tax a proportion of the generous employer-paid, nonretirement fringe benefits. *POLICY PROPOSAL No. 23:* Initiate a 3 percent tax on the value of nonretirement fringe benefits (collecting $19 billion over 1994–1997).

This chapter has suggested tax changes to increase the rate of gross private domestic investment above 19 percent of the GNP. An equally important issue is how American companies will utilize the extra funds. Most economists advocate an investment plan with emphasis on modernizing capacity, rather than expanding capacity. MIT professors Piore and Sabel suggest some industries should mimic the Italian model of flexible specialization, with fluid networks of small companies offering unrivaled product quality or skilled service. For other sectors, the Japanese model of velocity production with high-volume, around-the-clock factories may be the more appropriate prototype for modernization.

Investments range from capital spending to research and development. American business increased capital spending from $390 billion in 1987 to $425 billion in 1988 and $500 billion in 1990. Industry invested $70 billion in research and development in 1991 (compared to $23 billion of nonmilitary government research and development [R&D]). R&D can come up with effective yet simple new production methods (e.g., turning glass bottles into chips, then fiberfill, then insulation for parka coats). American R&D should probably focus on a number of 21st-century markets: (1) solar energy, (2) photon computers to replace the old electronic data processing, (3) inherently safe nuclear reactor fuel capable of withstanding very high temperatures without risk of meltdown or discharge, (4) nanotechnology assemblers the size of a few molecules to grow food or shelter or create a computer, and (5) advanced information technology including expert systems and artificial intelligence. If the 1970s was a decade for robotics, the 1990s could become the decade of the thinking machine, where networks of machines continuously reset themselves and learn from experience (Tyson, 1989).

American attitudes toward R&D must exit the 1950s and enter the 1990s. The traditional American attitude, modeled after the German chemical industry, views R&D as a steady river from basic research to applied research to products on the shelf. The Japanese have been successful with a German psychology model of R&D as a total Gestalt network of technological fusion from 10 to 20 to 30 disciplines, simultaneously working as a team with little regard to status hang-ups, or labeling which individuals come from the applied, basic research or marketing departments. Under the Japanese R&D concept of technological fusion, a hospital surgical operating suite engineer works with a crystallographer and an optics expert from a camera company to make a better silicon chip.

To support the notion of technology fusion, and in the spirit of government minimalism (more real investment, less bureaucracy), America should merge the departments of Commerce, Agriculture, Transportation, and Energy into a single cabinet-level Department of Technology. This department would be charged with closing the international R&D gap whereby America spends only 1.9 percent of the GNP on R&D, in contrast to 2.5 to 4.1 percent in Western Europe and Japan. One might even suggest a lower rate of capital gains taxation for high-technology R&D firms to foster risk-takers and regain our competitive edge.

CORPORATE TAX POLICY AND
CORPORATE DEBT

Corporate savings and debt are two important issues for tax policymakers. American corporate savings in the form of retained earnings accounted for only 45 percent of all private savings by 1992. Tax reform in 1986 broadened the corporate tax base (e.g., it abolished the investment tax credit) while decreasing corporate tax rates to net $122 billion additional dollars over five years. In the five years prior to the 1986 tax reform, corporations had the incentive to improve the financial returns of their shareholders by retaining income and converting it into capital gains. Prior to 1986, capital gains were then taxed at a lower rate than dividends or interest (investors could deduct 60 percent of long-term capital gains from income). The 1986 tax law: (1) eliminated this incentive to retain income and generate capital gains, (2) provided corporations with the incentive to minimize retained income because personal tax rates were set below corporate tax rates, and (3) provided an incentive to rapidly increase corporate debt because the corporate tax rates were above the personal tax rates.

Corporate tax rates are important in absolute terms and relative terms. In absolute terms, if corporate taxes are set too high, the government's gains in revenue in the short run are lost in the long run. Corporations drained of international savings and investment will be unable to grow, create new jobs and new taxpayers, and expand corporate profits. Corporate tax treatment is important in relative terms in two respects. First, corporate tax rates set too high relative to personal tax rates will create the incentive for the firm to save less and pay out more to their shareholders but utilize more debt (rather than equity) to expand or acquire other firms. Second, corporate tax policy should offer a relative bias in favor of new activity, rather than simply offer windfall rewards to past activity.

In this last respect, the 1986 tax reform bill was reckless for punishing new activity (elimination of the investment tax credit initiated in 1981) yet providing windfalls for most corporations by decreasing top corporate tax rates from 46 to 34 percent. Through appropriate deductions and tax avoidance under this 34 percent published tax rate, most corporations pay an effective tax rate under the 28 percent level paid in personal taxes by their shareholders. (The effective tax rates for aggregate nonresidential corporations declined by one-third between 1985 and 1987.) The decline in the corporate rates provided a windfall to the owners of existing capital stock, but elimination of the 6 to 10 percent tax credit reduced the incentive to initiate new investment. In the interest of fairness, we should consider *POLICY PROPOSAL No. 24:* Disallow deductions for half of business meal and entertainment expenses (saving $13.7 billion in 1994–1997).

INVEST OR DECAY

A more enlightened tax policy would realize the abuses of a too liberal investment tax credit law (1981–1986) and minimize the revenue loss while optimizing the incentive effect to create new economic activity. A number of economists with a wide range of political perspectives, from left to right (Summers to Feldstein and Boskin), have suggested a New Incremental Tax Credit (NITC). *POLICY PROPOSAL No. 25:* Institute a $5.7 billion annual subsidy to new economic activity (providing no subsidy to existing capital) through a tax credit applied to the real (inflation-adjusted) change in a firm's net capital stock from year to year. In contrast to the 1985 Investment Tax Credit's (ITC) high costs ($35 billion), this proposed NITC policy would offer no rewards to those who create passive losses or below-average rates of economic growth. Governor Bill Clinton was an early supporter of this proposal (*Wall Street Journal*, November 11, 1991).

A whopping 14 percent of NITC credit would be expected to cost a mere $5.7 billion in 1994. In the interest of budget neutrality, if the incentive proves too effective, the revenue loss could be capped at a suggested $6 billion level. Congress could suggest financing the NITC by increasing corporate tax rates by 3 percentage points (to 37 percent; yielding $29 billion over five years) on corporate income above $75,000. (Currently corporate income of $50,000 to $75,000 is taxed at 25 percent, and lower levels of corporate income are taxed at 15 percent.)

America needs more investment activity and fewer "dead-in-the-water" firms that only invest enough each year to offset depreciation. The tax system must help enhance investment beyond annual depreciation (i.e., net private investment). Why? Because the tax system must reflect the basic fact that citizen productivity is determined by the quality of the tools (the available capital). Net private investment averaged 3.0 to 3.6 percent between 1950 and 1978, dipping to 1.9 percent from 1979 to 1982, before rebounding slightly to a period average of 2.6 percent from 1983 to 1990. Why should labor care about corporate investment policy? Because real incomes would be 16.6 percent higher in 1993 if the 1950–1978 investment rate had continued.

Corporate tax policy is often guided by the presentation of quasi-data—statistics that tell only half the story. For example, in 1950 corporate taxes represented 34 percent of federal revenues, declining to a mere 7.1 percent by 1983. Does this mean that corporations are undertaxed? Not if one considers that 1983 was a bad year for corporate profits, and the corporate percentage share declined rapidly as social insurance payroll taxes dramatically increased (swallowing 36 percent of federal revenues).

Corporate taxes as a share of revenues rose to 9.8 percent in 1987 and

11.7 percent in 1992. Corporate profits have been much improved in the late 1980s, measured by return on investment, in contrast to the 1971–1986 period. Congressional tax treatment of corporations has been anything but stable (17 major annual changes since 1955). A Congress in search of revenue and concerned with the explosion in certain corporate takeovers (i.e., leveraged buy-outs [LBOs] with borrowed money) considered disallowing interest payments on corporate debt used to acquire other corporations in 1981.

For example, the federal government stood to lose $4.6 billion from the tax deductibility of interest payments on $18 billion of corporate debt resulting from the December 1988 RJR Nabisco $25 billion LBO deal. The takeover winner, Kohlberg Kravis Roberts, put only $15.2 million of its own funds into the $25 billion deal, which is analogous to putting a $150 down payment on the purchase of a $250,000 home. (The remaining funds, not debt-financed, came from $1.5 billion in cash put up by big investors and $5.7 billion in shareholder securities.) The deal involved $5.3 billion in junk bonds (high-interest, high-risk) and triggered Congress to consider limiting the use of pension-fund money to finance LBOs via junk bonds in 1989. RJR attracted $8.6 billion of equity, as the debt-to-equity ratio of 20:1 in 1989 declined to 3:2.

FINANCING RISKY BONDS

Junk bonds are simply postdated checks, five to ten years into the future, and have become increasingly popular since Chrysler was saved by this method of financing in the 1970s. A number of different junk bond types have grown up since 1980. Pay-in-kind securities are bonds that do not pay interest in cash, but rather in additional bonds, thereby gaining the nickname "bunny bonds." Pity the owner of bunny bonds if a severe recession destroys the company in question (owning more bonds in nothing still yields nothing of value).

Why do such bonds exist? Because bunny bonds are great for takeover raiders who buy up a business with postdated bunny checks (costing only the price of the paper yet offering big tax write-offs). With bunny money, the sellers (the raiders) of the bonds do not have to have any money up front, and they do not have to have any money to make annual interest payments (until the final year). Why have pension funds gobbled up junk bonds since 1984? Since 1984, firms are allowed to deduct interest of all types when it is due (even if it is paid in bunny bonds and not cash). This substitution of deductible interest charges in place of taxable corporate income "unlocks hidden value" in the language of Wall Street (thus reducing tax revenues). The taxman collects on this interest from investors whether they ever get the postdated cash or not (unless the investor is tax exempt).

Congress is considering making the "paper interest" payments taxable, even if they are paid to a tax-exempt organization. Such a policy would slow down, but not eliminate, the rate of corporate takeovers. Bunny bonds are the worst sort of junk bond. The toxic waste of bunny bonds are like poor S&L laws: they seem to be a fine paper game until all the postdated checks bounce or the company goes bankrupt in the future. The age of junk bonds, marked by $212 billion in volume in the 1980s, ended with the bankruptcy of Drexel Burnham Lambert in February 1990. Junk bond victims will not receive any direct federal financing, but the taxpayer will pay part of the bill to the extent that S&L banks owned much junk paper and government assisted failed banks.

HOW MUCH DEBT IS TOO MUCH?

One should consider two basic policy questions: are corporate debt levels out of control, and should we rein in corporate takeover deals? These twin issues are of interest to the general public because they often view takeover artists as the moral equivalent of "car thieves," too sleazy to earn money the honest way (producing products for people).

American nonfinancial corporations' debt increased $1.5 trillion over the 1980s, from $824 billion in 1980 to $2.32 trillion in 1989. Corporate defaults increased from $49 million in 1980 to $15 billion in 1989. Corporations are not like Third World countries or Uncle Sam. They cannot print money or restructure their debt. Corporations in financial distress can suspend dividend payments to shareholders, but they cannot avoid default or (un)-friendly acquisition when incapable of meeting their debt service.

One obvious policy change could reduce corporate debt levels. *POLICY PROPOSAL No. 26:* Corporate taxes should be levied on gross corporate profits, including interest expense, thus eliminating the tax advantage of debt. Takeovers will still proceed, but only for reasons of economic efficiency, not because there exists any preferential tax treatment for debt. This policy eliminates the strong incentive to overutilize debt. Reversing the incentive toward debt financing (increased by $1.5 trillion in the 1980s) may reverse the decline in equity positions. The equity position of American business has decreased by $323 billion over the seven years 1983–1989.

The foregoing three policy proposals are interrelated. If the federal treasury is tougher on corporate tax rates and interest deductibility, it must be a "kinder" force in treating capital gains to bring forth increased equity positions. Removing the tax magnet from savings, dividends, and capital gains will allow more equity flow into nation-building activities like R&D.

A world economy run on corporate and household debt predates the classic aphorism "neither a borrower nor a lender be." Father Polonius today works for an American corporation with debt equivalent to 40 percent of the GNP, and his son (Laertes) does two-thirds of his buying with borrowed money. Do they live in a house of cards? Three basic points must be considered. First, the vast majority of the extra burden of interest payments was acquired by the segments of corporate America best able to handle it (with interest absorbing 40 to 60 percent of cash flow and debt-to-equity levels of 0.7 to 1.1). In stark contrast, cyclical industries—corporate giants like Boeing, IBM, and Ford—have debts that amount to less than 11 percent of their total capital. Second, the debt-heavy industries (tobacco, textiles, food, and chemicals) are the least recession-sensitive sectors of the economy (their pretax profits fell only 6 to 19 percent during recessions since 1957). Third, relative to other nations, the American non-durable goods industries have less debt burden than the competition. Corporate debt represents 40 percent of the American GNP, in comparison to 58 percent in Canada, 60 percent in Germany, and 91 percent in Japan.

Debt is analogous to anticancer drugs in a duality of being simultaneously good and bad; too much can kill you, but a balanced amount is clearly necessary for survival. One is still left with a feeling that a larger fraction of American corporate debt is wasted on acquisition activity, leveraged buy-outs, and other unproductive activities that erode the health of the body public. Whether corporate debt does the economic body good or bad can be judged in relation to the assets that stand behind the debtor.

CORPORATE TAKEOVERS: GOOD OR BAD?

In summary, takeover activity is financed by corporate debt, and debt is preferred (cheaper) to equity because interest payments are tax deductible (dividends are taxable). By this logic executives rationalize that they maximize shareholder wealth by utilizing the maximum amount of debt capacity. To acquire corporate debt harms the federal treasury but helps shareholders, with the caveat that the borrowed money goes to acquisitions or new products that enhance capital assets. Horizontal mergers and acquisitions, involving similar corporations (in the same line of business), typically produce complementary marketing activity, synergies in R&D, and thus a stronger resulting corporate parent. Four good news items concerning takeovers follow:

1. Leveraged buy-outs have not suffocated American investment in plants and equipment (up 33 percent in the four peak years for LBOs in the 1980s).

2. Takeover victors profit by weeding out bad managers in poorly oper-

ated companies (wedded to outdated technologies and personnel practices). Without resorting to takeovers, the tax system could stimulate efficiency indirectly by offering a 50 percent tax exemption for income from productivity-incentive pay systems or worker profit-distribution plans.

3. Takeover victors make the hard decisions to cut overhead, reduce staff in line with workload, and jettison (sell) divisions that yield no synergies or profits to the corporate parent. Takeovers created over 11 million jobs, while the investment-grade *Fortune* 500 companies eliminated 3.9 million jobs (1980–1992).

4. Takeovers improve the morale of the victor, offering an executive ego massage to empire builders.

PREDATOR OR SCAVENGER?

Economists are what psychiatrists label "conflicted" when it comes to analyzing takeovers. They want stability, yet they want to dump excessive perks, bad CEOs, and inferior companies. We obviously do not have stability when lawyers and investment bankers earn $413 million in commissions on the RJR Nabisco deal to split apart a company that was brought together for just 38 months. The public should consider six bad news items concerning takeovers:

1. The takeover winner often does not understand the industry it has bought into, rapidly damaging the company and decreasing competition in the long run.

2. Takeover victims may become too lean and incapable of investing in either R&D innovation or expansion.

3. Takeover targets desiring to avoid acquisition will sometimes "destroy the company to save it," acquiring a white knight savior (investment partner) and a vast amount of debt.

4. Takeover victors in a vertical takeover are incapable of finding buyers for unwanted assets and eventually file for Chapter 11 bankruptcy (e.g., the huge Revco Drug Store went Chapter 11 in July 1988).

5. Takeover deals are often not undertaken for good economic reasons, but instead are done for unbridled greed and big fees for bankers, brokers, lawyers, and promoters (this conspiracy viewpoint was parodied in the 1988 movie *Wall Street*). *New York Times* columnist William Safire (March 9, 1989) summarized issues 3, 4, and 5 as follows: "When the profit motive is used to kill the goose that lays the golden eggs, capitalists must scramble."

6. In theory, the successful takeover may replace hired managers with real owners, but typically the corporate raider is equally detached from the workers and the workplace.

In some horizontal mergers the new owners have improved morale, entrusted their workers with a gain-sharing plan (to improve productivity, decrease costs, and then share the rewards), and invested more funds in R&D and new products. The effect of takeovers is positive in the minds of most economists if they discard poor managers, restructure bloated corporations into more sensible, smaller lines of business (fewer vertical mergers), and do no harm to competition. A 1991 *Northwestern Law Review* article by lawyer Gregory Sidak and economist Susan Woodward found that the 1986 anti-takeover law in Indiana cost shareholders 5.8 percent of the value of their holdings. (The typical 1990s takeover titan takes a long-run stake in the economic vitality of the firm.) Some takeovers are worth the price plus transaction costs, while others are a failure for all (except the lawyers and promoters).

Over time, after numerous life-cycle costing studies and time-series analyses, we shall have a definitive answer to the net economic impact of takeovers. Until that time, business journalists will continue to sound like the Chinese historian who summarized the French Revolution by stating that with only two centuries passed "it's too early to tell whether this thing will work." Some takeovers have acted as the kiss that turns the frog into the handsome prince. But how in the aggregate do the benefits compare with the costs? To some people takeover artists are bloodless scavengers cleaning out the bestiary; for victims they represent predators that should be roped in by changing tax laws. Reduced taxation of dividends will encourage savings and investment and reduce the need for corporate debt. The next section surveys consumption taxes as a strategy to cut the deficit, stimulate savings, and reduce household debt capacity (personal bankruptcy).

CONSUMPTION TAXES: LEECH OR GOOD MEDICINE?

Following the 1981–1982 recession, consumer spending averaged 3.95 percent in the 1980s. A tax on consumption is viewed by policymakers as a vast source of tax revenue. Consumption taxation makes savings and investment better options. In a macroeconomic sense, if we overtax savings and have no national sales tax to discourage consumption, Americans will continue to overspend and undersave. In summary, if tax makers designed a cow, it would consume milk and belch hay.

In a best case scenario, a 2 point addition to the national savings rate could be produced after a 3.5 percent consumption tax yielded a 2.5 percent one-shot decline in consumer spending. This one-shot decline in consumer spending need not send the economy into a tailspin if the resulting savings is well invested in R&D, new products, debt reduction, and deficit reduction. A tax on consumption could be achieved with a national sales tax or a broad business tax on the value added in the production process.

The value-added tax (VAT) is very popular in Europe (originally developed in France in 1955). Europeans realized that a central government could become too highly dependent on personal income taxes or payroll taxes, which are fully sensitive to economic fluctuations. In contrast, a VAT is more dependable (stable) and easy to administer, and it is levied on most transactions other than at the retail level. A sales tax is only imposed at the point of purchase, but a VAT is applied to the product or service at each stage of the production process (in proportion to the value added).

The British doubled their VAT in 1979 to finance their cuts in the income tax rates. VATs represented 32 percent of total revenues in Britain in 1990. The Japanese came to realize they had to reduce consumption and therefore initiated a 3 percent VAT as of April 1989. A 3 percent VAT in 1995 in America could generate $32 to $40 billion, depending on the exemptions (e.g., food).

The idea of a direct consumption tax, such as a national sales tax, has zero popular support in America. Buy less and save more is a painful prescription even in time of war. Any new tax must be indirect (e.g., a value-added tax implicit in the posted prices) and must be earmarked to popular government programs (education and health care). The public's attention must be focused on the positive impact of revenues provided to these programs, plus the positive impact of collecting a sales tax from "those foreign importers" (while avoiding a protectionist trade war). The public attributes of a consumption tax must be pro-savings, pro-health, pro-education, pro–free trade, yet soak the rich importers.

The successful speech to justify a consumption tax might include the line: "Our new VAT will force those rich Japanese and Germans to pay for our Medicare and college educations." This is consistent with international trade rules; for instance, Japan places a VAT on imported goods. Also the VAT will hit drug dealers and other members of the underground economy, through the goods they purchase.

The VAT produces a challenge for conservatives. The long-run fear of a VAT is that it may insulate politicians from public accountability. A whole host of taxes can be implicit in the price of goods and services that people buy, providing liberal paladins with the financing to initiate new social programs. For libertarians, an invisible tax like a VAT is dangerous if it fuels government growth and increased control of the economy. On the positive side, a VAT can improve capital formation by making consumption more expensive (and less desirable) than personal savings and investment. A VAT must be earmarked for necessary government programs. VAT collections must return the national savings rate to healthy levels, not resuscitate the liberal inclination toward big spending and bureaucracy.

The preamble to the September 1992 bipartisan budget commission report, chaired by Senators Nunn (D–Ga.) and Domenici (R–N.M.), calls for $1.10 in VAT for every $3 in spending cuts. The two senators cite a 17th-century quote from Thomas Hobbes: "It is fairer to tax people on what they extract from the economy, as roughly measured by their consumption, than to tax them on what they produce for the economy, as roughly measured by their income." The beauty of the VAT is that it operates on the theory that we should tax in proportion to what people take out of the economic refrigerator. America currently lets the public "pig out" but then overtaxes those who save and stock the refrigerator.

A VAT must be carefully crafted so as not to exacerbate the trade deficit. Consequently, the VAT could not be levied on exported goods. Certain necessary (non-luxury) items such as food could be exempt from taxation to minimize the regressive nature of any sales tax (i.e., minimize the unfair burden on lower income groups). Lastly, American tax officials should learn from the Japanese experience how to minimize administrative costs so that VAT collection expenses do not consume more than 10 to 12 percent of VAT revenues. Care must be taken to make sure the reporting requirements for a VAT are not too onerous for small businesses.

Some political leaders have a preference for financing deficit reduction without spending cuts (in the language of President Johnson, "all taxes, no spending cuts; all hat, no cattle"). Members of Congress see the VAT as a good new revenue producer because the tax avoids the public eye. Under a VAT businesses, not the taxpayers, send the tax receipts to the government. The tax is embedded in the price of goods and services, so the taxpayer seldom complains. This revenue-enhancement strategy has worked well in one American state since 1977. In Michigan firms send their check for 2.35 percent of the value-added base to the state government. VAT is a subtle levy on production, in sharp contrast to a direct sales tax or income tax. Since politicians can seldom be shamed into limiting the rate of growth in visible taxes, they must be forced into a bargain that will link tax hikes to spending cuts. *POLICY PROPOSAL No. 27:* Enact a VAT of 3 percent—excluding housing, health care, and food from taxation—and require Congress to pass an equivalent amount of spending cuts for each dollar of VAT. A VAT would cost the IRS $1.6 billion to administer annually, but a 6 percent VAT would collect $157 billion over 1994–1997.

If the VAT discourages costly consumption and encourages consumer savings, the policy proposal would force Congress into the same bargain (spend less, save more). The VAT has bipartisan support from Democratic Senators David Boren (Okla.) and Sam Nunn (Ga.) and Republican Senators Pete Domenici (N.M.) and John Danforth (Mo.). For economists the advantage of the VAT is that it is the most efficient tax possible, it is difficult to avoid, and it has the lowest negative impact on output of any possible type of tax. If we do not limit our politicians, the VAT in America could rise to European levels.

SIN TAXES AND THE GAS TAX

When is a tax not a tax? When it is a sin tax or gas tax, the government officials call it a user fee. A number of specific goods could be taxed at a higher rate to cover the health care costs generated following consumption of "sinful" products (e.g., alcohol and tobacco). The average retail price of a pack of cigarettes has increased from 59 cents in 1977 to $1.94 in 1993. Only 26 cents of the increase went to increased taxes; 97 cents went to profits for sellers and tobacco producers. American cigarettes would still be 35 percent cheaper than the Canadian price if we added an additional $1.52 per pack tax to the current 48 cents. The increased federal tax would collect an additional $27.2 billion in 1994. Judging by the Canadian experience, the price increase would reduce tobacco consumption per capita by 30 percent in five years (1999). What would the fiscal benefits be for the entire society following a 30 percent reduction in consumption? The tax hike would save the current generation of smokers $160 to $180 billion over the next four decades (1994 dollars).

Alcohol tax hikes could be substantial. Studies by Will Manning et al. (1989) at the Rand Corporation suggest that drinkers are paying a much smaller fraction of the cost for their activity compared to smokers. They report that drinking costs society 48 cents for every ounce of alcohol, but the user fee is only 22 cents per ounce. The users are not paying their way. Doubling the tax on beer and malts to 56 cents per gallon would increase federal revenues by $1.64 billion. Doubling the tax on wine and cordials to 32 cents per gallon would raise $0.313 billion, and doubling the tax on distilled liquor to $25 per gallon would raise $2.2 billion.

Special interest groups will claim such taxes penalize 90 percent of the users who are not causing damage or incurring unnecessary health care expenses. However, such innocent individuals may in the future be a member of the "irresponsible" group, and we should start saving in advance through federal excise taxes to reimburse society partially for the economic and social costs of their behavior. These tax suggestions will pass because consumption of these products has decreased among the demographic group that runs the nation: university-educated men and women.

Increased taxation will decrease consumption. If increased taxation hikes the price of alcohol by 10 percent, average consumption may be reduced by 3 percent. However, for those addicted to alcohol, the reduction on consumption may be very small (or nonexistent). Health policymakers should not oversell the benefits of excise taxes: a 3 percent decline in consumption may yield only a 1 to 2 percent decline in alcohol-associated mortality (102,000 per year).

Since the Whiskey Rebellion of 1794, American policymakers have fought to make "sin" taxes less unfair and burdensome to the poor. Excise taxes eat up a higher proportion of income for poor Americans. One needs to provide some offsetting assistance for the poor without resorting to "food stamps" for smoking and drinking. Certain states offer tax rebates to the poor to compensate that group for regressive state sales taxes or sin taxes.

An offset is also needed for a consumption tax on gas. Car owners earning under $15,000 per year and driving more than 75 miles to work per week could receive a $100 tax credit. The gas tax hits households harder (as a percent of income) among the working poor and in high-use regions (north-central and southern states). The Tax Reform Act of 1986 cut taxes by over $584 million for those earning under $15,000 per year. However, adding to the gas tax 9 cents per gallon ($155 per household per year) would more than wipe out this tax reduction. Depending on the assumptions concerning the degree of leisure driving and the price elasticity of demand among the working poor, gas taxes could represent 6 percent of family income in rural households if we raise them to 27 cents per gallon.

A more general solution to the regressive nature of consumption taxes would simply involve a large income tax credit, depending on location and vehicle ownership. The $15,000 household could pay $1,400 in consumption taxes (including VAT) and receive a $1,200 tax credit. The $45,000 household could pay $2,900 in consumption taxes, get back $1,200, and be a net contributor of $1,700. The consumption tax could even become progressive if the tax credit was phased out for the $50,000 to $100,000 income brackets.

The economic benefits of the gas tax are easily identified. Each 1 cent increase in the gas tax reaps $1.08 billion in federal revenue. Increased gas taxes will dampen consumption, enhance energy independence, and play a small part in reducing carbon dioxide emissions and the risk of a greenhouse effect. A tax increase at the pump is carefully targeted to raise revenues, promote conservation, and not benefit OPEC. By contrast, Gary Hart's 1988 policy proposal to increase the oil import fee from $4 to $10 per barrel was pure insanity. Americans would pay $61 billion more for oil each year, but the benefits would go to those least in need ($39 billion to American oil companies). Raising the price of imported oil has a dollar-for-dollar impact on the market price of domestic oil, producing a windfall of profits and adversely affecting citizens in northern states dependent on home heating oil.

WHEN POLITICS BEATS ECONOMICS

Consumption taxes or a VAT will never excite the hearts and minds of the average taxpayer or small businessmen. Small businesses hate the concept of any potential depressant on sales. They see little value in reduced consumption and increased savings. Cynics have suggested that America will need to experience a second depression to revitalize the savings ethic. The typical worker hates the idea of paying more for drinking, smoking, driving, and shopping. Few citizens speak for the public interest: a platform for more savings, more investment, and more long-run economic activity. Abstinence and conservation are not popular themes. Most economy-minded members of Congress support the concept of a VAT, but they still remember the fate of Representative Al Ullman (D–Or.), powerful chairman of the Ways and Means Committee. He identified real problems, offered practical solutions, and lost his job. In 1980 he lost his firmly secure House seat after suggesting a VAT to the voters back home. The politics of the situation is so obvious as to be overlooked by most political thinkers. If the politician claims he or she will rape the rich with higher taxes, that does not make the average worker feel compensated for getting nailed by the taxman at the liquor store, gas pump, or shopping mall.

Democratic advisers and paladins have long supported a VAT. In 1980 MIT economist Lester Thurow advocated a 7.5 percent VAT with a $1,000 per family tax credit (to net $95 to $100 billion). In 1988 Democratic presidential candidate Bruce Babbitt won praise from only the press and the economics profession by advocating a $40 to $45 billion VAT. The medicine (consumption taxes) will never be popular, but if the patient (the economy) gets sick enough through a prolonged recession, the necessary taxes may become the law of the land.

Tax policy can be utilized to promote a number of social ideas, like recycling. By placing a tax on new paper, but not recycled paper, tax policy can promote conservation. Some nations offer tax breaks to companies that recycle used auto chassis. In Norway and Sweden, the national government taxes new cars, but this tax is 100 percent refundable with interest earned when the car is scrapped. America must rediscover thrift.

There exists an organized constituency against each of the new taxes outlined in this chapter. Opponents of the gas tax claim that Wharton Econometrics simulations suggest an additional tax could cost 60,000 to 150,000 jobs. Proponents of the gas tax suggest that citizens from Germany to Japan pay much higher prices at the pump ($1.85 to $3.75 more per gallon) without any harm to their GNP, and increased workers in the energy-efficiency business would compensate for any losses linked to higher taxes at the pump.

Fiscal policy should be more sensible and more aggressive in raising revenue. The federal government needs to be more creative in collecting revenue. *POLICY PROPOSAL No. 28:* Establish user fees that cover the marginal cost for air traffic control services, thus collecting $6.4 billion in 1994–1997. Users of air services would still have a good deal because they would have to pay only for marginal costs, rather than the higher figure of average costs. Moreover, President Reagan would never have had his conflict with striking air traffic controllers if their work was not underpriced, undervalued, and undermanaged by the Federal Aviation Administration.

NO NEW "INVESTMENT" TAXES

A federal government in search of revenue enhancement has begun to learn a lesson from state government. New taxes targeted for specific goals, so called "investment" taxes, enjoy widespread public support. State tax increases targeted for education passed in 14 states during the 1980s. The public needs assurance that their taxes go to wise investments in education, transportation, economic development, and health care for the needy. The public will not support untargeted taxes for general goals like reducing the federal deficit. Deficit reduction is a focused goal for economists, but it is viewed as unworthy of support by the general public because the goal appears too unfocused (i.e., the beneficiaries are not immediate and easily identified individuals).

Many analysts draw a distinction between good and bad taxes. Good taxes are an investment in our future and make America more productive (e.g., education, research, and development). Good taxes do not impair useful, productive activity. Sin taxes are good taxes in that they may reduce substance abuse while improving productivity per hour and hours worked. Taxing Social Security benefits at a parity level with private pensions will cause some healthy elderly to supply more hours of labor. This is a good tax because it strengthens America (even though older Americans would still work much fewer hours per week than the Japanese elderly).

The jury is out as to the utility of 29 state's lotteries to raise revenues. The lottery movement has two strikes against it. First, lottery money does not seem to supplement other sources of tax revenue. For example, the Florida State Lottery "for education" funds only 5.6 percent of the 1993 state education budget. Florida voters still believe the lie that the lottery has increased educational funding per capita in real dollar terms. The second problem with lotteries to finance government programs is that they sanction the belief that thrift and hard work are less important than luck or chance. The diligent, hard-working Japanese contrasts with the stereotype of the gambler worshiping at the altar of chance. However, gambling is a regressive, albeit voluntary, source of government revenue.

CONCLUSIONS

In a macroeconomic sense, our overriding concern should be the net impact on growth, employment, and inflation. Consumption taxes are slightly increasing the price of a number of items so that we may reduce the price of another item, borrowed money. Tax revenues will reduce the deficit, promote savings and investment, and convince our independent Federal Reserve Bank to ease interest rates and promote economic growth. The Federal Reserve cannot reduce interest rates without rapidly increasing inflation in the economy. The federal government is simply soaking up too much of private savings because the deficits are too high, and citizens need the incentive to save more. If we tax consumption sufficiently, saving 2 points more, the cheaper borrowed money can cause 100 flowers to bloom in the economy, since faster economic growth always springs from lower-cost financing. A rebirth in inflation would erode the incentive to save.

Inflation yields what our economy needs least, increased consumption at the expense of investment and savings. Instead of being self-centered and empty of commitment, the average citizen with the help of a better incentive system can be more savings-centered. Financing investment does not sound like a social statement, but it is when it provides more jobs, more training, more independence from foreign investment, and more economic growth for all. Liberal politicians who claim America is undertaxed have no capacity to explain why, in the 45 years since 1947, the income of the average family of four has expanded 8.4-fold, but the income taxes paid by that family have expanded 247-fold. Americans do not need more taxes; they need a better and more fair distribution of the tax burden, with reduced government bureaucracy and unnecessary spending. In the next chapter trade policy will be discussed. Tax and trade issues are interrelated. For example, in 1962 President Kennedy passed a 7 percent tax credit for any new business investment "to help alleviate our balance of payment problems with other nations."

REFERENCES

Adams, C. (1993). *For Good and Evil: Impact of Taxes on the Course of Civilization.* New York: Madison.

Agell, J., Persson, M., and Friedman, B. (1993). *Does Debt Management Matter?* Oxford: Clarendon Press.

Auerbach, A. (1991). "Retrospective Capital Gains Taxation," *American Economic Review* 81:1, March, 167–77.

Auerbach, A., and Hines, J. (1988). "Investment Tax Incentives and Frequent Tax Reforms," *American Economic Review* 78:2, May, 211–16.

Bernanke, B., and Campbell, J. (1988). "Is There a Corporate Debt Crisis?" In *Brooking Papers on Economic Activity*, Vol. 1. Washington: Brookings, 83–125.

Bernheim, D. (1991). *The Vanishing Nest Egg: Reflections on Savings in America.* New York: 20th Century Fund.

Bernstein, H. (1992). "The Savings Concern: Should Small Potatoes Dominate the Feast," *Journal of Post Keynesian Economics* 14:2, Winter, 281–82.

Bohanon, C., and VanCott, T. (1986). "Labor Supply and Tax Rates: Comment," *American Economic Review* 76:1, March, 277–79.

Boskin, M. (1988). "Consumption, Saving, and Fiscal Policy," *American Economic Review* 78:2, May, 401–7.

Boskin, M., and Lau, L. (1989). "An Analysis of Postwar U.S. Consumption and Savings Behavior," Stanford University Mimeograph.

Dubin, J., Graetz, M., and Wilde, L. (1987). "Are We a Nation of Tax Cheaters? New Econometric Evidence on Tax Compliance," *American Economic Review* 77:2, May, 240–45.

Feldstein, M. (1989). "Tax Policy for the 1990s: Personal Saving, Business Investment, and Corporate Debt," *American Economic Review* 79:2, May, 108–12.

Hall, R., and Rabushka, A. (1985). *The Flat Tax.* Palo Alto, CA: Hoover Institution.

Hamermesh, D., and Rees, A. (1984). *The Economics of Work and Pay.* New York: Harper and Row.

Hayashi, F. (1993). "Japan's Saving Rate Trends," University of Tokyo, Department of Economics, Monograph.

Hoover, K., and Sheffrin, S. (1992). "Causation, Spending and Taxes: Sand in the Sandbox or Tax Collector for the Welfare State?" *American Economic Review* 82:1, March, 225–47.

Kaus, M. (1992). *The End of Equality.* New York: New Republic and Basic Books.

Kiesling, H. (1990). "Economic and Political Foundations of Tax Structure: Comment," *American Economic Review* 80:4, September, 931–34.

Lampert, H. (1990). *True Greed: What Really Happened in the Battle for RJR Nabisco.* New York: New American Library.

Lee, D., ed. (1986). *Taxation and the Deficit Economy: Fiscal Policy and Capital Formation in the U.S.* San Francisco: Pacific Research Institute for Public Policy.

Lindsey, L. (1990). *The Growth Experiment: How Tax Policy Is Transforming the U.S. Economy.* New York: Basic Books.

Malabre, A. (1987). *Beyond Our Means: How America's Long Years of Debt, Deficits and Reckless Borrowing Now Threaten to Overwhelm Us.* New York: Random House.

Manning, W., Keller, E., Newhouse, J., Sloss, E., and Wasserman, J. (1989). "The Taxes of Sin: Do Smokers and Drinkers Pay Their Way?" *Journal of the American Medical Association* 261:11, March 17, 1593–98.

Manning, W., Newhouse, J., Winkler, J., and Wasserman, J. (1991). "Effects of Excise Taxes and Regulations on Cigarette-Smoking," *Journal of Health Economics* 10:1, May, 43–64.

Mishkin, F. (1986). *The Economics of Money, Banking, and Financial Markets.* Boston: Little, Brown.

Ohmae, K. (1988). "Is Japanese Savings Rate Really High?" *Japan Economic Journal* 26:1312, May 14.

Pechman, J. (1990). "The Future of the Income Tax," *American Economic Review* 80:1, March, 1–20.

———. (1985). *Who Paid the Taxes, 1966–85.* Washington, DC: Brookings.

Pereira, A. (1993). "Dynamic General Equilibrium Analysis of Corporate Tax Integration," *Journal of Policy Modeling* 15:1, February, 63–89.

Sabel, C., and Piore, M. (1984). *The Second Industrial Divide.* New York: Basic Books.

Steurle, C. (1990). "Tax Credits for Low-Income Workers with Children," *Journal of Economic Perspectives* 4:3, Summer, 201–12.

Summers, L. (1987). "A Fair Tax Act That's Bad for Business," *Harvard Business Review* 65:2, March–April, 53–59.

———. (1981). "Taxation and Corporate Investment: A Q-Theory Approach," *Brooking Papers on Economic Activity* 1, 67–127.

Thaler, R. (1991). *Quasi Rational Economics.* New York: Russell Sage.

Thurow, L. (1985). *The Zero-Sum Solution: Building a World-Class American Economy.* New York: Simon and Schuster.

Tyson, L. (1989). *American Industry and International Competition.* Ithaca, NY: Cornell University Press.

U.S. Congress. (1993). *Assessing the Decline in the National Savings Rate.* Washington, DC: Congressional Budget Office.

U.S. Congressional Budget Office. (1993) *Reducing the Deficit: Spending and Revenue Options.* Washington, DC: U.S. Government Printing Office.

U.S. Department of Commerce. (1990–1993). *Survey of Current Business.* Washington, DC: U.S. Government Printing Office.

Whitehouse, H. (1992). "Pension Funds Impact on Our Declining Economy," Statement to the House Banking Committee, February 5.

Wolff, E. (1991). "Capital Formation and Productivity Convergence Over the Long Term," *American Economic Review* 81:3, June, 565–79.

Young, H. (1990). "Progressive Taxation and Equal Sacrifice," *American Economic Review* 80:1, March, 253–66.

4

Trade Deficits and Economic Restructuring

Competitiveness is the wrong word, because it implies that through some stratagem Americans can reassert economic supremacy in the world.

—Alice Rivlin, 1992

We buy from Japan and Germany and other nations the things we used to make and sell them. . . . Then at the end of the year, because we spend more than we collect in reduced taxes, we borrow back those dollars, paying billions more of our dollars in interest, increasing our debt, decreasing our ability to invest in our children, our schools, perpetuating a mad economic cycle.

—Governor Mario M. Cuomo, 1991

In 1992 the American merchandise trade deficit increased from $92 billion (1991) to $102 billion. Over half of this deficit was with Japan. American strategy to trim the trade deficit with Japan involves two basic options. The brave approach would be to negotiate a free-trade deal, eradicating with a stroke of the pen all the Japanese distribution and zoning laws that keep American products out of their market. The second option would be to continue the Republican results-oriented approach to managed trade. Under this second strategy, numerical, monitorable market share targets are set (e.g., Americans must have a 20 percent share of semiconductors sold in Japan). After five years this 20 percent target market share was achieved in 1992.

In the period 1950–1992, the United States' proportion of the world's goods and services declined from 41 to 19 percent. In 1970 the United States was responsible for the development and design of 75 percent of the advanced technology in the world. By 1992 our American market share had declined to 35 percent. In 1984 America lost its position as the world's leading exporter to West Germany, and Japan supplanted Uncle Sam for second place in 1987. America taught other nations to grow, and they learned their lessons well. Rather than long for the days when we totally dominated the world, America would do well to relearn respect for productivity, product design, customers, and the futility of isolationism and protectionist trade barriers.

Prudent families judge their financial standing partly by comparing what they owe with what they are owed. By that measure America has entered troubling times, but one should not use the overutilized term "period of crisis." A wealthy family usually maintains an enormous debt capacity and a substantial mortgage. In the mid-1980s America became the world's largest net debtor nation, with debts soaring to $600 to $820 billion in 1992. In the late 1980s, the American ratio of debt to gross domestic product (GDP) has grown from 11 to 17 percent. This is still substantially better than Brazil's ratio of 48 to 59 percent, Argentina's ratio of 66 to 73 percent, and Chile's ratio of 115 percent.

America imports more than it can pay for with earnings from exports. The nation consumes beyond its means and borrows abroad to pay the difference. We run a substantial trade deficit, with trade imports far in excess of trade exports. America would have to run a trade surplus of about $36 billion to meet its international interest obligations (not including principal payments). The figure of $36 billion may seem vast, until we compare it relative to what a few points of productivity gains would add to a $6 trillion American gross domestic product. Productivity gains can easily pay the interest payments and the principal as well. The total installment payments (interest plus principal) make American citizens imperceptibly poorer, in effect subtracting $435 from potential per capita income in 1992.

Estimates of our standing as a debtor nation ranging from $600 to $820 billion derive from how American and foreign holdings are valued. Under the high estimate, the government defines the value of the asset as the price at time of purchase, thus understating the value of America's overseas holdings, especially for investments purchased in the 1950s and 1960s. Compared to this historical cost method, America's international debt stands at $820 billion in 1992. However, if we use current replacement costs, the international debt is only $600 billion (up from the $464 billion Commerce Department estimate in 1989). If we are going to continue to add to this $600 to $820 billion mountain of international debt by running additional trade deficits, we must rely on American economic growth and technical efficiency (i.e., output/input = productivity) improvements to pay the bills. We cannot expect to run a trade surplus any time soon. Those who think that running a trade surplus is a worthy national economic goal should recall that America had a substantial trade surplus during the depression in the 1930s. A growing world economy will always need more dollars and more sales to Americans. Our policy prescription should involve a mild reduction in import consumption and enhanced exports of American goods (fueled in part by domestic productivity gains, quality improvements, and price reductions). Another way to look at the dark side of America running a trade surplus involves the consideration of foreign labor markets. If we suddenly eliminated the trade deficit in 1990 and ran a small trade surplus, then 2.8 million foreign jobs would be lost in Europe, Mexico, and South America. On the political front, democratic governments might be overthrown, and further debts owed to American banks might go unpaid.

If political instability threatened, foreign investors would increase their already substantial dollar or yen investments to act as a hedge against their local currency risk. This capital influx helps explain why the American standard of living is still second to none. The American living standard is still 5 to 15 percent superior to the German and Japanese levels. The problem is that it exists on borrowed money. There are some 1990s Jeremiahs who predict that a rapid capital outflow of foreign investment would cause the American standard of living to collapse. This author doubts this scenario will come to pass, but the evidence for this viewpoint is included in a number of popularist books. An economist who forecasts doom always sells better.

NO SHOCK EFFECT FROM TRADE DEFICITS

For most Americans the deterioration in our trade position in the 1980s and 1990s has been relatively painless. But the pain is insidious. Citizens did not get a bill in the mail for their $435 of lost per capita income during 1992. The shock effect of the American trade deficit is compared by academics to the shock effect of the Soviets' launching of the Sputnik in 1957. But in fact few decision makers, and fewer workers, are listening to the pleas of academics.

The trade deficit is "slightly shocking" not because of its absolute size, but because of its unprecedented context. The trade deficit rose up like a weed during a robust, record-breaking, nine-year economic recovery after the 1982 recession. The extra net imports implicit in the trade deficit make it seem that the American economy has grown by a cumulative amount of 7.3 percent more over the ten years (through 1992) than it actually has. Like some *Star Trek* voyager, citizens experience the mirage of a standard of living that is $1,780 better than it would be without any trade deficit. However, to steal the party punch bowl (as all good economists should), remember that this foreign debt has to be paid.

If the American economy grows at a mere 2.75 percent in the 1990s, we shall dedicate 0.6 percent of each year's total GNP to pay this foreign debt. America cannot simply say the foreign debt problem is harmless, a simple trade of green paper dollars costing pennies to engrave for foreign cars and other consumer goods. The policy problem comes in two areas. First, what happens if the American economy experiences a second big downturn in the 1990s? A prolonged recession might cause the installment payments to rocket up to $2,000 or $2,800 per capita, in which case the mirage of a better standard of living was in fact a bad deal. Only those who died before the debt came due actually enjoyed the swap of VCRs and foreign cars for pieces of green paper printed by the United States Treasury.

Second, we used too much of the foreign debt to acquire items that do not earn an economic return necessary to pay our bills (e.g., BMWs, Hondas, Hyundais, wine, clothing, and shoes). The best money we imported involves investment in American corporations, through stock ownership or equity positions, because those funds will earn an economic return all through the 1990s and beyond. Japanese and German investors were able to keep our rate of investment in plant and equipment in the normal zone of 17 to 18 percent during the period 1984–1993; otherwise that figure might have declined by one-third (to 12 or 13 percent). Such investment in America probably saved 1.2 to 1.4 million American jobs and allowed our unemployment rate to dip below 6 percent in 1988 and not go above 8 to 9 percent in 1992.

The Japanese did us a favor in the short run by making $83 billion in direct investment in America through 1992. These funds were used to build 10 rubber and tire factories, 7 auto-assembly plants, 250 auto-parts suppliers, and 39 steel mills in Middle America. In 1991–1992 some 45 percent of the Japanese cars sold in America were made in America. Is Japan our major problem? The annual trade deficit with Japan has been $36 to $49 billion in the 1990s, which is only 1.8 to 2.4 days of output in the American economy. If we exclude automobiles, the deficit with Japan is only $4 to $7 billion higher than our deficit with China.

The trade deficits are somewhat like an opportunistic virus that will do severe harm to the body politic if the patient experiences a mild cold (a mild tailspin or recession). In the last section of this chapter, we shall survey whether a national program of preventive medicine should be undertaken to reverse three decades of scientific-educational complacency. This does not involve socialism or "industrial policy," rather it involves America relearning the lessons we taught Japan from 1947 to 1969.

The standard of living of present and future generations of Americans is not linked just to our consumption patterns, but rather to our borrowing and investment position. In theory, foreign holding of American debt is no more destabilizing than American holding of the debt. Whether our debt position poses a threat to our economy depends on: (1) how big the total debt is relative to this rich nation's debt capacity and (2) how many jobs are lost because we underinvested in capital formation (and consumed like pigs at a trough). The average American worker consumed $3,260 more in 1989 than in 1981. Ultimately, $1,280 of that came from foreign borrowing and $1,180 came from real economic growth. The balance came from $840 of lower domestic investment!

The American trade deficit for the entire 1970s was merely $19.7 billion. The trade deficit is like the wind chill factor: few people can define it, but the public has a vague feeling it is important in some circumstances. The trade deficit is not a problem if annual economic growth equals 4 to 5 percent, but it is a problem if economic growth limps along at 1.5 to 2.5 percent or stagnates. The American trade deficit of goods and services widened from $123.3 billion in 1984 to $148.4 billion in 1985, $166.3 billion in 1986, and a maximum of $171.2 billion in 1987. It then declined to $144 billion in 1988, $108.6 billion in 1989, $100.9 billion in 1990, $65 billion in 1991, and $37 billion in 1992. The aggregate figures hold some interesting trends. The American trade balance in manufactured goods declined from a $11 billion surplus in 1981 to a $139 billion deficit in five years!

The 1992 $102 billion merchandise trade deficit is cause for alarm. We must improve this figure rather than wallow in the knowledge that our service surpluses shrink the net trade deficit. The services that produce this statistical gain involve royalties on American movies, legal fees, and tourism. Consequently, to improve this service sector balance of trade we could make more movies in Canada and Mexico, cheapen the dollar to increase tourism, and expand the utilization of American lawyers. In short, service sector balance of trade is not as critical as a merchandise sector trade imbalance.

NEW PROTECTION AGREEMENTS

The 1993 North American Trade Act (Lustig et al., 1993) did not eliminate all barriers and quotas. If America is to mimic the competition in foreign lands and offer some quotas, we should do it with an optimal economic strategy. The United States could sell quota slots at public auction to mimic the tariff rates charged by foreign nations in the name of equity (equal protection for American industry). *POLICY PROPOSAL No. 29:* Sell import quotas for apparel, sugar, and textiles at auction to the highest bidder (collecting $12 billion in revenues over the years 1994–1997, according to the Congressional Budget Office). There are two benefits to this approach: (1) for an equal dosage of protection, auction tariffs are much less damaging to economic growth than inflexible quotas and (2) American industry is not overprotected (i.e., not overinsulated from economic trends and innovation in technology).

The most revolutionary trend comes in the realization that trading goods no longer accounts for most of the daily financial flows across national boundaries. Loans, equity investments, shareholder investments, and real estate deals—so-called "pure cash flows"—dominate the trade figures. One way to summarize the net flow of funds, including the value of goods and services, involves tracking the current account deficit. In the American context, as a net debtor, the current account deficit measures the amount of money our nation must raise in other nations by borrowing and selling to finance our national economy. The current account deficit increased from $141.4 billion in 1986 to a maximum of $160.7 billion in 1987, before declining to under $100 billion in 1992.

When buyers import goods or services from Japan, they may purchase with dollars or use Japanese yen purchased from a local bank. If Japanese exporters accept the dollar for payment, they may convert the dollars to yen at the national (central) Bank of Japan. The national bank will then exchange the dollars with the United States Treasury. A transaction that reduces the reserves of the United States Treasury is a debit in the balance of payments account, and a transaction that increases these reserves is a credit. The rule of double-entry accounting ensures that a nation's current account balance is financed by equal and opposite movements of capital. The laws of economics plus the political relationships between governments determine exchange rates, interest rates, and prices. For example, the joint actions of the "Big Seven" national banks helped to prop up the value of the dollar as it declined in 1985–1988. Balance of payment accounts include three basic components: (1) international transfer payments, including gifts and grants from governments and individuals, (2) capital transactions (e.g., capital inflow when foreigners purchase an American asset), and (3) current transactions—the import or export of goods and services (e.g., shipping, insurance, tourism). Annual unilateral transfers have declined from a peak of $15.7 billion in 1986 to $8.5 billion in 1992.

To most readers this section seemingly exhausted the viewpoints one could possibly take on the trade balance issue. This is not true. One school of thought from the Jimmy Carter "malaise school of economics" argues that the flood of imports and consumer materialism caused the trade deficits. Contrary to conventional wisdom among liberals concerning "me generation" materialism, when expressed by our wallets (not the media), the American population was import-directed prior to the Reagan years. Americans just needed the overvalued dollar in the early 1980s to finance the pent-up demand to buy like crazy. What evidence exists for such a wild generality? Imports as a percentage of our GNP declined in the nine years after 1980. In 1980 imports were 9.4 percent of the GNP, declining to 8.5 percent in 1987 and 5.1 percent in 1992. Our exports were the biggest problem. They slipped from 8 percent of the GNP in 1980 to a minimum of 5.1 percent in 1986, rebounding to 6.3 percent in 1992.

Trade deficits improve (decline) if exports increase or imports decrease. America needs to continue expanding exports and not rely excessively on the rhetoric of smashing down imports as things not "made in the U.S.A." We have already done the job of holding down imported goods and services.

HELPING THE DOLLAR

The six largest foreign national banks contributed $110 billion of their own reserves to shore up the value of the dollar in 1986–1987. The dollar experienced a steady downward slide from February 1985 to April 1988. Foreign private investors only began resupplying net new capital at 1984 rates of investment after the dollar became stable and slightly increased in value in the late spring of 1988. If the dollar support strategy had not worked, the Federal Reserve may have had to mark up interest rates substantially to attract a sufficient supply of foreign funds to finance our twin deficits (trade and federal). The international investment community still remained wary of any country that bought $100 of goods and services for every $82 to $87 it was able to sell abroad.

The correlation between the rising monthly merchandise trade deficit and the declining value of the dollar (against six industrial countries' currencies) was a remarkable 0.91 from February 1985 to April 1988. The world economy was fortunate that the decline of over 40 percent in the exchange value of the dollar did not occur overnight. A one-day, 40 percent drop in the dollar would be economically equivalent to a 40 percent tariff. Japanese executives were the most resourceful at dealing with a steady decline in the dollar. They were willing to forego some price hikes and sacrifice profits to maintain market share.

A 39-month falling currency helped to create an American export boom, although the stimulus was two years slower in coming than most experts had predicted. According to the 1973 "J-Curve" theory of economist Stephen Magee, as a nation devalues its currency, its trade deficit will first get worse and then steeply improve (thus creating a J shape). The first part of the theory worked as predicted; the American trade deficit worsened from $123.3 billion to $166.3 billion in two years. The two pieces of bad news were that: (1) the J-curve stubbornly refused to turn around—taking an unexpected 23 additional months after a 16-month, 30 percent devaluation of the dollar against the yen and the German mark, and (2) the rise was never "steep," as a trade deficit of over $100 billion still exists many years after 1985.

Why does two-thirds of the 1987 trade deficit still exist? This core trade deficit is not related to exchange rates. What the rising dollar did not cause in the early 1980s, the declining dollar cannot cure after 1988. In the language of marketing and economics, American citizens' taste for foreign goods is downward sticky—once they have enjoyed these goods, price becomes less of an issue (so the exchange rate is less of a factor). We are not about to try the Cuban solution for eliminating a trade deficit: renounce all bills, fail to pay, and watch the unfinanced deficit fall like a wine glass glider. Some Japanese authors have suggested that the American curve has gone flat, and Americans and their economy shall never again be as vibrant and dynamic as they once were (the "sick uncle" theory). This cynical theory predates the 1991–1992 slide in the Japanese stock market and the rebirth of productivity gains in some American industrial sectors. America has caught the "British disease," with a number of symptoms, including poor productivity and the need to turn repeatedly to devaluation of the currency to get its trade deficit reduced (or brought into balance).

This analyst would counterargue that we Americans have not repeatedly turned to devaluation; rather, we did it on a one-shot basis to compensate for an overvalued dollar in 1981–1984. This overvalued dollar killed our export industries, including farming, because we had priced ourselves out of the market. This 40 percent overvalued dollar in January 1985 was equivalent to a 40 percent export tax on American products, so exports declined. If the trade deficit was created in large part by the overvalued dollar, then what caused the overvalued dollar, and what helped pay for American consumption of imports? The answer is the out-of-control federal deficit and the 1981 federal tax cuts. Foreign money flooded into America, thus making the dollar overvalued. Why did foreign money run to America? Because America had to borrow so much to pay for its federal government that real interest rates, the interest earned on investment after inflation, were frequently two- to threefold better in the United States than in foreign capitals. If we ever cure our twin deficits, federal and trade, there is no reason why home mortgage rates could not float down to 3 to 4 percent.

MAJOR AND MINOR CULPRITS

Most economists are prisoner to the rule of Procrustes: they automatically and unconsciously redefine any problem to fit the world view of their specialized training. This author will follow in that tradition and state that the major culprit for the trade deficit problem has macroeconomic roots in federal taxing and spending. In devaluing the dollar, we made imports expensive for American citizens, thus diverting demand ("let those newly rich Japanese and Germans buy more of their own domestic products and send their tourists to visit the bargain basement U.S.A. and buy cheap but quality American goods"). American industry sold more to foreigners than to fellow Americans. Devaluation of the dollar indirectly fueled an increase in American demand for domestic production. Therefore, domestic unemployment declined and none of the predicted recessions forecast through 1986–1988 came true. However, our deficit-induced recession made a poor beginning for the 1990s.

This macroeconomic viewpoint simply states that a federal budget imbalance played a major role in the creation of a large trade deficit (attracting foreign buyers of federal bonds, overvaluing the dollar, harming exchange rate–sensitive exports, and fueling a buying spree of foreign imports). However, a minor (30 to 40 percent) share of the blame perhaps rests with individual American corporations and the work ethic and educational skills of the American worker. A number of analysts and businessmen published in the July–August 1987 issue of the *Harvard Business Review* argue that the trade deficit problem remains a microeconomic problem. As the exchange rates stabilized in the late 1980s, these microeconomic forces may explain why trade deficits remain high. According to the microeconomic viewpoint, America needs a better educational system and innovative management to create high-productivity, high-wage, flexible production capacity. Such activities cannot be done through protectionist trade policies that are anathema to flexibility. If the steel or auto plant is out of date, we cannot force our outdated products on buyers. Thus we must keep capital mobile and the work force flexible.

America is very good at the first 15 percent of the product life cycle, the invention and initial development stage. However, unless American companies cut new product life cycles by 300 percent, Japanese firms will continue to out-innovate them easily. In the words of George Stalk, the handicaps of American product development are the frequent, lengthy delays caused by management or government, which inevitably create an outdated vision of consumer tastes. The Japanese get their products out quickly. For example, Mitsubishi's time-based focus left American air-conditioner companies ten years behind. The Japanese emphasize quick delivery to the market and flexible manufacturing at low cost with greater product variety. As a strategic weapon, time is equivalent in importance to quality, productivity, capital, and even initial innovation. The typical American factory develops new products at functional centers, whereas the Japanese gain speed by utilizing "factory cells" that are cross-functional, multidisciplinary teams.

In visiting Japan since 1974, the author has observed numerous design errors by America's senior managers. Americans try to sell cars overseas with the steering wheel on the "wrong" side of the car or washing machines that are four inches too wide to fit through Japanese doors. If it is not poor product design, it often involves cultural insensitivity in marketing strategy (e.g., knock-on-door daytime sales visits in Asian nations notorious for their self-effacement of women). There may exist some secret protectionism by "devious Orientals," but not in these examples. No American plant worker is to blame if the design and promotion efforts are ill-conceived. Our export market zones for growth may not lie in Europe; we may need to open new "virtual markets," such as India. We should also relearn a lesson we taught to the Japanese, sometimes called the Duesenberry Demonstration Effect. Customers will not know they always desired the item/concept until it dangles in front of them (e.g., snowmobiles in the mountains).

Some American auto companies have brought their product up to Japanese or German standards. The Ford Motor Company in the 1980s began to realize that 80 to 90 percent of the quality and productivity problem was management's responsibility. Ford relearned the quantitative quality-control measures that American professors exported to Japan in the 1950s. Today Ford can run 210 engines through the line with few defects. In the mid-1980s they would run 290 engines per hour through the line and have a 50 percent defect rate. It was a discovery to many that quality and productivity improvements were complements (to be done together). These improvements have been accomplished by Americans. Japanese-owned and -managed plants in America and Mexico have also demonstrated the folly in blaming the victim, the line worker, for system failures designed by senior company officials.

America's comparative advantage in stimulating a rebirth of good design and hard work may be our melting pot tradition. To paraphrase Walt Whitman, America is the race of races, and we can utilize the energy of a number of Koreans, Russians, Vietnamese, Mexicans, etc. This stands in stark contrast to the Japanese, who force their 670,000 Korean naturalized citizens to carry special identity papers. The Japanese Ministry of Education orders all local school boards not to hire Korean teachers, even those with 25 years experience. The 400,000 Vietnamese boat people will add a lot more to the American GNP than they subtract in education, training, and welfare costs. Those Japanese who argue for purity and homogeneous nationalism should read the writings of Tom Paine on the American ideal, an "asylum of mankind," 210 years ago. Our melting pot may do a better job of financing the aging of the American population than an "asylum free" Japan.

The Japanese miracle may be undone by a younger generation with less drive than their elders. Japan in the 21st century may experience a decline analogous to a slow loss of oxygen. Japanese citizens will be 41 percent pensioners in 2022, in contrast to only 26 percent of Americans. America in the 1990s will be utilizing Japanese engineers and venture capital, as we assisted them in the past. In two to three decades, America may have to return a favor and reenergize the Japanese economy a second time.

The Japanese are not solely efficiency oriented; they have some traditions that would amaze Americans. Each woman who wraps your food items, each man who caries your groceries contributes to the high price of food. This also helps explain why unemployment is extremely low (2 percent). Unless Japan finds a way to raise imports in the 1990s, unemployment will rise. Japan cannot become a low-wage country similar to Britain. Even when indexed against American wages, the Japanese worker who formerly earned $5 per hour less than his American counterpart in 1985 earned $4 per hour more in 1990. This is because the Japanese economy is more productive, and the yen has a better exchange rate in contrast to 1985. Japan in the 1990s will have to target the new wealthy class, not exports to Americans, for an increase in domestic sales to fellow citizens, a booming housing industry, and rapid growth in recreational activities.

In surveying the 1992 *International Dun and Bradstreet* survey, the Japanese appear to offer another advantage for building larger firms. In Japan scale breeds more investment in research and development. In other words, bigger companies tend to have more than proportionate increases in the amount spent on R&D. The trend is exactly the opposite in our nation. In America increases in firm size are correlated with less than proportionate increases in the amount spent on research and development. Ideas are more frequently generated by small business in America. But these ideas tend to drift across the Pacific to big Japanese firms that build electronics and other items at a low unit cost in 23 nations.

The Japanese are great imitators, and their patent laws are very liberal (Tyson, 1992). Japanese patent law reflects their copycat culture by allowing a firm to make a relatively small cosmetic change in the patent, claim it as their own, and then claim that it is all done to "avoid conflict and promote cooperation." Small businesses in high-technology markets are quickly swallowed up by larger companies in the Japanese system. The Japanese show no interest in imitating the American system of antitrust legal principles or patent infringement.

This seemingly unfair playing field, or legal field, argument appeals to American politicians who call for protectionism. The Japanese want 100 percent free trade for themselves, but they also want exclusionary barriers and taxes to keep out American imports. During the late 1980s Tokyo liberalized some import restrictions, and with the help of the Mansfield subcommittee on patent infringements, it reduced the unreasonable delays for bureaucratic and legal decisions. However, even the reduced level of Japanese protectionism offends our fundamental commitment to fair play. Subsidies and protectionism will cost the Japanese $306 per capita in 1992, in contrast to $130 per capita in America. Americans should still reflect on the fact that 17,000 American jobs have been saved through restrictions on imports, but at the cost of $150,000 per job (Center for the Study of American Business, 1993 estimate).

PROTECTIONISM—THE DEMISE OF OPEN TRADE

British economist Henry George fought higher tariffs in 1901 with the simple observation that what protection teaches us to do to ourselves in times of peace, our enemies seek to do to us in times of war. The average tariff on industrial goods dropped from 40 percent to about 5 percent in 1992. Democrat Paul Tsongas was wrong to suggest that we bring back protectionism in the name of industrial policy (i.e., "producerism"). The Organization for Economic Cooperation and Development estimates that the total worldwide cost of protectionism will be $260 billion in 1993.

In the 25 years following World War II, America led the world as an advocate of free trade. To the public, open trade meant prosperity and protectionism meant depression. Congress's passage of the mid-1930s Smoot-Hawley tariffs was widely believed to have caused a worldwide trade war and deepening depression. Protectionism was reborn in the American context when President Nixon's protectionist trade bill was passed in 1971 in reaction to "our onerous $2 billion trade deficit." Six days of the 1987 trade deficit equalled the entire 1971 trade deficit. Protectionism became an industry-specific form of welfare. All Americans paid higher prices so that they could protect some small group of American workers from foreigners and their imports. Yet during the period 1971–1988, open trade ranked just below religion and far above reading on the list of American activities constantly praised but sporadically practiced. In 1980 a whopping 20 percent of goods produced in America were protected from foreign competition, and by 1989 that proportion had doubled to 40 percent.

It is inaccurate to say America has a clear choice between free trade and protectionism. Protectionism is often justified by short-run thinkers who emphasize retaliation. For example, under the July 1986 trade deal, the Japanese were supposed to guarantee that their exported computer microchips were not "dumped" upon the American market at too low a price. In the opinion of our Commerce Department, the price continued to be too low, so in retaliation the Reagan administration slapped $310 million in tariffs on the Japanese. This message may be seen as bad news by some austere conservatives. But such thinking need not result in a rebirth of the Walter Mondale concept of "industrial policy," with many new bureaus of government and massive new federal spending. Instead, government can become a part of the solution to our trade problem by changing tax policies and directly supporting more education programs for all ages, including adult education and job training. Results will take time, but a problem created over many years is clearly immune to a quick fix.

Attitudes toward competition and protectionism have become a national Rorschach test. If one asks voters what they believe competition means, they list: enhanced productivity, efficiency, a better standard of living, and higher quality goods and services. If one asks a liberal politician, one hears a much different list: better protectionism, good quotas, fair retaliation, and more restricted imports in the war to save American workers. Such politicians neglect the fact that the American worker is also the American consumer. When we purchase lower priced, higher quality foreign goods, the American household improves its standard of living.

THE COMPARATIVE ADVANTAGE
OF OPEN TRADE

The comparative advantage model of David Ricardo is still the primary textbook theory for competitiveness. In this English economist's classic 1817 book, he argues that nations with a cost advantage in growing food should grow food and export it and should purchase clothing from countries that can cheaply make it. Updated to the 1990s, this means we should sell personal computers to Italy and buy their shoes, or sell food to Japan and buy their VCRs. Consumers in all nations would then experience a comparative improvement in their standard of living. But special interests in each nation provoke their politicians to quell the tides of free trade. The politicians defend their short-sighted salvation of inefficient domestic industries with a number of arguments. Protectionists argue that free trade would mean lost jobs, even in the nation with the lowest production of electronic goods. The Japanese Ministry of International Trade and Industry imposed export quotas in effect to reduce available supply, so the market would drive up chip prices to satisfy the American chip makers. However, this is a zero sum game. What is good for American chip makers in propping up the price is bad for American users of the chip who have to pay it. Sometimes protectionism is a means of retaliation pursued after careful economic study.

It may not be politically feasible to achieve the pre-1971 era of open trade. Unions and owners of protected industries disregard the insidious nature of protectionism: the negative side in lost jobs and higher prices is slow to develop, but the damage is real. Pursuit of protectionism to save jobs is similar to a dog chasing its own tail. According to Hufbauer and Rosen at the Institute for International Economics (1986), American consumers paid an estimated $53 billion in higher prices in 1984 because of our import restrictions. By 1993 that figure had risen to $87 billion. Many Americans are coming to realize that the better solution for failing industries would be an improvement in productivity and product quality. This is good news for American conservatives. However, to paraphrase why Congressman Joseph Kennedy (D–Mass.) voted against his party's Gephardt Trade Bill on April 30, 1987: (1) Protectionism doesn't address the real causes of our trade deficit, (2) more protectionism means more trouble, and (3) productivity growth can never be achieved by cutting education, research, and job training.

Japanese politicians have discovered the need for hope over fear and for freedom over protectionism. Japanese politicians feared unemployment in the countryside because the central government allotment of representatives counts one farmer's vote to be equal in worth to 3.6 votes from urban dwellers. Japanese rice farmers fought to the end to keep American rice out of Japan. But starting in 1993, the Japanese will allow rice imports. Net job reductions, with free trade, is an unwarranted fear. Witness the massive growth in employment in that paragon of free trade, Hong Kong. Protectionism limits (quotas, tariffs) are as irrational as the suggestion that the orange grower can only buy as much lobster as the lobster man buys in oranges. Who cares if Maine has a $139 million trade deficit with California? Maine would only begin to care about the issue if California began to purchase a significant portion of their state. If Maine citizens want to swap land to get fruit, why should economists care? We do not. But if trade is between nations, nationalism rears its ugly head.

INNOVATION, NOT PROTECTIONISM: BRAINS INSTEAD OF WALLS

The basic 1817 principle of comparative advantage will always ring true: if each good or service is supplied by the best-value producer, all will be richer. The public benefits from products that last longer, run better, and need less servicing. Protectionism saves jobs in noncompetitive industries at much too high a price. The post-1982 import quotas on Japanese cars cost the American public $156,000 for every job slot saved. During the period 1980–1988, employment in the American auto industry increased 11 percent to 1.75 million. Without the import quotas the employment level in domestic auto production would have slipped 11.2 percent to 1.4 million

American workers. To save those 347,000 jobs, the American public paid excess costs of $53.9 billion. But these huge costs were so indirect and unreported that few citizens outside the economics profession complained about this $323 expense per car.

Protectionism smacks of defeatism and represents special interest politics at its worst. People working for weak, stagnating firms are duped by high union wages into putting off learning other skills. The human misery of protectionism goes beyond the work force of the sheltered industry. Protectionism for one industry ripples throughout the economy. For example, quota protection raised the American price of steel, undermining the competitive price of industries that use steel (auto, truck, and machinery). American steel makers reduced weekly capacity by 30 percent to under 100 tons of steel in the period 1982–1989. This should not be a cause for concern. What counts from a competitive standpoint is not bulk but the ability to innovate, enhance quality, and price-compete.

The small, lean firm is often in a better position to do research, development, and cost control. Consequently, America's 54 steel mini-mills have doubled their capacity to 22 tons per year with specialized products, leading technology, and the flexibility to listen to customer reaction. In a different context, Professor Eric Von Hippel suggests in his 1988 book *The Sources of Innovation* that the best market research may come from simply copying user-initiated innovation. He suggests users are responsible for 60 to 90 percent of innovations. Innovation is seldom a dazzling space shot. Rather, most innovations are won by the turtle instead of the hare. Attention to detail and suggestions from users are examples of the old maxim: experience is the best teacher. America's competitive problem is simply that we have closed our ears for three decades. The Japanese had their ears open and sold the product innovations users demand in our marketplace.

One should return to a basic question posed earlier. What is wrong with America? Do we not work hard? We worked harder over the last 20 years as evidenced by the Harris poll that found the workweek increased to 48 hours in 1992, up from 40.6 hours in 1973. Self-reported leisure time had declined in that period by ten hours. As a subgroup, professionals work 52 hours weekly, with small business owners working the most, at 58 hours weekly.

If we are not lazy, then are we ignorant? The educational system certainly needs improvement, but we are not in as bad a shape as many Americans think. It may surprise many Americans that ten years after graduation, the Japanese test just as poorly as their American counterparts. The Japanese work very hard in high school, but they work less than American college students. The Japanese have two main advantages. A very large proportion learn the pre-med style ethic of hard, focused, systematic work for the beloved company. Secondly, the Japanese have a much smaller underclass because school dropouts are infrequent. In eschewing a rigid Japanese-style tracking system, American educrats (education bureaucrats) hoped to promote equity and not give up too early on the slow learners. If we do not begin to reform the American educational system and catch up with our past failures (or new immigrants) in adult education classes, our economic and moral power will dissipate.

We do not need more "industrial policy." There is a selection bias in favor of publishing your success stories, rather than your failures. The Japanese Ministry of Industry and Trade has had numerous recent failures, suggesting that the central government need not underwrite more industrial research and development. For example, the Japanese plans for fifth-generation computers produced nothing of note in the late 1980s, causing Mitsubishi to move their basic research lab to the greater Boston area in 1990. The Japanese attempt to use public and private funds to gain a foothold in the jet production sector has also been an unconditional flop. Consider a third example of failure. The Japanese failed to come up with the breakthroughs in superconductivity. They ignored the one combination that American university researchers found: copper-barium-lanthanum. The Japanese failed to try this combination because they followed narrow, conventional wisdom: copper oxides are magnetic and therefore do not permit superconductivity.

Limited tunnel vision in R&D attitudes produces failure. In addition to these three Japanese examples, the American VCR industry failed to realize that consumers might want recordings lasting longer than 59 minutes. Narrow vision is enhanced by industrial policy and restricted federal funding. Breakthroughs are produced when private funds, and public funds for basic research, are given to researchers with limited constraints.

Corporate officials should not restrict the process, but they can reserve the right to limit the scope of less successful research teams and close down R&D projects that continue to fail. Bureaucrats should leave researchers alone, and corporations should trim unproductive R&D teams. Too many American corporations have an inability to trim the number of R&D projects and initiate new study teams. R&D is a crap shoot, but too many corporations attempt to operate an excessive number of crap games. A federal industrial policy is nothing more than a national program for underwriting more, less successful, R&D crap games. The nation needs federal funds for basic research, but we do not need a Japanese-style Ministry of Industry and Trade.

FORTRESS AMERICA FEARS BEING
BOUGHT OUT

Rapid change often brings out the worst in people. The dean of American political reporting, Theodore White, warned in a summer 1985 *New York Times* editorial that the Japanese were dismantling American industry. Someone should tell the advocates of protectionism that in a dynamic economic world we should not lament the demise of an American steel plant any more than we lamented the demise of a hand calculator plant in the late 1970s. There will always be a better, new idea that comes along to employ an inefficient plant's work force. People who made hand calculators can now manufacture personal computers.

Another childish response to rising competition was to complain that the opponent and the scorekeeper were cheating. The scorekeeper in this context was the Institute for International Economics (IIE), a think tank in Washington that estimated the cost of Japanese protectionism as closely approaching (within $2 to $6 billion) the value of Japanese products that we keep out of our country by similar means. Those who advocate protectionism would begin to impute the motives, and thus the accuracy, of IIE estimates because the institute receives funding from Germany and Japan. Even Congressman Richard Gephardt (D–Mo.) had to admit that Japanese protectionism contributed only 10 to 15 percent to the 1986 U.S.-Japan trade deficit.

In the 1993 context, some extremists still call for an across-the-board 10 percent tariff to keep out foreign imports. Such a tariff may reduce imports by $34 to $38 billion in a static model, but 50 to 55 percent of this improvement would never be realized in a dynamic world because: (1) the dollar would be overvalued by 5 percent and (2) our interest rates would add an additional 0.33 to 0.36 points. The real GNP for America would decline by 0.56 to 0.59 points (which is a lot in a $6 trillion economy). Protectionist trade tariff wars are a very bad idea. No one wins a trade war or a nuclear war. Trade wars subject the best industries in a country to retaliation. Consumers should be allowed to benefit from the fruits of high quality and high productivity, wherever they are produced.

Xenophobic visions shaded a number of good books on trade policy, including Clyde Prestowitz's *Trading Places* (1988) and Martin and Susan Tolchin's *Selling Our Security* (1992). Each book has an overblown view of the extent to which foreigners control the American economy. This is not to deny the direction: foreigners are purchasing more of our assets and our debt. One cannot deny the fact that Japan had sold us a number of products and bought up pieces of Hawaii, Manhattan, and CBS with the proceeds. People read about billion dollar purchases and fear for the ownership rights to America. However, the Japanese overpaid for their American invest-ments. After one includes the effects of the declining dollar, the Japanese earned a mere $59 million in interest and dividends in 1991–1993 on $2.26 trillion direct investment in the United States. With these fiscal returns, it is surprising that they buy our real estate. For example, the Japanese group that purchased the Pebble Beach golf course for $840 million in 1991 had to sell it at a $500 million loss 2 years later.

The United States has about $52 trillion in national wealth, with about $18 trillion in financial claims on physical capital and $34 trillion in natural and human resources. From 1983 to 1989, America's net foreign investment position shifted negatively by $0.7 trillion to Japan and West Germany. The key word is "net," because we own firms and do business in their respective countries. IBM has $7 billion in annual sales in Japan, and Coca-Cola has a 62 percent market share in the Japanese soft-drink market. American multinational corporations produce and sell goods for the Japa-nese and the Germans that we do not count as exports. In the 1980s compa-nies lost their country of origin as trade and capital flows broke outside conventional economic models.

JAPAN: RICH INVADER OR GOOD BANKER?

Financial influence is shifting to Japan because its citizens save more of their money and spend less than Americans do. Even if there is a more massive movement of capital, should it be viewed as a threat to American self-determination? Would the citizens of Maine lose self-determination if Texans and Californians jumped from owning 2.9 percent of their state to owning 6 percent of it? Perhaps they would feel some embarrassment about these "outsiders," but they would not want to give the money back, throw their citizens out of work, and cut their standard of living by, say, 15 to 20 percent. As Karl Marx observed in the 1860s, the investment of rich nations ends up providing "the secret foundations" for new, more powerful local economies. America should not play the Marxist game and dwell on the negative side of such "capital stock imperialism" (rich Japan over debt-ridden America). America is garnering 60 percent of Japan's overseas invest-ments, because the Japanese view our country as a great place with the best return on investment. America is not selling itself like a prostitute, nor should we be Marxist and carp about those rich imperialists in foreign lands.

In December 1981 America reached its historic peak as a net creditor in world markets. We had a $141 billion surplus by borrowing from abroad and liquidating some foreign assets. At the end of the 1980s, we had a $600 billion deficit. The $741 billion we lost over the period 1982–1989 is 280 percent larger than all foreign interest payments by all the less-developed debtor nations. Should America hold a fire sale and declare bankruptcy? No, because this is not an immense sum for the richest nation on earth. But if we waste $100 billion a year over the next two decades, we will get into real problems. The trend over time is more critical than a country's creditor or debtor status.

Consider the mythical country of SAM reporting enhanced productivity in utilizing capital assets worth $18 trillion, and a second country, MITT, experiencing a minimal improvement in productivity with assets of $11 trillion. If citizens in MITT acquire $1.02 trillion of capital in SAM, MITT is a net creditor while SAM is a net debtor ($100 billion). This $100 billion is small in comparison to the $7 trillion ($18 trillion minus $11 trillion) spread in assets between (Uncle) SAM and MITT (Japan). With a few more productive years, SAM could again have double the productive wealth of MITT. In ten years America could be that SAM if we improve our productivity by restructuring our educational system, tax incentives, and banking system.

The Japanese banking system runs a close second behind the educational system in explaining the country's economic boom. The author was amazed during visits to Japan that bankers made house calls, because savings and investment are considered patriotic duties. Japanese banks treat the companies they lend to as long-term clients, so the debt provided by the bank is considered a defacto equity contribution. Japanese bankers do not merely lend; they invest for the long term. In direct contrast to this are the short-term incentives driving American banks and the banks of other English-speaking nations. American bankers are no longer encouraged to bail out ailing companies or assist companies through difficult periods. Unlike Japanese banks, which would never divorce a financial mate, American banks are forced by overzealous federal bank regulators (since 1988) to dump companies as soon as possible after a weakening in a company's financial position is uncovered. The unfortunate recent result of this has been a plethora of bankruptcies, some of which might have been unnecessary if only the lenders had been encouraged to help, rather than dump, their customers.

INVESTMENT IN AMERICA

The political debate over trade deficits always ignores one simple financial law: currency that outflows to foreign lands to buy imports always flows right back. The Japanese do not sit in the closet and play with our green paper; they spend it in four possible ways: (1) purchases of goods and services, (2) purchases of American government debt (at a premium interest rate relative to buying Asian treasury bills and bonds), (3) small-scale port-folio investment, and (4) substantial control of American assets through direct investment. From an economic vantage point, too many dollars have flowed back through category 2, paying for our out-of-control government deficit. Our $600 billion debtor status would be more bearable if larger portions of the borrowed foreign resources had gone into capital investments that earn a multiyear stream of cash flow to pay off the debt. However, as we stated earlier in this chapter, the foreign funds did not increase the capital investment rate above 18 percent of the GNP; instead, the rate stayed flat while foreigners began to own one-third (or 6 of those 18 points) of the GNP. Of America's $17.6 trillion worth of capital assets in 1990, only 7 percent was owned by foreigners after factoring out American ownership of foreign assets (13.4 percent of the gross, 7.1 percent net). Foreigners now own about 13.4 percent, or $2.36 trillion, of American assets, and Americans own $1.11 trillion in assets abroad. The $1.11 trillion figure may be an underestimate, since the figure would be higher if every asset Americans held abroad was priced by our Commerce Department at present value rather than original cost. In any case, America is still a capital-surplus nation, just not as strong a capital-surplus nation relative to Japan as we were in 1980.

The second type of foreign investment into America goes toward the purchase of treasury bills and bonds. None of this cash inflow creates new jobs, plants, or service organizations. The purchase of our government debt simply allows our politicians to defer tough decisions regarding reduction in federal spending. Foreign ownership of the federal debt simply forces future taxpayers to subsidize consumption by today's taxpayers and enhance the wealth of foreign investors.

The third type of foreign investment is portfolio investment, bank deposits, and securities in volumes not large enough to gain influence over American companies. In this case, American companies are still totally under American management control. The reader should note that bonds, treasury bills, and portfolio investment confer control over nothing but paper.

The fourth kind of foreign investment, direct investment, implies some degree of economic control (minority or majority impact on company decisions). According to the Commerce Department, direct investment in America from Japan amounted to $4.6 billion in 1992 and $17 billion in 1988. This sounds like a lot of money, but this figure is merely 10 percent above what Britain directly invested in America during the years 1988–1992. The Netherlands directly invested the same amount, and yet few nationalist cries were heard to protect America from the Dutch.

America should avoid nationalist impulses and take a more mature, long-run viewpoint. Direct investment from Japan or Germany brings technology. Today's technology from foreign investors will improve our productivity and fuel tomorrow's export outflow from America. We can pay back our trade deficit with our exports. Exports are how Japan and Germany paid us back from 1951 to 1981. In summary, more direct investments bring more technology, which seeds future growth in exports. Americans do not suffer from any oversupply of new technology, new ideas, or new money. American unions should give the Pearl Harbor analogy a rest and consider their enlightened self-interest. Investment in America brings higher wages for Americans. To discourage Japan and Germany from investing would lower our real wages. From 1969 to 1992 real manufacturing pay has increased by a meager 24 percent in America, compared to a 148 percent gain in Japan.

After considering the facts, if anyone is still a confirmed Japan-basher, he should read the classic 1966 popularist book by Jean-Jacques Servan-Schreiber, *The American Challenge*. This nationalist diatribe argued for European restrictions on American direct investment in European companies. If the politicians had followed such advice over the past two decades, Europe would have six million fewer jobs and lower average wage rates. Congress should not set an arbitrary restriction on direct investment from foreign lands just to insulate us from growth benefits that would be achieved from outside money and technology. The only benefit from such actions is that America could prop up a macho pride and claim "we gain a few percentage points more of domestic control over a weakened economy." To use a boxing analogy, would you rather own 99 percent of a weak fighter or 85 to 90 percent of a great fighter? Foreign investment can bring better management, different technology, more jobs, higher wages, and more competitive retail prices. The Japanese have been so good at using American workers that when our citizens buy Matsushita electronics or a Honda, they get more American workmanship than if they bought a Ford or an RCA product. Restricting foreigners from investing in America also risks creating a domestic banking crisis if foreign investors suddenly withdraw their resources.

The most eloquent defense of foreign investment is over 200 years old but is just as relevant in our era. Our first secretary of the Treasury, Alexander Hamilton, wrote in 1789 that foreign "investment should not be viewed as a rival, but ought to be considered a valuable luxury to build these United States." Allowing the payback for our deficits to come off the American balance sheet through direct sales of assets will not make America a poorer place. This statement is true if America uses this exportation of wealth to create even greater wealth through enhanced financial performance. Japan and Western Europe have benefited from their earlier exportation of wealth, and there is no apparent reason to think that America is not up to the task. To choke off investment in the name of nationalism is to bring America down to the level of Cuba and Vietnam, and to set us up for decline.

FACT OR FICTION?

Closing this chapter suggests a brief summary of some basic myths concerning America's economic standing. *Myth no. 1:* The country is a weak giant engaged in "deindustrialization." Industrial production in 1992 was 38 percent above the 1980 level. Yet we have 2.5 million fewer workers involved in industrial production. Is this a paradox? No, it is the definition of productivity—doing more with less. If we generate 38 percent more with fewer people, this demonstrates an improvement in labor productivity. A 38 percent improvement in industrial productivity clearly shows that America is staying competitive. The net debtor status and trade deficit are not as critical to our economic health in such circumstances, because slow industrial production is not the American disease. From 1983 to 1992 our industrial production increased by 42 percent, compared to 39 percent in Japan, 21 percent in Germany, and 15 percent on the average in Western Europe. The 20-year trends tell the same story within the American economy. Manufacturing was not reborn in the late 1980s, because it never died in the first place. Between 1970 and 1992, manufacturing output increased 79 percent, almost as strong an increase as the 84 percent growth in services.

Myths should be counterbalanced against some basic truths. *Truth no. 1:* The American labor force is somewhat deindustrialized, but the dream of many blue-collar workers was that their sons and daughters could wear white collars in service jobs. In 1920 one-third of American workers wore blue collars. By 1955 the proportion declined to 25 percent and then declined steadily to 13.4 percent in 1992. By 2015 the number of blue-collar jobs in America will be down to 12 million, in contrast to 23 million in 1974. We should not be any more concerned about losing blue-collar jobs than we were about losing saddle makers in response to the automobile. To further this trend, our educational system must emphasize adult courses, and government and industry must help finance job retraining programs.

Myth no. 2: Inflation must plague the American economy if we export more goods and services to reduce our trade deficit. In 1988 former Senator William Proxmire (D–Wis.) considered the $2.6 trillion federal debt, the $3.2 trillion household debt, and the $4 trillion corporate debt as a "monster constituency for inflation." By this logic selling more goods abroad must leave Americans competing for a smaller supply of goods at home;

therefore, we must incur an acceleration of inflation (too many buyers chasing too few goods). In fact, Americans began to save a little more and travel less as the devalued dollar brought down the trade deficit in the late 1980s.

Truth no. 2: A lower trade deficit can mean that America is producing more in relation to consumption, working smarter but spending less. The key word is "can." If America continues to regain the twin virtues of productivity growth and greater rates of savings, inflation will remain in check.

Truth no. 3: Letting foreign interest rates decline is in relative terms like allowing American interest rates to go up, but without the pain for American citizens. In simple terms, in an age when investors search the world for good deals, having foreign rates decline 0.75 points is approximately equivalent to having our rates go up an equal amount.

Myth no. 3: Unfair foreign protectionism and dumping of products caused the American trade deficit. In fact, the big federal deficit generated high exchange rates (an overvalued dollar) and high interest rates. The dollar appreciated 63 percent between 1980 and 1985, our products became less competitive, and exports declined. American-owned assets in foreign lands benefited from this trend (e.g., Taiwan's top exporters are American-owned RCA and General Instruments). American overseas production was 17 percent of our total output in 1992. By contrast, Japanese overseas production increased from 4.3 percent of its total output in 1984 to 8.9 percent in 1992.

Truth no. 4: Managed trade, with government support for critical information networks composed of corporations and university research teams, is the only efficient form of industrial policy. This strategy has worked well for the Japanese in the development of new technologies, but it totally violates American antitrust laws. Superconductivity and other forms of high-tech should be exempt from certain antitrust laws (as was done in the insurance industry's exemption from companies and universities to share information). Our laws are 50 years out of date if we wish to compete with the Japanese and the Germans. American industry is handicapped like a boxer with one arm tied behind his back. We must encourage information sharing without succumbing to monopolization, price-fixing, and other anticompetitive activities.

Americans cannot stand guard at our borders, whip in hand, to fight those "yellow people" and protect hopelessly inefficient domestic companies. Racism and "lemon socialism" (industrial policy for failures) are poor policy prescriptions. We should welcome foreign ideas and foreign money, because they ultimately enhance our standard of living. For example, American banks have much to learn from Japanese banks about assisting business in a long-term, mutually beneficial relationship.

Truth no. 5: Our banking laws (Glass-Steagall) and regulations should be changed to encourage bankers to view companies as long-term relationships and to allow banks to be defacto equity holders in American companies. Easing up on the regulations that force banks to dump weakened companies quickly would allow the bankers to embrace a long-term philosophy, thereby preventing unnecessary bankruptcies and loss of workers' jobs. Allowing banks to purchase stock in its customers, as Korean and Hong Kong banks are allowed to do, would bring down American businesses' cost of capital, which is significantly higher than the cost of capital in Asia. Studies have demonstrated that Japanese and South Korean companies enjoy a lower cost of capital than their American counterparts due to the faithful, long-term relations with bank/partners and also the banks' direct ownership interest in the local companies.

Myth no. 4: State governments offer more privileges and lower taxes to foreign investors, when all capitalists should be working under equally onerous handicaps in paying for growth in government infrastructure. The better alternative is for equal opportunity among all companies in any country, but with all working under reduced handicaps. In other words, the bidding war should continue to attract private capital and reduce the wasteful portions of the public sector. Americans should rejoice when Komatsu and Honda beat Caterpillar and General Motors. Each of these two Japanese companies has demonstrated that there is nothing wrong with the American worker (while a lot is wrong with American corporate officials, bureaucrats, and unions). Komatsu construction equipment and Hondas made by American hands are of such high quality that they are being exported out of America! American product quality suffers from poor design and inflexible union shop rules, not inferior assembly-line workers.

A CHANGING ENGINE OF PROGRESS

In summary, world investment (resources, expertise, technology) will drive the international economy in the 21st century. Trade tariffs and unions are becoming less policy relevant, as legal rules, exchange rates, and tax policy increasingly determine economic growth rates. Trade is less a barter swap of goods for goods and increasingly a function of investment options (e.g., "you will receive more VCRs and Hondas if we can invest more in America"). In 30 years one-quarter of the pensions of rich foreign nations may reside in American investments. This is a vote of confidence in America and our melting pot labor force, not an insult to American sovereignty. Macroeconomics textbooks will provide no guidance in this new world. As Peter Drucker (1986) has observed, there is no theory for an international economy fueled by world investment rather than by world trade. Brains and investment have won a sneak-attack victory over barter and trade barriers. America has not been sold, but it has been reenergized and challenged. May the walls against efficiency and technology continue to fall. The supremacy of capitalism and the American standard of living depend upon rising investment and declining asset-protectionism. In analyzing the North American Free Trade Agreement, one should consider that lower tariffs with Mexico changed a $5 billion 1989 trade deficit into a $5 billion 1992 trade surplus. (This agreement passed Congress in late 1993.)

In his seminal book *The Competitive Advantage of Nations*, Michael Porter (1990) presents the metaphor of a national "diamond" of four basic ingredients determining economic health: (1) factor conditions like education, (2) domestic rivalry between competing firms, (3) clusters of critical mass expertise and skill within a geographic region (e.g., Silicon Valley), and (4) the nature of domestic demand (smart customers, or dull customers tending to get dull products). The reader will encounter a more up-to-date review of the effects of education and training in chapter 5 of this book. Chapter 6 will survey the need for increased rivalry between American firms for enhanced productivity, innovative products, and better research on process technology.

To summarize this chapter, protectionism, government-funded research as an "industrial policy," and mega-mergers will do nothing to improve the economic position of the American economy. Even in global markets, Porter states that domestic rivalry in quality, productivity, and innovation is still critically important. Competitiveness resides within industries, not national borders. America should look within industry not for protectionism, but to improve our trade deficit. Our lack of competitive goods in some sectors is the problem, not the mythical "cheating" Japanese or "nasty" Germans. We should stop blaming the competition and instead reform the tax laws and redouble our efforts to improve productivity and develop innovative products.

REFERENCES

Adams, R. (1993). "Fashions in Macroeconomics," *Journal of Post Keynesian Economics* 15:4, Summer, 609–18.

Bagwell, K., and Staiger, R. (1990). "A Theory of Managed Trade," *American Economic Review* 80:4, September, 795–99.

Bhagwati, J. (1988). *Protectionism*. Cambridge: MIT Press.

Caves, R., Frankel, J., and Jones, R. (1993). *World Trade and Payments*. New York: HarperCollins.

Christopher, R. (1984). *The Japanese Mind*. New York: Fawcett-Columbine.

Clark, K., and Fujimoto, T. (1992). *Strategy, Organization, and Management in the World Auto Industry*. Cambridge: Harvard Business School Press.

Cohen, L., and Noll, R. (1992). *The Technology Pork Barrel*. Washington, DC: Brookings.

Cooper, R. (1992). *Economic Stabilization and Debt*. Cambridge: MIT Press.

Destler, I., and Henning, C. (1989). *Dollar Politics: Exchange Rate Policymaking in the United States*. Washington, DC: Institute for International Economics.

Dollar, D., and Wolff, E. (1993). *Competitiveness, Convergence, and International Specialization*. Cambridge: MIT Press.

Doroodian, K. (1992). "Another Look at Trade," *Quarterly Review of Economics and Finance* 32:2, Summer, 129–39.

Drucker, P. (1986). "The Changed World Economy," *Foreign Affairs* 64:4, Spring, 768–91.

Fitzgerald, E. (1993). "The American Ostrich Strategy," *Journal of European Business* 4:2, March-April, 60–62.

Frost, E. (1987). *For Richer, for Poorer: The U.S.-Japan Relationship*. New York: Council on Foreign Relations.

Garten, J. (1993). *A Cold Peace: America, Japan, Germany, and the Struggle for Supremacy*. New York: Times Books.

Gold, P., and Nanto, D. (1992). "Trends in Trade with Japan." Washington, DC: Congressional Research Service.

Greenfeld, S., and Dyck, H. (1993). "Free Trade in the Americas: The NAFTA Debate Heats Up," *Business Forum* 17:4, 17–21.

Hufbauer, C., and Rosen, H. (1986). *Trade Policy for Troubled Industries*. Washington, DC: Institute for International Economics.

Jorgenson, D. (1988). "Productivity and Economic Growth in Japan and the U.S.," *American Economic Review* 78:2, May, 217–22.

Lawrence, R., and Litan, R. (1987). "Why Protectionism Doesn't Pay," *Harvard Business Review* 65:3, May–June, 60–67.

Lincoln, E. (1991). *Japan's Unequal Trade*. Washington, DC: Brookings.

Lustig, N., Bosworth, B., and Lawrence, R. (1993). *North American Free Trade: Assessing the Impact*. Washington, DC: Brookings.

Magaziner, I., and Reich, R. (1989). *Minding America's Business*. New York: Vintage.

Mansfield, E. (1988). "International R&D in Japan and the U.S.: A Comparative Study," *American Economic Review* 78:2, May, 223–28.

Mayer, T., Duesenberry, J., and Aliber, R. (1992). *Money, Banking and the Economy*. New York: Norton.

McCombre, J. (1993). "Economic Growth and Trade Interlinkages," *Journal of Post Keynesian Economics* 15:4, Summer, 471–505.

Meltzer, A. (1989). *Keynes's Monetary Theory: A Different Interpretation*. London: Cambridge University Press.

Morris, C. (1989). "The Coming Global Boom," *The Atlantic* 262:10, October, 51–64.

Nau, H. (1990). *The Myth of America's Decline: Leading the World Economy into the 1990s*. New York: Oxford University Press.

Peterson, P. (1987). "The Morning After," *The Atlantic* 260:10, October, 43–52.

Phelps, E. (1990). *Seven Schools of Macro Economic Thought*. New York: Oxford University Press.

Porter, M. (1990). *The Competitive Advantage of Nations.* New York: Free Press.

Preston, R. (1991). *American Steel: Hot Metal Men and the Resurrection of the Rust Belt.* Englewood Cliffs, NJ: Prentice-Hall.

Prestowitz, C. (1988). *Trading Places: How We Allowed Japan to Take the Lead.* New York: Basic Books.

Reich, R. (1991). *The Work of Nations: Preparing Ourselves for 21st-Century Capitalism.* New York: Knopf.

———. (1987). "The Rise of Techno-nationalism," *The Atlantic* 259:5, May, 62–69.

Rivlin, A. (1985). Statement before Congress by the Director of the Congressional Budget Office, May 11.

Salvatore, D. (1992). *National Trade Policies.* Westport, CT: Greenwood Press.

Scheinkman, J. (1989). *General Equilibrium, Growth and Trade.* New York: Academic.

Schultze, C. (1992). *Memos to the President: A Guide through Macroeconomics for the Busy Policymaker.* Washington, DC: Brookings.

Stares, P. (1992). *The New Germany and the New Europe.* Washington, DC: Brookings.

Stein, H. (1986). *Washington Bedtime Stories: The Politics of Money and Jobs.* New York: Free Press.

Thurow, L. (1992). *Head to Head: The Coming Economic Battle among Japan, Europe, and America.* New York: Morrow.

Tolchin, M., and Tolchin, S. (1992). *Selling Our Security: The Erosion of America's Assets.* New York: Knopf.

———. (1988). *Buying into America,* New York: Times Books.

Trefler, D. (1993). "Trade Liberalization and the Theory of Endogenous Protection: An Economic Study of U.S. Import Policy," *Journal of Political Economy* 101:1, February, 138–59.

Tyson, L. (1992). *Who's Bashing Whom? Trade Conflicts in High Technology Industries.* Washington, DC: Institute for International Economics.

Von Hippel, E. (1988). *The Sources of Innovation.* New York: Oxford University Press.

5

Improving Productivity for a
Better Standard of Living

Productivity is the first test of management's competence. One should get the greatest output for the least input effort, better balancing all factors of the process to achieve the most with the smallest resource effort.

—Peter F. Drucker, 1964

When you are through improving, you are through.

—Bo Schembechler, 1979

The budget deficits produced a slower-growth economy. If Americans are to live better in the future, they need to save more and channel those savings into productivity-enhancing investment.

—Alice Rivlin, 1992

Invest in people.

—Bill Clinton, 1993

Productivity, labeled technical efficiency in the jargon of economics, is the ratio of output to input. If a unit of output, like a standardized radio or a haircut, is produced with fewer inputs (i.e., fewer employees or capital inputs) from one year to the next, one can measure an improvement in annualized productivity. Changes from year to year are seldom large, but the cumulative approach is important. For example, if our national productivity in the period 1973–1993 equaled the 1946–1970 postwar boom period, then our gross national product would be 44 percent higher in 1993. The quantity of work is not our problem; we need to work smarter, not harder. In 1993 American workers will work 156 hours more per year than in 1972. This represents one month more of working (135 hours) and commuting (21 hours). Working more hours is not equivalent to creating more output per hour of work. We need a better trained and equipped work force to make substantial gains in productivity. Otherwise our standard of living will begin to lag behind that of the Germans, who work 38 fewer days per year than Americans (Schor, 1991). American work weeks have increased largely thanks to the contribution of women. In the period 1973–1993 our GNP rose an average of 2 percent only because of those additional 31 million female workers.

There are a number of misconceptions concerning American productivity. The American public believes that manufacturing labor productivity is very low. In point of fact, in the 1980s American factory labor productivity, output per hour, increased 38.4 percent. This rise in productivity is the best rate of improvement since the 1940s. If labor on the factory floor is not the critical problem, what is wrong with American productivity? The problem resides in two areas: productivity in the service sector is very slow to improve (consequently, overall national nonfarm productivity increased only 1.2 percent per year since 1973) and capital productivity could be marginally improved if the federal government would pass some of the capital formation reforms suggested in chapter 3. This last point should be obvious: if you give workers more up-to-date equipment, they will produce more.

A second myth in the conventional wisdom is that American productivity is vastly inferior to Japanese productivity. In point of fact, the Japanese rate of annual improvement in productivity exceeds America in most industries, but a shortfall still exists. In 1949 it took a Japanese worker one hour to produce what an American worker could produce in ten minutes. In 1992 it took a Japanese worker one hour to produce what an American worker could produce in only 47 minutes. In the 1980s the Japanese growth rate in the GNP exceeded the American rate by only 0.74 percent. An extrapolation of this growth rate would mean that the Japanese GNP will finally equal the American figure in the year 2120. However, Japanese multifactor productivity, taking into account labor and capital productivity in one composite measure, will surpass the American rate in the late 1990s. Americans may still boast in 1993 that we can produce a 1949 standard of living (goods and services) in 46 percent of the time it took in 1949.

When a recession occurs we must strive for a "soft landing." The definition of a soft landing includes low inflation with continued economic growth (often low growth of only 1 percent). This last economic downturn was our first "growth recession"—the so-called double-dip recession with a 1.8 percent drop in GDP under President Bush (1990–1991) where the growth rate of the economy (1991–1992) was so slow that unemployment rose only a little. However, many sage economists would suggest that slow growth is a frail weapon against inflation (or unemployment) in the late stage of a business cycle. The 1982–1989 eight-year cycle rivals the recovery/expansion that lasted 106 months from February 1961 to November 1969.

Each political party has experienced spurts of job creation (averaging 3.4 percent during President Reagan's last five years in office and during the Carter administration). Job growth averaged only 1.8 percent per year during the Nixon-Ford years and 0.3 percent per year under President Bush. Democrats in the 1990s are highly motivated to rebuild lagging industries such as construction, manufacturing, mining, and wholesale trade.

RESEARCH AND DEVELOPMENT FOR ENHANCED PRODUCTIVITY

A more productive manufacturing process often involves product redesign, job redesign, and eliminating unnecessary units of activity. The traditional American model of research and development involves the "ladder paradigm," by which the brilliant individual idea evolves into applied technology and eventually the finished product. The paradigm makes for great history, as evidenced by the life of Thomas Alva Edison and the invention of the light bulb. However, a superior model for product development since the 1950s involves the "cycle paradigm" as practiced by the Japanese and Koreans. For example, the VCR may have been invented in America, but the Japanese captured the market by applying the cycle principle of fast, continuous, incremental improvements in design and production. In most cases the developing and manufacturing teams work together to design a product that can be made easily. This approach yields improved labor productivity and capital productivity. Moreover, under the cycle paradigm, market research is quickly translated into action (e.g., American companies tried to continue selling one-hour VCR tapes, whereas the Japanese firms listened to consumers and produced three- to six-hour tapes).

The example of the VCR reveals a basic truth in the new industrial world: there is no connection between basic research discovery and manufacturing supremacy. America can continue to invent things that will make the Japanese rich. *POLICY PROPOSAL No. 30:* American companies should copy the Japanese and spend two-thirds of their research dollars on process technology and one-third on new products. This ratio is currently reversed, and America is spending too much on new products. The current American position is consistent with the myth of industrial policy: the dream that if only America nationalized some research and development functions under a Japanese-style Ministry of International Trade and Industry (MITI), better American products would pop off the assembly line. This viewpoint is a byproduct of the obsolete ladder model view of production, the myth that research and development is an independent variable that drives production. However, in the more productive cycle model, research and development is a dependent variable, better financed by private industry. Halal (1986) points out the benefits of firms performing basic research and problem-solving but states that we do not need a MITI. Most Japanese managers report that their success is less than 10 percent due to the MITI and over 50 percent due to flexible applications of the cyclical model.

According to the Massachusetts Institute of Technology Commission on Industrial Productivity (Berger et al., 1989), American companies must adopt a cyclical paradigm, flexible manufacturing, and customized products. Bureaucratic roadblocks to a free internal flow of information and compartmentalization of tasks allow too many American design teams to neglect the manufacturing process, making it more costly and time consuming to come up with a quality process. It is good for quality and efficiency to have multifunctional teams design a new product and develop the process technology.

A textbook example of an American firm adopting the cyclical model is the Ford Taurus. Ford employees worked simultaneously (not serially) to design, engineer, manufacture, and market a new car model quickly. Ford's American-based assembly plants require 3.3 workers per car per day (equivalent to Japanese labor productivity), in contrast to 4.9 employees at General Motors (GM). This difference in technical efficiency costs GM $4.3 billion annually in cost efficiency, driving its profit margin per car under $110. Quality has improved at Ford thanks to the emphasis on process technology. The percentage of Ford cars pulled aside for repairs before being shipped to dealers declined from 38 percent to 1.7 percent in the late 1980s.

A textbook example of a failure to invest in process technology and utilize the cycle paradigm is provided by the GM Fiero. GM underinvested in the process technology for this new car in the early 1980s and borrowed parts from other cars, including the front suspension from the Chevy Chevette, resulting in engine fires and the unusual placement of the engine behind the passenger seat. GM ignored its own extensive market research and tried to sell the Fiero as a commuter car, despite its lack of critical power steering to allow for easy parking. In 1984 Toyota trusted GM's market research and listened to the American consumer. Toyota began to retrofit its MR2 cars with power steering. Mazda also listened to the public and in 1986 began introducing the Miata with power steering. Japanese firms and small flexible firms in Italy never miss the chance to learn from customers and suppliers (Dertouzous et al., 1989). Underinvesting in process technology and ignoring the customer explains why GM's market share of the auto industry declined from 46 percent in 1980 to 31 percent in 1993. The Fiero plant closed in 1988.

MORE IS NOT BETTER, BETTER IS BETTER

As a former member of the GM board, Ross Perot said that attempts to change GM's corporate culture were like trying to teach an elephant to tap dance. Firms do not always have to spend more to enhance productivity. Ford does more with less investment than GM because it emphasizes human organization, cyclical design, and manufacturing. This approach beats the GM investment in $40 billion worth of robotics. The smart allocation of research dollars, process technology, and incentive-pay program dollars determines success. For example, the *Business Week* January 1993 survey named Merck the best managed corporation and highlighted the fact that it reinvests 11 percent of its revenues into research and development. Merck pharmaceutical does a great job with its R&D funds, in sharp contrast to GM.

GM may spend $4.1 billion on research and development, but it would benefit from reallocating $1.4 billion dollars of new product funds into well-designed process technology. In addition, to paraphrase Ross Perot, GM would benefit from a technology review process that jettisons memo writing in favor of common sense: don't insult the customer by being cheap on a 3-cent deficient gasket that leaks oil on the garage floor.

America may have been successful from 1875 to 1975 with standardized products, developed along the ladder paradigm from brilliant inventors, but we must now adopt the cycle paradigm. American business has to move away from the GM style of management by memorandum and adopt the cycle style of ad hoc communication. Firms running on the cycle paradigm of flexibility in northern Italy and Japan use current information the week it is received, channeling the data directly to the engineers rather than through channels of bureaucracy. The principle is simple: information flows to where it is most useful.

Although the cycle paradigm will improve industrial productivity, service sector productivity provides a different set of problems and possible solutions. Whereas manufacturing productivity has improved 3.4 percent per year since 1979, service sector productivity has grown at a snail's pace, only 0.29 percent per year. According to Brookings economist Martin Bailey (1990), some of the lag in service sector productivity may be due to an insufficient measurement of quality improvements (e.g., the obvious time savings from automated airline tickets with seat assignment). But, given the service sector's size and scope, continued growth in productivity is imperative to raising living standards. Services employ 59.5 percent of the work force, compared to 23.5 percent for government and nonprofit institutions such as hospitals, nursing homes, and foundations, 15.5 percent for manufacturing, and 1.5 percent for farming.

The Clinton administration has established worker training as the key federal strategy to enhance productivity. Democrats point to England under a conservative government as the textbook example of what happens to a nation that underinvests in training programs. Thatcher's industrial program after 1982 did little to stem the rollback in British investment in human capital. In England the proportion of manufacturing workers in training declined from 4.5 percent in 1979 to 1.9 percent in 1992 for males, and from 2.4 percent to 1.9 percent for females. Comparable data suggests an equally serious problem in France and the United States. The French, however, have found a workable solution by allowing business to deduct all worker training expenses, which are offset by the imposition of a 1 percent national sales tax (Thurow, 1992). The Japanese government gives equally generous support for worker training. While no nation complains about an overtrained work force, the problem of measuring outcomes and service sector productivity is a universal issue.

SERVICE SECTOR PRODUCTIVITY

One reason why American service productivity may lag far behind factory or farm productivity involves technical difficulty in measuring output. Service output is easily measured for haircuts but not for physician office visits or financial advising. For example, physician visit productivity declined during the 1980s, yet hourly productivity on a deflated revenue basis was constant (Pope, 1990). This suggests that physicians packed more care into each office visit in 1990 than in 1980. Thus, any increase in physician requirements attributed to lower visit productivity is actually the result of greater intensity and technology per visit (Eastaugh, 1991).

An American, W. Edwards Deming (1982), was instrumental in improving postwar Japanese productivity by utilizing quality-control techniques and the "theory of continuous improvement." These techniques have spread to some American factories but are slow to evolve in the service sector of our economy. Too many service industries spend millions on electronic snooping schemes to catch the truly productive or antiproductive worker (e.g., the poor typist or lazy telephone operator). Deming argues for continuous improvement in small increments for the entire distribution of workers, rather than focusing too much time and effort on the worst employees. Productivity improves most when you concentrate on the average worker, not the atypical worker, by focusing on learning and rewarding and not on finding and penalizing bad employees (e.g., Shingo, 1992).

Service industries can also benefit from Deming's ideas concerning job redesign. Team meetings among workers can focus on expanding the creative side of the process, to make tasks more varied, flexible, interesting, and thus more productive in the long run. It is good business for service sector managers to try to inject more variety, fun, and feeling of control into job design. Creative job design can engender loyalty and commitment to the employer, which is superior to the materialist ethic of "everyone for themselves." The core paradox is that to enhance productivity the firm must offer incentive compensation, not to "buy off" the employees but rather to give them a fair share of the financial gain. Incentive pay tends to reduce adversarial relations and mistrust and engenders the team spirit of "all for one and one for all." If we do not close the social deficit and offer education and incentive pay for productivity, we can not expect our workers to do more.

INCENTIVE COMPENSATION: PAYING FOR PERFORMANCE

There has been a rapid growth in incentive payment schemes to pay for education plus quarterly or annual bonuses for incremental improvements in productivity, profits, or sales. Pay for performance means that, rather than linking pay levels to position titles, pay can be linked to contribution. Contribution can be measured for the individual, work team, or department. The best programs offer incentive pay for most workers, rather than the traditional bonus option for senior managers only. The company gets better results in terms of productivity if it offers incentives for the average hourly paid production worker earning $24,000 per year or the service worker making much less than the chief executive officer. A top executive does not deserve the entrepreneur's reward for having a bad year or doing the bureaucrat's job. One worker summarized his view of rational incentives as follows: "It takes fewer carrots to get the smaller bunnies moving, at least relative to the big, fat bunnies." His employer, Raht Manufacturing in Wisconsin, used a productivity gain-sharing system to pay $1.56 per hour in bonus pay on average in 1989 (a 15 percent enhancement to standard pay levels of $10.37 hourly). This approach can also work for service industries. Some hospitals have experienced 10 to 15 percent gains in annual productivity by employing gain-sharing programs (Eastaugh, 1987). Such productivity enhancement is usually linked to quality improvement. As Tom Peters (1987) has observed, "quality improvement is the primary source of cost reduction." Things done right the first time do not need to be redone at additional expense; therefore, a quality process for service delivery is quicker and less costly (e.g., shorter hospitalization).

One unpublished 1993 survey reports that only 14 percent of Americans believe that they would benefit personally if their company became more productive. The comparable figure to the same question in Japan is 92 percent. In order to stimulate business interest in incentive pay consider *POLICY PROPOSAL No. 31:* Make half of the productivity-based incentive pay tax-exempt. This reform would send a simple, powerful message to the workplace: compensation should be tied directly to contribution. Allowing the government to tax half of the improved level of contribution is sufficient. Americans are not undertaxed, but we do need some assistance to unleash our productive capacity.

Some unions are opposed to gain-sharing in the hope of standardizing wage rates. Gain-sharing is seen by some as a threat because it increases wage flexibility and encourages above-average job performance. Should gain-sharing programs also offer loss-sharing programs? Unions are resistant to this idea, but it has theoretical merit in the opinion of most economists. One public manager, the mayor of Minneapolis, took this approach and fined himself $1,130 because his city sewer workers were loafing in 1987. The Phillies' Lefty O'Doul's batting average declined from .398 to .368 in 1930, resulting in a pay cut of 6.6 percent. Currently few employers have tried to introduce risk, with a downside of lower wages, into their incentive pay program. One of the few exceptions is the trial system of DuPont's 19,000 fiber plant employees: if they achieve only 80 percent of the performance goal their pay will be 3 percent less than that of their peers in other companies, but if they achieve 100 percent of the performance goal their pay will be equal, and if they achieve 150 percent of the goal their pay will be 12 percent higher. DuPont will evaluate the success of this program in 1994. In times of industrial recession, the "big bunnies" should take the biggest pay cuts; in the mid-1980s Nucor Steel executive pay declined 68 percent and worker pay declined 19 percent.

In summary, incentive compensation or gain-sharing is one mechanism to stimulate worker support for productivity enhancement. The manufacturing sector and the service sector could both benefit from increased reliance on incentive pay. Tom Peters (1987) has gone so far as to suggest that one-quarter of employee compensation should be incentive-based.

James Coleman (1990) advanced a rewrite of the theory of rational choice. According to him, people act in purposeful ways, like imperfect versions of the economist's concept of utility maximizers. The most basic question for such socioeconomics theorists is, what can be done to encourage people to innovate and to use their best efforts to produce what society needs and what employers and consumers demand? Productivity enhancement has many elements, ranging from incentive pay to changing the way people are treated (job design). The most productive employees want a stake, financial and psychological (see Kanter, 1986; Pinchot, 1985).

If the 20th century was the era of paternalism and wage standardization, the 21st century may become the era of performance and self-direction. If how much the institution can pay out in dividends or raises is a function of worker productivity, then worker contribution should have a bearing on how much pay the individual worker earns. Work teams should get an explicit share of any gains made from their improvements in productivity, and additional bonus checks should be cut for employee suggestions that prove effective. If the firm does not offer incentive pay, employees will generate fewer ideas and they may lower daily job performance and sometimes sabotage new ideas in the trial state of implementation. But if a new idea may enhance your paycheck or ease stress in your workday, then there is little effective resistance to innovation (Eastaugh, 1985). Gain-sharing can help build commitment and creativity among workers and managers.

URBAN DESIGN

There are two basic theories about optimal urban economics growth: (1) total specialization—high concentration in one industry and (2) broad specialization in a select small number of industries. Prior to World War I, the British economist Alfred Marshall was an advocate of total concentration in one industry. This theory, concerning the economics of learning by doing, was formalized in a 1962 paper by Nobel prizewinner Kenneth Arrow. Arrow argued that urban growth would be best in a one-industry town, like Detroit in the heyday of American cars or Pittsburgh when it was the steel capital of the world. Parents would teach pride and workmanship to their children, and any industrial spying or stealing would stay within the few firms in the one central city for that industry. Marshall had also gone one step further and argued that monopoly concentration in a one-industry town was better for regional economic growth than competition, because the externalities generated within a city would stay within it.

The current world of global competition, where intellectual capital has no geographic boundaries, is better captured by Harvard Professor Michael Porter (1990). Porter uses the example of strong domestic competition within the Japanese economy to argue that competition and cross-fertilization of ideas is essential to regional economic growth (e.g., Silicon Valley in the 1970s and 1980s). Jane Jacobs, in the classic 1970 book *The Economy of Cities*, offers a second variant of this theory. Jacobs still argues that the most important cross-fertilization of information does not come from the core industry (Porter's viewpoint; computers in Silicon Valley or education in Boston). She believes that the best transfer of ideas comes from a broad variety of industries, in a city or town with broad specialization. Boston, Washington, D.C., and Palo Alto, California, have a broad degree of specialization in information technology, health care, and education think tanks. Innovation happens when people from different fields get together, often for social reasons. The synergy that results is seldom "planned interdisciplinary research" funded by government but is often an unplanned event. The interaction of a variety of effective specialists yields new products and services. The classic humorous example of innovation is provided by Jacob's much-cited example: the bra was developed from dressmakers' ideas, not by underwear designers.

Which theory is better for predicting economic growth? In an April 1991 National Bureau of Economic Research paper presented by University of Chicago economist Jose Scheinkman and Harvard professor Andre Achleifer, the authors support the second theory that competition rather than concentration stimulates growth. They found that: (1) city/industries grow more rapidly when the rest of the city is broadly specialized and (2) competition rather than concentration favors economic growth. Perhaps Detroit would benefit from further diversification away from the auto industry and Baltimore could benefit from further diversification outside of health care.

PRODUCTIVITY AND HEALTH STATUS

Traditional economic studies of productivity involve either process learning-curve studies or product life-cycle studies. In these two traditional modes of productivity analysis either process or product is the subject for study, but few authors have looked at both topics simultaneously. In a landmark study of the automobile industry, Harvard professor William Abernathy (1978) concentrated on both: the process and product ramifications of technology and work design. He came to the conclusion that productivity enhancement is not solely beneficial but rather has costs as well as benefits.

Process studies, time-motion studies, and work speed-up techniques can reduce morale and do little to improve productivity. However, when properly done such process studies can reduce motion-related injuries from running equipment, unnecessary units of activity such as paperwork, and walking time (e.g., hospital nursing; Eastaugh, 1985). Does technology always help enhance productivity? Not unless the process technology screens out preexisting or newly generated unnecessary activity. For example, in the 1980s Americans spent $230 billion on 22 million computers, but the productivity gain in doing real work was outweighed by the avalanche of worthless activity, memos, and unnecessary reports. Even after cost cutting in 1990, IBM's overhead as a percentage of revenues was 29 percent, or double the comparable percentage among competitors like Amdahl and Fujitsu. IBM lost ground to the Japanese because its international bureaucracy demands more unnecessary memos, reports, and organizational charts each and every year. Examples like this explain why an MIT study group suggested trimming corporate bureaucracy: "building a flatter hierarchy for enhanced organizational effectiveness" (Berger et al., 1989).

Productive improvement involves working smarter not working harder. Unfortunately, when poorly designed by the consultant or poorly implemented by management, the cost in terms of stress and declining morale can be substantial. Middle-aged Americans in the peak productivity age group are already "stressed out" and in need of a kinder, gentler productivity-enhancement approach. It is not a gentle approach to emphasize electronic snooping and invasion of employee privacy. Incentive carrots work better than the snooper's stick. The middle-aged worker responds well to cash incentives designed to upgrade productivity. The current "triple-squeezed" generation of middle-aged individuals reacts to monetary incentives because it needs money for children's college education, for taking care of parents, and for retirement (fearing a shortfall from private pensions and Social Security). Fear of illness and the need for incentive bonus pay are great motivators for the "triple-squeezed" generation. These workers are the most important group in the work force. By contrast, the pool of young workers (ages 16 to 24) entering the job market will decline from 26 percent (1972) to 12 percent of the work force by the year 2000.

Because the standard of living rises, the net impact of productivity enhancement is always cost-beneficial for society. Other nations have more pressing economic problems. The problem of absenteeism is acute in the nations of the former Soviet Union and Romania, where the rate typically exceeds 35 percent. The classic joke there is: "They pretend to pay us, and we pretend to work." In the next section we shall review one mechanism by which corporations can offer employees better incentives, cut absenteeism, and contain overhead costs (e.g., health care expenses). Whereas underdeveloped countries need to improve investment in their health care sector to create the necessary conditions to expand work force productivity, there is no evidence that consuming an additional $100 billion of health care annually would enhance the productivity of America, Japan, or northern Europe. Shifting the burden of health care away from the employer, either by increased cost sharing or global cost controls (outlined in chapter 7), would create the resources necessary to fund worker training programs. We must redirect resources so that training programs are not more available inside prisons than in industry.

SHARING HEALTH CARE EXPENSES

In the past dozen years the nation's health care costs have more than tripled, rising from $180 billion in 1979 to over $810 billion in 1992. Since 1986 corporate health care spending has exceeded after-tax total profits and will top $210 billion in 1993. Employees are a critical asset, and health maintenance is a business cost in need of control. Employment-based health insurance is necessary to attract and retain skilled workers and reduce sick days. American business is not just concerned with current employees, but also with the escalation in retiree health care costs. Appropriate accounting of this future liability may reduce profit margins of American corporations by 10 to 12 percent. Union contracts often specify provisions for the health care expenses of retirees and their dependents not covered by Medicare. The sum total of General Motors' and Ford's future liability to retirees and their dependents exceeds $12 billion. Health maintenance organizations (HMOs) and utilization review have done little to slow the costly inflation problem (Eastaugh, 1990).

A business has three basic options for controlling health care expenses: cost shifting, usage reduction, and management efficiency. The strategy of managing costs more efficiently has been done in the late 1980s largely through self-insurance, negotiation of discounts, and coordination of benefit rules for phantom coverage. The cost shifting strategy has taken two basic forms: (1) increasing the employee's premium contribution and (2) "cost transfer" off the insurance plan and onto the employee's or retiree's pocketbook through increased cost-sharing requirements of increased deductibles, coinsurance, and copayments. The first method, cost shifting of premiums, fosters increased price sensitivity at the annual point of selecting an insurance plan. Unfortunately, this mechanism provides the consumer with no incentive to cooperate, or stimulate, the more efficient utilization of services. Method two, cost sharing, affects behavior at the point of consumption of service. Cost sharing not only shifts the burden onto the employee, but it also reduces the cost of care by deterring unnecessary services (usage reduction). Thus, cost sharing reduces total costs and does not just shift the burden.

EXCESSIVELY LOW COST-SHARING
REQUIREMENTS

Consider the use of cost-sharing requirements in the most costly segment of the health economy, the hospital. In Japan and Korea, out-of-pocket payments represent 30 to 40 percent of hospital revenue. However, in the mid-1980s American business made such a timid use of cost sharing that out-of-pocket payments declined from 5.3 percent of hospital revenues in 1983 to 4.8 percent in 1986 and to a record low 4.5 percent in 1987. The nation incurs a competitive disadvantage by requiring too small a dose of cost sharing in its health coverage plans. The good news is that out-of-pocket hospital expenses are rising, from $8.8 billion in 1985 to $11.3 billion in 1988 and a projected $21 billion in 1993, according to the federal Health Care Financing Administration Office of the Actuary. But our cost-sharing requirements would have to increase twofold to achieve parity with the Japanese and the Koreans. This author would not prefer achieving parity, since too high a level of cost sharing might deter some necessary care and erode the quality of care in theory.

In the collective bargaining process, employers should strive to increase cost-sharing requirements and finance quality assurance activities to protect and promote the quality of care (Eastaugh, 1987). During collective bargaining, labor representatives are interested in how much cost transfer is required to purchase a certain amount of usage reduction. This trade-off can benefit all concerned in the long run, with the exception of the provider's pocketbook. (Health care providers like competition in what they buy, not what they sell.) The employer must seek to curtail, through cost sharing, what is labeled "moral hazard" in the jargon of economics. The economist's term "moral hazard" does not imply any moral turpitude. An employee's response to excess insurance coverage is rational behavior: demand more service when you pay less.

Cost-sharing options developed a kinder and gentler provision in the 1980s. To prevent a possible catastrophic fiscal impact from employee cost-sharing requirements, many companies instituted a maximum out-of-pocket provision, such as $2,000 per family. This provision can also be set to promote equity between blue-collar and white-collar workers (e.g., the maximum out-of-pocket expense cannot exceed 10 percent of salary).

CONCLUSIONS

If America can improve its rate of productivity growth by doubling the 1.2 percent annual gain, most of our pressing economic problems—federal and trade deficits, relations with Japan—would substantially decline. Why target a 2.4 percent growth rate in productivity? Because a mere 1.4 percent gain in productivity would cause the wealth of the average American to shrink (after factoring out funds paid to investors). The impact of sluggish growth in productivity is slow and insidious. This prolonged wasting disease of low productivity gains has acquired the label "the British disease." A 1.4 percent gain in American productivity would produce an additional

$792 billion in goods and services and $228 billion in additional tax revenues in the next three years (1994–1996).

Until the 1980s, Britain was a nation more concerned with styles of life than with productivity. The nation did not face the basic truth that raising productivity was the only way to raise standard of living, with the exception of working longer hours. The United Kingdom from 1905 to 1980 experienced a slow decline of 0.54 percentage points per year in annual productivity gains relative to the competition, making Britain in 1988 an inferior economy in comparison to Italy and five other nations. Our corresponding gap is twice as large (1.2 percent gains in productivity, rather than 2.4 percent), so we need wait only 40 years (not 80 years) before we become a second-rate economic power. This chapter has suggested some avenues for a return to steady prosperity. Can we bounce back? Definitely yes! The British achieved annual productivity growth in the 1980s that was merely 0.2 points below the Japanese rate of improvement. With a 2.2 to 2.4 percent annual growth in productivity, combined with a 1.1 percent growth in the work force, the American economy could raise the GNP by a healthy 3.3 to 3.5 percent per year. The joy of a small, steady improvement in productivity is also a slow improvement in the standard of living and the national savings rate. Prior to the 1940s, the scarcity and location of natural resources were the critical industrial issues, but process technology, incentive rewards, and human organization are the critical issues in the new world.

Financing a productivity revolution will require increased funding for education. Half of the Clinton administration's planned new resources for education can be financed by efficient administration. The General Accounting Office (GAO) is currently conducting a study on alternative ways to finance student loans by making the funds flow as direct federal loans. Rather than wait for the study results, Congress should consider *POLICY PROPOSAL No. 32:* Replace commercial bank loan guarantees with direct federal loans for students. During the period 1994–1997, we will waste $5.8 billion if we continue the present policy of having students apply through their schools to borrow from commercial banks.

The Clinton administration's proposal to restructure college loans would save money, trim administrative profit-taking by banks, and allow more students to enroll in post–secondary school education (college or vocational training). The "allowance" student loan bonus of 3.25 percentage points above the rate of interest on 91-day Treasury bills wastes the taxpayers' money. In the long run, President Clinton is trying to replace the current student loan program with a system by which college graduates could repay loans by working for one or two years in public service jobs or directly through a payroll deduction based on income.

REFERENCES

Abernathy, W. (1978). *The Productivity Dilemma: Roadblock to Innovation in the Automobile Industry.* Baltimore: Johns Hopkins University Press.

Bailey, M., and Winston, C., eds. (1990). *Microeconomics.* Washington, DC: Brookings.

Bartley, R. (1992). *The Seven Fat Years and How to Do It Again.* New York: Free Press.

Baumol, W., Blackman, S., and Wolff, E. (1989). *Productivity and American Leadership: The Long View.* Cambridge: MIT Press.

Beer, M., Eisenstat, R., and Spector, B. (1990). *The Critical Path to Corporate Renewal.* Cambridge: Harvard Business School Press.

Berger, S., Dertouzous, M., Lester, R., Solow, R., and Thurow, L. (1989). "Toward a New Industrial America: MIT Commission on Industrial Productivity," *Scientific American* 260:6, June, 39–47.

Binder, A. (1990). *Paying for Productivity: A Look at the Evidence.* Washington, DC: Brookings.

Botkin, J., and Matthews, J. (1992). *Winning Combinations: The Coming Wave of Entrepreneurial Partnerships between Large and Small Companies.* New York: Wiley.

Coleman, J. (1990). *Foundations of Social Theory.* Cambridge: Belknap Press of Harvard University Press.

Conner, R., Hudson, J., and Mayne, J. (1993). *Learning from International Experiences.* New York: North Holland.

Deming, W. (1982). *Quality, Productivity, and Competitive Position.* Cambridge: MIT Press.

Dertouzous, M., Lester, R., and Solow, R. (1989). *Made in America: Regaining the Productive Edge.* Cambridge: MIT Press.

Drucker, P. (1964). *Managing for Results.* New York: Harper and Row.

Eastaugh, S. (1991). "Financial Methods for Paying the Doctor: Issues and Options." In *Paying the Doctor*, ed. J. Moreno. Westport, CT: Greenwood Press, chapter 5.

———. (1990). "Sharing the Burden: Containing the Health Care Bill," *Business Forum* 15:4, December, 35–41.

———. (1987). *Financing Health Care: Economic Efficiency and Equity.* Westport, CT: Auburn House.

———. (1985). "Improving Hospital Productivity," *Hospital and Health Services Administration* 30:4, July-August, 97–111.

Gomory, R. (1990). "Of Ladders, Cycles and Economic Growth," *Scientific American* 262, June, 140.

Griliches, Z. (1992). *Output Measurement in the Service Sectors.* Chicago: University of Chicago Press.

Halal, W. (1986). *The New Capitalism.* New York: Wiley.

Hutchens, R. (1989). "Seniority Wages and Productivity: A Turbulent Decade," *Journal of Economic Perspectives* 3:4, Fall, 49–64.

Johnson, C., Tyson, L., and John, F. (1991). *Politics and Productivity: How Japan's Development Strategy Works.* New York: Harper Business.

Kanter, R. (1986). *The Change Masters: Innovation for Productivity in the American Corporation.* New York: Simon and Schuster.

Lu, D. (1990). *Kanban, the Just-In-Time Production Systems (JIT).* Cambridge: Productivity Press Books.

Manning, W., Newhouse, J., and Duan, N. (1987). "Health Insurance and the Demand for Medical Care: Evidence from a Randomized Experiment," *American Economic Review* 77:3, June, 251–77.

Miller, D. (1990). *Icarus Paradox: How Exceptional Companies Bring about Their Own Downfall.* New York: Harper Business.

Norsworthy, J., and Lang, S. (1993). *Empirical Measurement and Analysis of Productivity and Technological Change.* New York: North Holland.

Osterman, P., and Batt, R. (1993). "Employer-Centered Training for International Competitiveness," *Journal of Policy Analysis and Management* 12:3, Summer, 456–76.

Peridog, M. (1991). *Achieving Total Quality Management: A Program for Action.* Cambridge: Productivity Press Books.

Peters, T. (1987). *Thriving on Chaos: Handbook for a Management Revolution.* New York: Knopf.

Pinchot, G. (1985). *Intrapreneuring: Why You Don't Have to Leave the Corporation to Become an Entrepreneur.* New York: Harper and Row.

Pope, G. (1990). "Physician Inputs, Outputs, and Productivity 1976–1986," *Inquiry* 27:2, Summer, 151–60.

Porter, M. (1990). *The Competitive Advantage of Nations.* New York: Free Press.

Schor, J. (1991). *The Overworked American.* Boston: Basic Books.

Shapiro, E. (1991). *How Corporate Truths Become Competitive Traps.* New York: Wiley.

Shingo, S. (1992). *The Shingo Production Management System: Improving Process Functions.* Cambridge: Productivity Press Books.

Thurow, L. (1992). *Head to Head: The Coming Economic Battle among Japan, Europe, and America.* New York: Morrow.

Vedder, R., and Gallaway, L. (1993). *Out of Work: Unemployment and Government.* New York: Holmes Meier.

Watanabe, C., Santoso, I., and Widayanti, T. (1992). *The Inducing Power of Japanese Technological Innovation.* New York: Columbia University Press.

Wheelwright, S., and Clark, K. (1992). *Revolutionizing Product Development: Quantum Leaps in Speed, Efficiency and Quality.* New York: Free Press.

Wolff, E. (1991). "Capital Formation and Productivity Convergence over the Long Term," *American Economic Review* 81:3, June, 565–79.

6

Education and Productivity Enhancement for a Better Tomorrow

We can not always build the future for our youth. But we can build the youth for our future.
—Franklin D. Roosevelt, 1933

It takes a whole village to raise a child.
—African proverb

Failure to prepare is preparing to fail. Do not mistake activity for achievement. The purpose of discipline isn't to punish but to correct.
—John Wooden, 1971

Our national work force is like an army: it cannot function with lousy lieutenants any more than it can function with comatose corporals.
—Lester Thurow, 1992

President Clinton offers a clear vision of why deficit reduction is but one part of a total economic plan. A total economic plan is about people—their skills, their hopes, their savings, and their education. American's educational system has room for improvement judging by the job performance of recent college graduates (the lieutenants), the corporals from the local community college or adult education programs, and the privates who sometimes fail to finish school. We must do a better job of teaching people to finish high school. We must do a better job of teaching people to calculate, think, compute, create, and communicate. Schools must ask a basic question: If we were not already doing activity X, would we start?

The link between educational quality and productivity is well established. For example, Wisconsin economist Michael Olneck (1993) has calculated the degree to which declining test scores (1967–1981) translated into eroding national productivity. The 3 percent mid-1970s decline in

American productivity is explained: 1/15th by lower test scores of new entrants to the work force and 3/15ths by lower training/skills of older workers. America needs a better educational system for adults, preschoolers, and the 38 million students in elementary and secondary school. Education is not only good for national productivity, but it also acts as the keystone to individual fulfillment and is the preferred method for upward mobility. The old aphorism remains true: knowledge is power. America is a top spender on college education, but in 1993 we ranked tenth in the world for spending on education for children under age 18.

The 1983 federal report, "A Nation at Risk," prompted many states to improve their public schools. The presidential summit on education in Virginia in 1989 set benchmarks to measure future progress. The 1990 national governors' association offered a number of goals for the year 2000:

1. to improve the high school graduation rate from 72 percent to 90 percent

2. to make America first in the world in math and science

3. to make sure every school is drug-free and violence-free

4. to eliminate adult illiteracy (25 million adults)

5. to get every preschooler ready to learn by age five

Even though education has been a locally funded activity since the 1600s, the federal government could make the most impact on preschool programs for the poor. Goal five is positively achieved through expansion of Head Start. Almost 12 million children have enrolled in Head Start since 1965. Head Start programs were run in 23,000 classrooms in 1990 at a cost of $2,800 per child. Modest funding increases of $1.1 billion for Head Start during the period 1989–1991 have increased the percentage of poor children enrolled in the program from 22 percent in 1987 to 35 percent in 1989 and to 60 percent in 1991. Perhaps 100 percent of poor children will soon be eligible for Head Start. Goal three is often achieved through special programs, as evidenced by the success of Harvard-trained physician Deborah Prothrow-Smith's violence-prevention curricula in greater Boston public schools.

The current Head Start program may not be effective in the long term for two-thirds of children. A fully effective 1994 Head Start program would: (1) last longer, (2) include tutors for ages 6 to 15, (3) increase parental involvement, and (4) thus cost an additional $2,000 per child in 1994 ($5,800 total in 1994 dollars). In life-cycle costing terms a $9.7 billion Head Start program in 1994 dollars, including all eligible children and adding a tutors program, might prove a good public investment. In addition to funding more educational research and developmental activities, should the federal government massively infuse more funds into existing schools? Liberal Democrats answer "yes" and call for a fourfold increase in the proportion of the federal budget going to education from 2.25 percent to 9 percent. Currently, the federal government spends 2.25 percent of its budget to finance 7.3 percent of all education expenses in America ($394 billion). In the peak year, 1979, the federal government contributed 9.9 percent to education. State and local governments are spending $26 billion on education and only $1.53 billion on vocational and adult education in 1993.

The absolute amount of dollars invested is secondary to targeting those educational projects that really work. The nation needs increased funding in education research and development, which should in turn instill our students and educators with a renewed spirit of inquiry. Do we suffer from a retarded spirit of inquiry or a deficit of dollars? The problem does not appear to be dollars when one considers that we are spending $6,700 per pupil per year on public school education in 1993, compared to $4,300 per pupil in Germany and Japan. All three nations spend 4.5 percent of their gross domestic product on education expenditures. A number of basic problems have been identified in the American educational complex: (1) student apathy toward breaking down the Berlin Wall or learning any math and science, (2) slow diffusion of techniques exported from the most successful schools, and (3) few teachers visiting the classroom down the hall to improve teaching techniques. Reenergizing our students and teachers will involve some spending hikes, but the more critical element is a change in spirit (e.g., learning is fun, a better education is necessary, a spirit of inquiry fuels a good life better than a full wallet).

TARGET WHAT WORKS

Federal and state government cannot just spend more money on education without channeling the new funding to the most effective and cost-beneficial approaches and schools. Moreover, educators cannot expect to steward more public money without discovering models for the education process and demonstrating that the outcomes are cost-beneficial. The public should realize that all education does not happen within school walls, and many "school problems" are in fact "home problems." Education is a community enterprise that can include older women tutoring children and pregnant teens, summer jobs and one-on-one mentoring, and business partnerships offering instructors, equipment, and apprenticeships.

The drop-out problem has a cultural context when one considers the fatalism and alienation of the poor students most likely to drop out. They see dropping out as a right of passage, like going to prison. Specialized schools with a concentrated population of drop-out "possibles" have reported lower drop-out rates, however. When surrounded by their own kind, other alienated peers, and offered remedial education and special counseling, some students are less likely to give up (and feel lost, left behind). The family context must also be addressed. Too many students in the inner city are neglected or abused by their parents. Young people need to be reminded of the value of an education and the value of a future-oriented life view. In that context, Georgetown University basketball coach John Thompson has a deflated basketball in his office to remind students that "somebody without an education is at the same disadvantage as a ball without air in it." The next four sections could be subtitled "how to put air back into the American education basketball." Just as you teach basketball by playing basketball, our schools must begin teaching science by letting the students do science. Less teaching must revolve around rote memorization, and less testing must involve multiple-choice questions. Student-centered learning and performance-based tests (where the student performs actual tasks, like an essay or chemistry lab experiments) represent the best hope for American education.

Statistics on the failings of our secondary schools are not easily summarized. If one samples a one-year cohort of 18-year-old citizens, 14 percent are self-reported high school drop-outs. If one samples a time series of adults age 18 to 25, 27 percent are high school drop-outs. What is the quality of the high school graduate? A surprisingly 25 percent of graduates have the equivalent of an eighth grade education (or less), and 19 percent cannot read their high school diplomas. The problem is worse in certain areas of the country: 82 percent of the 22,000 graduates taking the exam for entry-level jobs at New York Telephone failed in 1990; one-third of the 7,400 IBM workers at the Vermont computer-chip factory in Burlington need retraining in eighth grade trigonometry to do their jobs; executives at Motorola report that only 22 percent of their job applicants can pass a fifth grade math test or seventh grade English comprehension test. The required after-school educational expenses add to the cost of American products. On a more basic cultural level, all of this means that much of the citizenry cannot think clearly, act wisely, or perhaps feel deeply.

The American Society for Training and Development reports that American business spends in excess of $30 billion on formal education programs for its employees. As is traditional with any special interest group, American business would like a tax break to finance these educational expenses. If corporations receive tax breaks for investing in equipment and plants, why shouldn't they receive tax relief for investments in human capital. The argument has some supporters in the current climate of declining numbers of young Americans (1.5 percent fewer Americans aged 20 to 29 each year) and diminished levels of job preparedness, but American business will be forced to make the investment in any case. American business cannot afford to be callous and say to the unprepared young persons that they deserve to be unemployed. We have too few workers in this new world to sacrifice any demographic group to long-term unemployment. The American labor force is shrinking; 9.9 million fewer citizens will enter the job pool in the 1990s in comparison to the 1970s. The quality of entry workers may have stopped declining, but we need a rapid upswing in quality to compensate for the decline in quantity.

COLLEGE-BOUND OR VOCATIONAL EDUCATION

Too many educational reform papers have focused only on higher education or college-prep class work. While the future captains of our work force do need more math, science, and language training, one-quarter of Americans need a better system of vocational education. All careers are not professional careers. A graduate of a good vocational program experiences a feeling of self-worth because for the first time he or she can see the fruits of labor. They become motivated and interested in their career. Some vocational education graduates will go further, acquiring college aspirations, because they have developed the attitudes and work habits necessary to produce college success. But 98 percent of vocational education students do not need four-year plans but do need attainable, shorter term goals and a taste of success. Vocational education programs are 50 to 80 percent less expensive than a year on welfare or a year in prison, the alternative "career" paths for many social drop-outs. *POLICY PROPOSAL No. 33:* The new welfare reform agenda should include tripling federal government spending on job training and education by 1997, to $3.1 billion, and adding $1.7 billion in tax credits for the working poor.

The federal government or the American business community might consider standardizing vocational education. For example, in Germany the school system offers certificates in 381 apprenticable skills so that employers can be sure that the entry-level worker meets minimum standards. German firms spend 2 percent of payroll on apprenticeship programs. If vocational education is more valuable and reliable for all concerned, more students sign up for it. An amazingly high 73.5 percent of German high school students spend their last two years of secondary school enrolled in on-the-job apprenticeships. Over 700,000 German students applied for apprenticeship positions in 1993. The apprentice system slowly evolved after publication of the 1963 report "The German Education Disaster." The apprenticeship might represent 20 to 50 percent of the student's school week (apprenticeship with the employer follows six hours of classroom work, six days a week). German officials and employers see this effort as an attempt to raise the level of technical workers per million citizens to the Japanese level (requiring a 49 percent growth in technical workers over the period 1993–2010).

One last issue concerns the possibility that too many students will forsake college for a vocational education. Contrary to demographic projections, American college and university enrollment is at an all-time peak (13.6 million). The American bias for a college education minimizes the danger that tenth graders will be prematurely steered into vocational education.

American business leaders increasingly complain about high school graduates without basic skills and college graduates incapable of writing or critical thinking. The annual direct price of our suboptimal American educational system costs the nation $25 billion in direct costs (e.g., mistakes) and another $100 billion in indirect costs by lower earnings capacity. Inferior educational returns tend to translate eventually into declining financial returns, for a family or for a nation. Poor educational performance may produce a second-rate labor force in America. In 1992 America had 50 percent more technical workers per million citizens in comparison to Germany, but Japan had 18 percent more than the U.S.A. It is difficult to become a technical worker if you cannot read or imagine a job waiting at the end of the training program. Germany has had a vocational craft tradition since Bismarck in 1888. Its name, *Ausbuilding,* means both education and training. America ranks 14th in literacy, far behind Australia (number one) and Japan. We must do a better job at all levels of the education system, including adult literacy programs and remedial education. American firms should contribute more than 1.9 percent of corporate giving to schools. President Clinton would like the federal government to contribute $960 million over the next four years to create 300,000 youth apprenticeships.

LAND OF EQUALITY

The concept that "education can set you free" is a modern American ideal. That ideal contrasts with the European tendency to gear the educational system to the elite. In America 73 percent of all secondary students qualify for entry into higher education (compared to only 8 to 9 percent in 1905), which is in sharp contrast to more elitist educational systems with 26 to 29 percent entry rate into post–secondary school education (France, Germany, the United Kingdom). The duration of education programs is also a critical issue, especially when one reflects on the fact that 23 percent of elementary school students have to repeat a grade. America must work to do a better job in the lower grades, ensuring that students are not "passed up" from grade to grade.

For 3,000 years the older generations have engaged in excessive hand-wringing about poor education systems. American officials may overstate our problems in certain areas. For example, we may not be outside the top five ranking nations in international comparisons of math and science knowledge. The control groups for the published rankings are biased; the best students (top 300 to 800) in each European country are compared to the average American student taking advanced placement courses (13 percent of the class of 1992). If America ranks 8th in physics, 19th in chemistry, and 12th in biology, it may be because we are comparing our top 13 percent of students to the other nations' top 1 percent. This good news item is short-lived, however, because relative to Japan, American scores are inferior, and the Japanese are equally egalitarian with their school system (87 percent of high school students are eligible for college, and their average student beats out the American average student).

Extending the quantity of school hours per year is often suggested by educators. They would experience a longer pay period, but the American public seems to resist the extension of the school year. For example, Polk County, North Carolina, extended the school year from 180 to 200 days in 1984 and 1985. Educationally, the longer school year may have been a success, as student test scores increased modestly, more so than the state-wide average gain. However, the reform was a political failure, resulting in legal suits from parents enraged over any shortening in their vacation schedule. Given the unpopularity of the longer school year, any subsequent changes may have to be gradual (e.g., extending the school year five days every five years). Perhaps, however, the quality of education per hour is more critical than the quantity of hours within the school walls. Japanese students may perform better because they do 300 percent more homework and utilize private tutors after school three to four days a week. Japanese officials borrowed the national curriculum idea from France, the advanced placement math and science courses from America, and the rote-learning determination from their Asian neighbors. Americans do not want Japanese schools, but they do want more self-discipline without dampening self-expression, and they want more emphasis on individual responsibilities. It would not hurt to mirror the Japanese tradition of students doing more homework and teachers eating at lunchtime with students.

A standard core curriculum is also becoming more popular in college education. The University of Chicago, Stanford, Columbia, and Harvard have upgraded the breadth and rigor of their core curriculum since the 1980s, but too many colleges still spend two-thirds of the student's time on "joke courses designed by a game show host" (Sykes, 1988). In 1992, 32 percent of college graduates took no science or math classes while attending college, 45 percent had no literature classes, and 36 percent had no history classes. American college professors should not expect improvements in life-style values and "seriousness" if the curriculum is too simple and unchallenging. The Clinton administration is attempting to reopen the American mind, and educational system, by increasing federal investment in education by 15 percent in 1994–1995.

TEACHING SCIENCE

A national push to enhance the quality and quantity of the science curriculum in the public schools received a shot in the arm by two major events. First, the flight of the Russian satellite Sputnik in 1957 sent a wake-up call for Americans to emphasize science education in the 1960s. Second, public hearings reporting that the 1986 space shuttle Challenger disaster resulted from poor quality control and a ruptured $900 gasket stimulated public anger. Science teachers nationwide could use this case example to call for better science education and quality control in business and government. America needs more good engineers and scientists, who must be involved in quality control and accountability (e.g., witness the failure of the $1.6 billion Hubble space telescope in 1990).

If the late 1950s was a shot in the arm for science education, the protest generation's push for "creativity" in 1969 was a shot-in-the-head rebellion against disciplined instruction and against learning "hard subjects" with absolute correct answers. Students in the 1990s are correct to rebel against "trite requirements" to take "baby classes (like 'science appreciation') to learn this science stuff." The classes should be made more difficult and demanding. What matters is education, not schooling. Disciplined lessons learned translate across fields, so that a physics class might improve future economists in the way that organic chemistry classes improve future physicians (Deming, 1986).

Students cannot be expected to respect math and science skills if they are never exposed to the complexities of the subjects (Westheimer, 1992). Why should everyone be forced to learn a standard amount of math and science in school? First, every good citizen should be schooled in such subjects in order to make intelligent decisions in the voting booth or in community action committees. Nuclear power in recombinant-DNA research is a less "other worldly topic" if the citizen is well versed in physics and biology. The second reason we need increased emphasis on math and science is for international competitiveness.

We need to spot superlative science and math students in high school, reward their talent at science fairs, offer college and graduate scholarships, and offer sufficiently high salaries to keep the necessary manpower supply in the workplace. We must arouse and channel student interest in science and math. The production of creative scientists and mathematicians must invoke the apprenticeship concept from vocational education. Apprenticeships focus less on rote formulas than on analyzing the way a professional chooses a path/process to a real-world problem. The nation needs better quality math and science teachers. More than half of these teachers will have to come from industry, passing alternative certification programs before teaching at the high school level. In the 1990s education schools will produce only 8,500 to 9,000 math and science teachers each year, but the nation needs at least 20,000 per year. Scholarship funds would help attract potential teachers of all ages. A large fraction of the profit margins from athletic departments should go to academic scholarships, in amounts equivalent to what has been paid to "rent" the student athlete. George Washington University president Stephen Trachtenberg has been outspoken on this issue, suggesting that the kind of financial aid package offered to a really stellar player should also be offered to the academically stellar student.

The nation also needs more math and science instruction at the college level. Consider the amount of science and math required of an elite college student at the turn of the century. In 1899 Harvard College required a course in science or math or both every semester. The average liberal arts student in 1899 had 40 percent of his or her semester hours in math and science. In contrast, Brooke Shields, like 100 to 150 Princeton University students each year, graduated from college without taking a single class in science, history, math, or economics.

POLICY PROPOSAL No. 34: Double the required semester hours of science and math for the average college graduate from 9 to 18. This doubling of effort would represent only 14 percent of total semester hours, only one-third the amount of science and math required of a Harvard student in 1899, and only one-fourth the amount required of a Japanese student in 1990. Our science "pro" prospects will clearly need much more than this minimum dose, but this is a good first step in making America first in the world in math and science. Students will not respect the subjects if the rigor is minimal and the intellectual content substandard. The attitude that exposure to a substandard product is better than no exposure at all is a ridiculous argument, eroding the quality of education. Improving the average level of scientific skills will help graduates use the computer at work, form a logical written or oral argument, and nurture the self-knowledge that quantitative skills will increasingly form the basis for learning and living in the next century. The very process of learning will become more self-centered.

STUDENT-CENTERED LEARNING

One of the central problems with teaching today's students is that they have a short attention span and limitless impatience with any problem that cannot be answered in under 30 minutes. This short-term focus may be a by-product of television. As a nation we need more patient students willing to work 90 hours on a monthly project, yielding a few insights, before producing a decent partial solution. Math or science cannot be placed on a 30-minute TV time schedule, because it may take 90 hours of hard work before the student even has a glimpse of that first creative insight into the problem. Our multiple-choice tests reinforce a false impression in students' minds that answers are found in under two minutes (or the problem isn't worth the effort). Students should be encouraged to do two more hours of homework each evening, and two fewer hours of TV viewing. In a nation where kids can easily name nine mixed drinks and six drugs, but 42 percent cannot name three presidents, it's time to turn off the TV and engage the world. Ask a child to describe "joy," and he or she will tell you about a TV soap commercial.

American educators have been calling for a revolution in our educational system since 1957. For the majority of educators the concept of a revolution derives from the Latin word *revolvere*, or turning back, returning to first principles. The clarion call to teach basic skills, then teach critical thinking, is a reaction to failed experimental education programs that ignore "the three Rs" (reading, writing, and arithmetic) and attempt to jump to critical thinking without first establishing a foundation. In this decade computer-based, student-centered tools may eliminate the need for tracking, as students can learn the advanced material at their learning station while staying with their peers in an average classroom. A student wishing to learn a specialized subtopic will learn from a 3D interactive laser videodisc. The videodisc will challenge the student more than the constantly repeating "skill" drills that move onto new material at an imperceptibly slow pace. The federal government must assure equal access to these future computer-based instructional methods across all school districts. Computers can also educate and test teachers to make sure that they are technically proficient in their subject matter.

Lastly, one way to make student-centered learning more relevant is through the introduction of the new performance-based tests that go beyond multiple-choice questions and force students to perform actual tasks. Vermont and New York are pioneers in the field of performance-based testing, creating a more valid exam that is really worth taking. Because these tests are not machine-graded, the performance-based essay tests (writing or solving complex science and math questions) require more administrative expense. Within a few decades such essay tests will increasingly be graded by "thinking" computers that can critique both the answer and the student's thinking process.

In the 1970s it became popular for teachers to write lesson plans that avoided any controversy and any context where a student had to make a judgment. Duller-than-dull lesson plans and textbooks lead to mediocre imaginations and limited career paths for both the teacher and the students. The author's high school teacher in the spring of 1970 placed the issue into context: "I don't want to be found guilty of trying to educate any of you students if an issue could make one student in class feel bad." This "don't make anyone feel bad" approach to "cooperative learning" removed all reference to religion, gender, or race from history and social studies texts. No slaves in the 19th century? No religious persecution in the 17th and 18th centuries? This moral-free, value-free approach slowly eroded the traditional core content of education. A society with such insidious, insubstantial books and classes harms the value system.

REBEL—AND DO IT RIGHT

A school rebel in the 1950s might have attacked the textbook memorization of dates and geography, but a school rebel in the 1990s could rebel against the teacher by reading a history book published before 1970. Today's student rebel has traditional 1950s values and the hope that America can do better (the students may also hope that their teacher learns how to take a position, defend it, and stop talking about moral relativism—"for any culture, any action is okay"). Greed and apathy grow when a bland sanitized point of view is presented, whether the source of the fictional "unbiased" viewpoint is right wing or left. Unbiased books cannot be written until the issues are so ancient that they cease to matter.

Moral relativism grew from the emotional wellsprings to get religion out of the public schools. The decade after we threw religion out of the schools we allowed the educators to throw morality out as well. However, Americans are starting to realize that there are commitments beyond the life of the textbook—to tolerance, to respect, and to civic values—that must be reinforced at school. The three Cs are important values that belong in school: cooperation, consideration, and compassion. Teachers should unambiguously teach that cheating, lying, stealing, and violence are wrong. If teachers wants to go beyond such simple clarification and present a liberal philosophy that stealing is okay if you're poor, or terrorists need to be understood, not punished, then let them wait for law schools to teach such foolishness. It's equally absurd to expect children to rediscover morality or the principles of engineering if they have never been exposed to the subject. Stressing the fundamental priority of values is as important for the rich stockbroker's child as it is for the inner-city kid. Schools should teach skills but also offer some values; otherwise, ethical illiterates will come to dominate American society. President Clinton has suggested a Youth Opportunity Corps for troubled teens who drop out of school. They would be matched with adult mentors to help them develop skills and self-discipline (at a cost of $450 million).

Civility and values education are important because they provide specific common reference points for communication and also offer the cornerstone for character development. The basic messages to students in value clarification are: you are responsible, we need you, we have a code of conduct, there is a place for you. Moral relativism is a silly idea that should be retired from American curricula. Relativism mainly belongs in physics, where you can impress a class with the fact that Elvis weighed 255 pounds on earth, 13 pounds on Pluto, and 7,490 pounds on the sun. Teddy Roosevelt summarized the issue: "To educate a man in mind and not in values is to educate a menace to society."

A "do-the-right-thing" approach to education would tell the truth, and present bias, rather than attempt to present a sanitized view of the world. One could discuss slavery but also present the uplifting sides of black history (beyond stating that 40 percent of the cowboys were black). Citizens need to know their history, warts and all. A sanitized rewrite of history is for hoary old men trying to avoid confrontation and change. The prospect of biased but documented truth holds out the incentive to learn. The prospect of "moral relativism, given that everyone has an equally worthy opinion" only holds out the incentive to not work hard or take a stand. The Japanese laugh at American schools of noneducation, which emphasize personality development and moral relativity but refuse to teach Einstein's brand of physics. The Japanese press portrays Americans as "soft people" who avoid difficult intellectual effort.

Increased funding for education is not the answer if too much of current expenditures go to local corruption and patronage. A number of scandals have emphasized the need to root out corruption from public school boards. Detroit school board members voted educational funds to purchase Cadillac limousines. In some cases a higher government official must take control of the local schools. New Jersey Governor Tom Kean's 1,000 page report on corruption in Jersey City schools prompted the state to take over the local school system.

We need to fight apathy in the student and parent populations. The average voter doesn't care about school board elections but should. America needs to make the public part owners again in our schools. Parents should also be involved with their children's homework and the career counseling process. Parents have a limited amount of hours to tutor their children, but with the help of public subsidies, many families would benefit from a Japanese *jeukeu* (or second school day, to tutor students after 3 P.M). The second school may be partly funded through partnerships with local businesses. This forces the students to do their homework and/or face their future. Half of the time the second school might take a work-study approach. Since 1984 California has had a program for 33,000 former dropouts, teaching vocational skills at hospitals and local physicians' offices. The program gives the students some career goals, guidance from a mentor, and a clear reason to stay awake in class.

MOTIVATION AND ROLE MODELS

Role models are needed to teach students the necessity of preparation and application. A motivated teacher can perform wonders in the worst possible public school. J. Matthews (1989) tells the story of one teacher, Jaime Escalante, who spent nine years working as a janitor and cook so he could become a teacher. With aggressive didactic teaching techniques Escalante convinced his math classes that "underclass" need not translate into "incapable of learning." Instead, his students from one of Los Angeles's worst high schools set records in passing the advanced placement calculus test for college placement. Escalante was a classic example of the observation that "all progress depends on the unreasonable man," as he was very unreasonable and demanding. He demanded that his students do their homework, he demanded that they not place music or sports above his math class, and he was very unreasonable in not letting students drop his class. He required parents and students to sign a contract, which he also signed, stating: "When you come to class with desire, I will come to class with as much desire, if not more, to teach." He was not just an information dispenser; he was a "thought inspirer" and strong antidote to the defeatism prevalent among inner-city children.

The need for role models is even more acute in primary education, when the children are most likely to copy the behavior of the teacher. A number of special programs in Dade County, Florida, New York, and Washington, D.C., have been tailored to poor male students. A number of studies (e.g., *Teacher* magazine, 1989) suggest that high school drop-outs actually drop out psychologically and emotionally by the third grade. These new programs offer all-male classes male teachers to provide the minority students with the message that "you can still be a real man and be literate, nonviolent, and not a substance abuser." One *Washington Post* editorial writer, Carl Rowan, started a program to reward black males who were being beaten up by their peers for reading books and getting into that "white education thing." Educators can also do a better job of teaching values by example, including the value of work, personal integrity, and respect for your family and neighborhood.

Quality teachers try to do five basic things in the process of teaching: (1) teach each child, move around the classroom; (2) engage students in thinking for themselves, bringing the abstract down to earth with real-world examples; (3) emphasize integrity, character, and the value of adhering to principles; (4) the good teacher is a master of the subject, and likes the subject, so the subject becomes the center of attention in the class; and (5) the good teacher never stops learning the subject or the craft of teaching. A number of educators (Barth, 1990) have emphasized the importance of this last point and the need for teachers and administrators jointly to create a community of learners in each school. In so doing, the teachers reveal themselves to students as learners, and the value of education becomes more concrete and universal.

Good teachers convey the basic message that if the individual does not study, he or she will never achieve anything of consequence. In our society if you study, you become what you wish. The career stairs will not be easy for many, but education is the one way to smooth the splinters from ladders that remain no easy climb (to paraphrase Robert Kennedy). College-bound students should climb a more rigorous ladder. A student who aspires to teach a certain subject should major in that subject, and not major in education, while in college. Each of the two basic types of education schools has a pet fallacy. College-based programs fall prey to the fallacy of technique: assuming a good teacher can teach anything. University-based programs fall prey to the fallacy of "the knowledgeable can teach:" assuming the person who knows his or her subject well can teach it to anyone. The basic difference between the two groups is that the university-based programs have developed ways to deal with their fallacy; they teach the nonteacher how to be effective in the classroom.

Many current teachers resent the concept of hiring adults from industry to teach high school or special subjects. They argue that a "mid-careerist" scientist or engineer may know more about their subject, but they didn't go to education school and cannot actually teach students. The public balance seems to have shifted away from pedagogy and toward subject matter. Experts in their subject matter do not always make the best teachers. For example, the new math in the 1970s suffered because it was developed by mathematicians who wanted kids to learn the way professionals do. Parents, however, were unable to assist their children with homework assignments. It works better for the average student to learn arithmetic, then learn mathematics. We may repeat this same mess in the 1990s, as recent college graduates in chemistry, physics, and biology wish to teach fractual geometry and chaos theory before the student has learned the basic sciences. Fractual geometry is fine for the gifted high school student, but it is not necessary knowledge for most.

QUALITY AND QUANTITY OF TEACHERS

Does America need a higher teacher-to-student ratio? Perhaps the answer is yes, but not for the conventional reason. We do not need more teachers just to reduce class size. Indeed, the larger class sizes in Japan and Korea seem to suggest that better quality education need not require smaller classes. The reason we need more teachers is so that teachers can offer higher quality, graded homework, because employing more teachers will reduce the number of classes they teach per day and reduce bureaucratic meetings to free up time to grade papers and upgrade lesson plans. In Korea, Japan, and Hong Kong, the average teachers offer only three classes per day and spend four to six hours grading papers (based on a personal observation). We cannot expect American teachers to offer more challenging homework assignments if we never provide the time to grade the material. When we allow our teachers the requisite hours necessary to grade homework, they will have the capability to require students to do homework on a daily basis. A good principal and more challenging homework assignments may represent the two critical determinants for improving performance.

The concept that one idea fits all is as much a failure in fashion as it is in education. In a 1992 Gallup poll, school choice is favored by 65 percent of Americans and 71 percent of minorities. Choice programs will only work if there is a sufficient array of choices from which to select. Sweden, a nation with a socialist tradition, implemented a popular school choice program in 1992. According to the socialist party leader, a state monopoly makes no sense in education.

Absence of parental choice and a centralized school board bureaucracy work to demoralize teachers and lower academic performance, especially in poor neighborhoods. In theory, real choice/opportunity programs will startle disadvantaged parents into a new, higher level of concern for their sons' and daughters' development. Good parents can send their children to the better schools with that special program in science or history and civics. Schools will have to work hard to produce the first generation in two decades with a lively sense of social engagement: caring enough to read books, or run for political office, or sponsor a petition. America cannot survive as a world power if we continue to produce noncitizens, full of apathy and alienation.

The Japanese educational system relies more on competition and private schools. Almost 33 percent of Japanese senior high schools are private in 1993. Government pays for up to 50 percent of the cost of tuition to these schools. Attendance levels in private schools (up or down) are considered an informal check on how well the public schools are doing their job. The main difference between Japanese and American educational work load statistics occurs after school. In America 57 percent of high school students report that they do less than one hour's homework each school night, and 32 percent do none. In Japan students do 300 percent more homework, whether they attend a public or private high school. Class size is 20 percent higher in Japan, but capital investment per teacher is 420 percent higher.

American education has the lowest level of purchasing technology and capital investment of any service industry. Education has $1,400 in capital investment per employee, in contrast to $38,000 per hospital employee in 1993. Hospital care may or may not be overcapitalized, but consider *POLICY PROPOSAL No. 35:* American education should boost capital investment by 50 percent per employee to allow more individual-based computer learning and to stay competitive with the Japanese and Germans.

The education bureaucracy's concept of reform, born in the early 1980s, is teacher empowerment. Teachers involved in macro–decision making (e.g., budgeting) are more likely to work harder, implement the reform plan, and participate in accountability programs for monitoring teacher quality. Under school-based management teachers are players for the coach/principal. This approach minimizes lengthy bureaucratic meetings over central office policy and supplies, creating more time for parent-staff advisory meetings and education. Teachers operate with various styles: some are traditional/didactic, while others utilize game-like lessons to excite students (e.g., Jaime Escalante).

The best schools tend to have the highest level of autonomy and the lowest administrative expense per student. Bureaucracy is a problem throughout industrial nations, but the problem is particularly acute in American education. According to Al Shanker of the American Federation of Teachers, 45 to 50 percent of American education spending goes to administration, compared with 20 percent in Europe and 25 percent in Japan. *POLICY PROPOSAL No. 36:* Half of the careerist education bureaucrats should be fired. This fraction may even be an underestimate. For example, Catholic schools in New York have 82 percent fewer bureaucrats per student compared to Washington or Baltimore. Schools with more bureaucrats provide the worst service (e.g., the shortage of textbooks in Baltimore schools in 1989 was caused by debilitating educrats running "their" school system and preserving "their" books in storage at "their" warehouse. Eventually, in 1992–1993, 12 schools were placed under private contract management). Community empowerment is one method by which the

American public hopes to rid the educrat bureaucracy of waste and corruption (e.g., buy books, not unnecessary jobs).

The godfather of the community empowerment movement is Dr. Jim Comer, a professor of child psychiatry at Yale University. He has argued for three decades that everyone should have a stake in running public schools, through formation of school governance teams of parents, teachers, the principal, and other staff members. Bad quality schools are a disease, and the community empowerment movement believes that schools should be run for the children and the community, including employers. Schools should not be run for teachers, just as hospitals are not run for hospital employees. The ultimate beneficiary is the child, or the hospital's patient, not those who work in the institution. But if we do not allow some level of teacher empowerment and incentive pay, productivity and morale will continue to decline. Cynical competition strategy advocates counterargue that teachers are like cooks, as they do not cook better food if they feel better about their kitchen. This assertion should be subject to future research, but with a possible undersupply of teachers, morale and productivity are important issues.

THE CULTURAL CONTEXT FOR EDUCATION REFORM

The public is tired of education reform without improvement. The "team-teaching," "programmed learning," and "open-space" approaches did not do the job. Americans are results-oriented. Some nations dictate that children be what their parents were. In America we are what our children become. Educators and business leaders must be willing to sponsor experimental programs and promote the approach that works best for a demographic segment of the student population. Specially tailored programs are necessary and best understood in the context of our changing labor markets. Of the next 25 million Americans to join the work force, only 18 percent will be native-born white males.

A former schoolteacher himself, President Lyndon B. Johnson was fond of saying that a high school education is our number one antipoverty program. Only 0.5 percent of men and 1.5 percent of women 20 to 64 with only a high school education were in poverty in 1990. Leaders have always advanced the cause of education. In a classic speech in Chicago in 1964, Martin Luther King, Jr., stated the need for always doing more: "When your white roommate says he is tired and goes to sleep, you stay up and burn the midnight oil and read and learn." The reader should reflect on educational performance since King's death in 1968. America cannot afford to have a third consecutive "lost" generation that has no respect for others and shares no sense of a common cultural or physical place in history. Disrespect for education and others is not just a hindrance for the individual; it also harms society. Such self-indulgence creates drug dealers and white-collar criminals. Improving our educational system is our duty, and it is also an economic necessity. Our leaders must stop groaning about distorted value systems and the "hopeless underclass" and start investing more funds in education. Neither cheapness nor complacency are warranted. School reform is evolving like two intertwined strands of a DNA double helix: the inner strand tries to improve the productivity and effectiveness of teachers, while the outer strand of school managers and parent groups tries to promote involvement and improve resource allocation. Much reform remains to be done, especially in the area of teaching math and science: how to think symbolically and analytically, how to work independently and collaboratively.

Schools have a cultural importance. They are the last location where Americans come together as only citizens, rather than consumers. The single most difficult subject to teach is ethical values. The cacophony of teaching going on via socializing or via the media involves an unbalanced focus on materialism and greed. Materialism beats poverty, and there is nothing wrong with being upwardly mobile, but the classroom and the media must also foster responsibilities and civic duty. Without better citizens, no new school or social organization can make a dent in the nation's social deficit of illiteracy, homelessness, embezzlement, theft, fraud, and vandalism. If you don't think the problem is real, go to a museum and watch the rude children on a school trip push and shove the elderly. To reduce the social deficit, we need to change peoples' attitudes and pay for our rights with a coin of civil behavior and individual responsibility.

THE HIGH COST (AND HIGH VALUE) OF COLLEGE

University education has priced itself into the public eye. Family members were spending double the percentage of disposable income on tuition in 1990 in comparison to 1960. Students are working longer hours part-time, but the burden has increased. In 1960 a private college student could work 11 hours per week at 25 percent above minimum wage to cover the cost of tuition; the comparable figure in 1992 was 70 hours. Higher numbers of American students receive support for attending college under the Pell grant and loan program. Pell recipients increased from 1.8 million in 1978 to 2.6 million in 1980 to 3.2 million in 1989 and 4.3 million in 1992. In 1992 default of student loans cost the federal government $3.9 billion. Eligibility for grants was expanded so that a member of a family of four with up to $49,000 annual income might qualify. Eligibility for the guaranteed loan program had been liberalized so that any family, regardless of income, could qualify for these low-interest loans. Another problem is that Congress will not condition college grants or loans on student merit. College students receiving federal Pell grants and loans should be required to pass a test.

Faculty in private colleges have been forthcoming in expanding requirements and rewarding student performance (Westheimer, 1992). However, university faculty are not happy with their personal financial condition. Faculty salaries have barely kept pace with inflation but school empowerment grew by 194 percent in the 1980s, while tuition charges increased at more than double the consumer price increase. We see the paradox of rationing in a time of plenty in private college education. Certain schools announce a growth in endowment above the rate of inflation while simultaneously announcing that their admission standards will be harder for poor students requiring financial aid. Hopefully, federal assistance programs can reverse this trend and help the nation maintain the egalitarian spirit of upward mobility and equal access to high quality education. In this context the reader might reflect on the 1947 President's Commission on Higher Education concluding:

We have proclaimed our faith in education as a means of equalizing the conditions of men. But there is grave danger that our present policy will make it an instrument for creating the very inequalities it was designed to prevent. If the ladder of educational opportunity rises high at the doors of some youth and scarcely rises at all at the doors of others, while at the same time formal education is made a prerequisite to occupational and social advance, then education may become the means of deepening and solidifying class distinctions.

The prevailing social philosophy that fostered the 1960's Great Society programs held that: (1) an insufficient supply of employment opportunity existed and (2) impersonal impediments held back the poor. Creating more active poor people, with the hope for a better life, may require what Joel Schwartz calls the "remoralization" of America. Schwartz, editor of *The Public Interest,* advocates reinvention of a moral compass for the poor and the re-creation of a work ethic and social ethic of good behavior and private policy. Remoralization can be done with tutors from the same racial background, acting as role models to look up to and imitate. Public school students need morale boosting, given their surroundings: obsolete buildings, 140,000 guns brought to class weekly, and little personal experience with liberty and job selection. Work habits and dreaming of having choices are important because work is the basis of any stable society. Work teaches responsibility and therefore the value of liberty.

As we observed following the 1992 Los Angeles riots, no current social thinker has the magic "correct" approach to dismantling the culture of poverty and building up hope. At minimum we need four things: (1) enterprise zones to draw expertise and capital from the safe suburbs to the poor neighborhoods, (2) presidential leadership and a national commitment to defeat poverty, (3) education value via better schools, and (4) values education (remoralization in the home, in churches, in the street, in school, at the movies, and on television). Liberals may find the concept of moral education anathema, asking the tough question: Whose morals and whose values should be taught? But to avoid the subject is to let the subject die. We do not let Latin die, but more critically we cannot exist if we let morals die. Yet bad morals are taught everyday. The teacher allows cheating in class. Televised professional wrestling offers one basic message: the guy who cheats almost always wins.

Rich people in the suburbs cannot take the attitude that public schools in cities should be allowed to deteriorate. The social forces that erode the inner city also erode the suburbs. Morals must be taught in the schools, running a compromise between the zeal of the religious right that breeds intolerance and the politically correct left.

DEMAND THE BEST AND TEST BETTER

Parents may deserve a fair portion of the blame for poor school performance. Parents often complain that the teacher does not bring knowledge out in the child. The implication is that students need not work hard or apply themselves. Schools are made responsible for pulling the best work out of students, and the students need do only one hour of homework each evening. Learning for some parents must be made as passive and easy as watching television. Teachers must not get the student pregnant with new ideas, so classes become "dumbed down" in some schools. The student must have a pain-free pregnancy, getting an A or B with no effort. Parents will demand that students not be given bad grades because that hurts "their self-esteem." Students claim its popular to have a high IQ but not popular to work hard. Unfortunately, these students are entering a global workplace where Japanese and Korean students do seven hours of homework each day, and German students do four to five. Only American students have classes in self-esteem as an official method to wallow in self-praise, which produce a poor education for many. Washington, D.C., students report the highest rating for self-esteem in math—and the lowest math scores in America and 19 foreign countries. The best students are also harmed by unneeded self-esteem classes and insufficient homework. Students in Asia and Europe are not burdened by empty theories that self-esteem is the most important element in education. Michigan professors Harold Stevenson and James Stigler (1992) report that students think they should coast on innate ability, enjoy the success to come, and not bother to work hard. Teen movies like *Uncle Buck* or *Ferris Bueller* make fun of "dweeb" students who work. Students have an easy situation: 72 percent of college freshmen attend their first-choice school, and another 22 percent get into their second-choice school. Hard work and persistence need to become virtues again in American education. We need to stop thinking that only teachers need to persist. The students need to persist with class projects and lots of homework, and the parents must persist in helping their children learn.

In 1992 Yale University president Benno Schmidt joined business executive Chris Whittle to head a chain of proposed top-flight private schools. The proposed Whittle schools would get tough because students and parents do not respect schools that expect little of them. In return, these for-profit schools would have a longer school year (45 weeks), a nine-hour school day, and utilize computers and televisions up to three hours per day. Whittle students would spend three years more in school than average Americans. The Whittle schools would do this at the equivalent cost per pupil of public schools (an estimated $6,700 a year in 1996). In 1996 there may be only 100 Whittle schools, but they may provide a break-the-mold model for America's 109,000 elementary and secondary schools. Business will also finance education to a great extent. RJR Nabisco offers its employees a tax-deferred savings plan. The company will match annual contributions of up to $1,000 for each child's four years in high school. The plan cost $6.2 million in 1992 and also offered children 4,000 loans annually.

Creative financing options for education are also matched by a national push for better methods of teaching. We need to replace the multiple-choice tests with a very unique exam, the performance assessment. Instead of fill-in-the-blank questions, exams should consist of essays and real-life math problems and scientific experiments—and be graded by human teachers, not computers. Test companies like McGraw-Hill, Houghton Mifflin's Riverside Publishing, and Harcourt Brace Jovanovich have launched their own versions of performance-assessment exams. Whereas standardized tests have such importance that teachers build their lesson plans around them, the new exams may encourage more learning and less standardized memorization of bits of information.

Our inner-city schools need better quality teachers and better equipped classrooms. Inner-city schools need day-care programs, an ample supply of tutors (often using grandparents from the neighborhood), and pillars of hope (role models) to compensate for the insecure home environment, violent parents, drugs, etc. In all public schools, the annual school year could be lengthened by 20 days, but for poor students with an unstable family situation, the duration of the school day should be expanded so that the school can act as an oasis of hope, a place of learning and life planning. Year-round schooling offering three or four three-week vacations would reduce fatigue among the students and close the gap in quantity of schooling between America and Japan, where students are in school 60 to 70 more days each year.

America needs a better educated, more imaginative, and more curious citizenry to keep our economy internationally competitive. Certain schools need more funding, but they mainly need the intelligence, discipline, and vision to spend the funds appropriately. The public should work with the media to promote the idea of more discipline, fewer video games, more homework, and less TV viewing time. Strong solutions that address the complexity of the problem may have to include computerized monitoring of one to two hours of homework completion each day before TV viewing, recreation, or dating is permitted.

Our teachers must be up to the task of preparing students for a lifetime of learning in a new world where skills must be rapidly revised and continually renewed. The career ladder concept, involving a system of senior "master teachers" acting as mentors for their peers, seems to be the single most effective school reform in the last half-century. Teachers should view the perfect graduate as the individual who embraces education as an unfinished process, constantly seeking to acquire new knowledge and insights.

REFERENCES

American Association for the Advancement of Science. (1989). *Project 2061: Science for All Americans*. Washington, DC: AAAS monograph, January.

Arrow, K. (1991). *Issues in Contemporary Economics*. Volume 1, *Markets and Welfare*. New York: New York University Press.

Barth, R. (1990). *Improving Schools from Within: Teachers, Parents, and Principals Can Make the Difference*. San Francisco: Jossey-Bass.

Bell, T., and Elmquist, D. (1991). *How to Shape Up Our Nation's Schools*. Salt Lake City: Education Consultants.

Berlin, G., and Sum, A. (1988). *Toward a More Perfect Union: Basic Skills, Poor Families, and Our Economic Future*. New York: Ford Foundation.

Blair, L., Brounstien, P., and Hatry, H. (1990). *Guidelines for School-Business Partnerships in Science and Mathematics*. Washington, DC: Urban Institute.

Bloom, A. (1988). *The Closing of the American Mind*. New York: Simon and Schuster.

Bok, D. (1990). *Universities and the Future of America*. Durham, NC: Duke University Press.

Boyer, E., and Rice, G. (1990). *The New American Scholar*. Princeton, NJ: Carnegie Foundation for the Advancement of Teaching.

Boyett, W., and Conn, H. (1991). *Workplace 2000: The Revolution Reshaping American Business.* New York: Dutton.

Chubb, J., and Moe, T. (1992). *A Lesson in School Reform from Great Britain.* Washington, DC: Brookings.

Cornell Consortium for Longitudinal Studies. (1983). *Head Start.* Ithaca, NY: Cornell University, School of Human Ecology.

Cremin, L. (1990). *Popular Education and Its Discontents.* New York: Harper and Row.

Deming, W. (1986). *Out of the Crisis.* Cambridge: MIT Press.

Dewey, J. (1938). *Experience and Education.* New York: Macmillan.

Doyle, D., and Kearns, D. (1988). *Winning the Brain Race.* Indianapolis: ICS Press.

Finn, C. (1991). *We Must Take Charge: Our Schools and Our Future.* New York: Free Press.

———. (1987). "Education That Works: Make the Schools Compete," *Harvard Business Review* 66:5, September-October, 63–68.

Fuhr, D. (1990). *Choices: Public Education for the 21st Century.* Boston: University Press of America.

Goodlad, J. (1990). *Teachers for Our Nation's Schools.* San Francisco: Jossey-Bass.

Harvard Education Assessment Project. (1990). *Explorations with Students and Faculty about Teaching, Learning, and Student Life.* Cambridge: Harvard University Report, 94.

Hoffman, R. (1989). "Ignorance, Ignorantly Judged: A Nobel Prize Winner Suggests Comparing U.S. Students with Others Can Be Misleading," *New York Times*, September 14, A29.

Johnston, W., and Packer, A. (1987). *Workforce 2000: Work and Workers for the 21st Century.* Indianapolis: Hudson Institute.

Kozol, J. (1991). *Savage Inequalities: Children in America's Schools.* New York: Crown.

Kurshan, B. (1991). "Creating the Global Classroom for the 21st Century," *Educational Technology* 31:4, April, 47–50.

Levy, F., and Michel, R. (1991). *The Economic Future of American Families.* Washington, DC: Urban Institute.

Lieberman, M. (1989). *Privatization and Educational Choice.* Washington, DC: CATO Institute and St. Martin's Press.

Martz, L. (1992). *Making Schools Better.* New York: Times Books.

Mathews, J. (1988). *Escalante: The Best Teacher in America.* New York: Owl/Holt.

Nathan, J. (1989). *Public Schools by Choice.* Bloomington, IN: The Institute for Learning and Teaching.

Olneck, M. (1993). "Productivity and Education," University of Wisconsin, Madison, monograph.

Papert, S. (1980). *Mindstorms: Children, Computers and Powerful Ideas.* New York: Basic Books.

Piattelli, M. (1980). *Language and Learning: The Debate between Jean Piaget and Noam Chomsky.* Cambridge: Harvard University Press.

Ramler, S. (1990). "Global Education for the 21st Century," *Educational Leadership* 48:4, April, 44–46.

Runkle, D. (1991). "SMR Forum: Taught in America," *Sloan Management Review*, 33:4, Fall, 67–72.

Sizer, T. (1992). *Horace's School: Redesigning the American High School*. Boston: Houghton Mifflin.

Stevenson, H., and Stigler, J. (1992). *The Learning Gap: Why Our Schools Are Failing and What We Can Learn from Japanese and Chinese Education*. New York: Summit Books.

Sykes, C. (1988). *ProfScam: Professors and the Demise of Higher Education*. New York: Kampmann Regnery-Gateway.

Thurow, L. (1989). *Toward a High-wage, High-productivity Service Sector: A Background Paper*. Washington, DC: Economic Policy Institute.

Toch, T. (1991). *In the Name of Excellence: The Struggle to Reform the Nation's Schools*. New York: Oxford University Press.

U.S. Department of Education. (1991). *America 2000: An Education Strategy*. Washington, DC: U.S. Department of Education.

Weikart, D. (1989). *Quality Preschool Programs: A Long-Term Social Investment*. New York: Ford Foundation.

Westheimer, F. (1992). "Deciding How Much Science Is Enough," *Harvard Magazine* 94:5, May-June, 38–40.

Zigler, E. (1992). *Head Start: The Inside Story*. New York: Basic Books.

7

Health Care Reform: Enhancing Productivity and Solving the Access Deficit

If we do not face up to the health care cost crisis first, as priority number one, the deficit numbers will not improve. In the next eight years Medicare and Medicaid spending will grow, if unchecked, from 13 to 24 percent of the federal budget. This cost explosion must stop.

—Bill Clinton, 1992

Saving money will require a reduction in the number of beds and in the number of employees in the hospital; not their redeployment to provide yet another untested treatment. We need a leaner, trimmer health care economy.

—John E. Wennberg, M.D., 1990

We have no system for closing out excess capital. We don't let hospitals fail, which keeps the pathology in the system, and that drives the costs up.

—Eli Ginzberg, 1991

American health care is potentially what the Soviet Union was to economics: a costly failure at distributing service. Over 35 million Americans lack health insurance, and some 60 million are underinsured (Eastaugh, 1992b). Global budgeting as practiced in Europe and elsewhere offers American health policymakers an alternative approach for expanding access while controlling aggregate provider capacity. The health economy should not be viewed as completely independent from the general economy. The health sector is in some sense a microcosm of Baumol's model of unbalanced growth for the economy (Baumol et al., 1985). An oversimplified health economy might divide into three productivity-growth sectors: one stagnant (inpatient) and two progressive (ambulatory and long-term care). The share of the gross national product devoted to inpatient care will soon rise to above 7 percent. We will spend more on the "miracles of modern medical technology," but the hospital inpatient volume remains in a permanent recession relative to 1980 levels. The share of health expenditures invested on the stagnant inpatient sector may increase in the long run as our appetite for transplants and high-tech medicine expands. However, the progressive sectors' share of the labor force might increase with the aging of the population and the decline in hospital workers. Productivity improvements may have to underwrite the volume expansion in numbers of services.

National health care system reform has priced itself into the public eye. The cost of continued inaction has grown too expensive for small firms, export industries, 35 million uninsured Americans, and a public demanding equitable cost control. Reform of our system of high-cost care must be viewed in the context of our expanding federal deficit. In 1992 Senate Budget Committee member Pete Dominici (R–N.M.) suggested that Congress slow the annual growth of entitlement programs from 7.25 percent to 6 percent. A bipartisan coalition rejected this approach, arguing that it is unfair to limit growth in entitlements like Social Security until the administration works with Congress to contain health care costs.

The quid pro quo deal is seen simply as follows: to cap entitlement annual growth at 6 percent one should also cap national health care spending at 6 percent. This 6 percent solution is evident in all national health insurance plans introduced for implementation in 1994. They all specify a system of global budgets to set health care spending increases at 6 percent: the Dingell-Waxman Health Choice plan to create a government single payer system; the Stark-Gephardt bill to eliminate Medicaid and set up a government-administered plan that would provide a package equivalent to that offered by Medicare with additional benefits; and the Senator Mitchell (D–Me.) Pay or Play bill to mandate health insurance benefits for the employed that would limit total health care spending. The Mitchell plan would guarantee coverage to all Americans through employer plans and a state-administered public plan, called AmeriCare, which would use the Medicare payment system. Individuals who failed to enroll in a health plan would pay tax penalties. All three bills would require global budgets, imposing enforceable limits on price-times-volume, regionally and nationally. Without global budgets medical costs will crowd out public health spending, acute care will take an increasing share of workers' incomes, and more Americans will be left without health insurance.

Global budgeting offers implicit recognition of the fact that no nation is sufficiently wealthy to finance blank check spending. Hospitals and specialty groups of physicians could receive a budget with which to provide an expected level of services, just like our fire departments. Striking a fiscal balance between medical care and other societal demands requires knowledge of what the resources will yield, given different uses. Other provider groups (e.g., nurses) and consumer groups (e.g., the disabled) will have various nonmonetary reasons for not trusting global budgeting. They may fear that they will not receive their fair share of limited health care dollars, but this has not been a problem in Canada or Europe (Kirkman-Liff, 1991; Glaser, 1993; Eastaugh, 1992b). Congress is clearly familiar with the general concept of global budgets, as witnessed by the passage of the Medicare Volume Performance Standard program in the 1989 budget deal with volume increases through the behavioral offset. If Congress does not legislate, a "default formula" will set next year's conversion factor: next year's expenditure target, an average of the last five years' targets less 2 percent (Physician Payment Reform Commission, 1993).

In Canada and Europe the semantics as to whether global budgeting boards set a cap or a target is of some importance to various interest groups. Sickness funds and government officials prefer caps to targets because they are more predictable and simpler to implement. Providers prefer paid-in-full fee schedules, with expenditure targets, because they symbolize autonomy of their special profession: "We providers give costs in excess of the target back to the public, in terms of lowered future fees, because we are good people." Despite this difference in preference, the growth in technology and rapid rise in the number of physicians may pressure governments to include physicians in the global budgeting process as done in Germany. The budget process will be surveyed in the next section.

GLOBAL BUDGETS

Global budgeting boards (GBBs) are forums that enhance the fairness and equity of the rate-setting process. A GBB is a political process under which payers, providers, and consumers sit down and negotiate overall hospital sector budgets (Germany, Norway) and physician fee conversion factors in the case of one country, Germany. Restricting the total sum up front makes sense in medical care. Global-based budgeting for health care provides one approach for minding our Ps and Qs. We need to control both the Ps (prices) and Qs (quantity or volume of service) to cap the Es (expenditures). Global budgeting may be designed with a centralized form (Finland, Sweden, Norway), a decentralized form (Germany), or with a style that falls somewhere in between (Canada, Australia) (Glaser, 1993; Eastaugh, 1992c).

Only a budget will restrain costs. American cities with lots of managed competition have the same rate of cost inflation as locations with no competitive health plans. Managed competition does nothing to curtail spending except to offer an untested hope for price wars among plans. In the short run competition leads to a medical arms race as consumers demand technology. Budget caps would strengthen hundreds of private-sector insurance funds and offer real, disciplined partnerships among business, labor, government, and consumers at controlled costs. A national budget board offers a system that balances the need for rational technology growth, reasonable physician income, and reasonable hospital cost inflation. A consumer-dominated board will vote to set target inflation at the level of general wage inflation (2.5 to 3.5 percent), whereas a board dominated by health care providers and hospital managers will select a rate closer to 7 to 8 percent. Assume we target only the expenditure controls for hospitals and specialty physicians, at an annual rate of 3.5 percent. We can achieve universal coverage by 1996 with an additional $178 billion over the four years 1994–1997, of which $133 billion will be offset by consumer-dominated cost controls of hospitals and rich specialists.

Economists have suggested that global budget boards are a less costly substitute for American-style cost containment, which too often results in placing regulators and health care providers in adversarial positions, resulting in costly and contentious relationships, litigation, and "pork barrel" statutory exemptions (Fuchs, 1991; Eastaugh, 1987). The development and integration of global budgets and local budgets that are well defined, easy to apply, and that permit substantial local flexibility would create a common ground for expenditure allocation. For example, the decentralized German system of fee negotiations between hospitals and sickness funds requires final approval from state governments, but the overall management of the policy is typified by compromise and consensus building. Federal and state governments, sickness funds, labor unions, hospitals, and physician groups work to limit budgets through local councils.

The budget caps remain stringent for hospitals, but starting in 1992 the German expenditure caps for physicians have been replaced with flexible volume standards (Kassenarztliche Bundesvereinigung, 1992). If an investigation suggests a doctor orders more than 50 percent of the local service volume standard per capita, his fees will be rolled back if he cannot document the increase in clinical severity of his patients. Physicians' unions do this peer review. The German government does not actively participate in the details of running the medical sector, in contrast to the other five nations with global budgets.

Only America has an intricate and deceptive shifting of cost among payers to maximize the financial position of the hospital. In Europe, with multiple payers, a common global budgeting board process or a national office concentrates payment into a single process. Each German hospital negotiates a set of per diem rates each year with the sickness funds in its area. These flexible rates involve an estimate of the break-even volume for the hospital and an allocation of total expenditures into fixed and variable costs. To promote efficiency, since 1988 individual hospitals keep 25 percent of their total net profits, but they must also cover 25 percent of losses. This Maryland-style rate setting system, tested since 1979, is intended to create incentives for hospitals to contain costs (Eastaugh, 1992c).

In Australia, Canada, Norway, Finland, and Sweden if the actual revenue is higher than budgeted, due to higher-than-expected utilization, the surplus can be rechanneled into other health programs. These comparisons of actual and budgeted revenue are independent of the costs of the hospital. The hospital is responsible for costs in excess of the actual revenues and may keep any surplus if actual revenues are greater than costs, except in Norway. This structure creates strong incentives for operational efficiency and for the substitution of ambulatory care, especially in Norway and Sweden. Monies saved can be redirected to meet primary care and other health-related needs of the population, rather than being returned to some general fund. All hospital budgets are set and administered at the local or county level of government, and most health care revenues come from taxes levied directly by the county's publicly elected politicians. Thus, decisions about the size and distribution of health funds are made in a highly visible, politically accountable way.

ANALYZING THE COST SAVINGS

There has been a dearth of literature concerning how effective global budgeting has been in controlling costs. Canada and Australia, like Germany, Norway, Finland, and Sweden, have predictable global budgets for the entire hospital sector and for each hospital. This section provides a statistical analysis of 21 years of available data for nine countries without global budgeting and six countries with global budgeting, to ascertain the impact of GBBs on health care costs per person.

The financing scheme for medical care only partially determines health care costs per capita. To separate out the impact of global budget financing on spending, a careful analysis must also adjust for a number of factors. As with any time series comparison, the data must be reliable and valid. Published data is available from the Organization for Economic Cooperation and Development (OECD) Health Data Set publication (1972–1992). Five nations are excluded from the analysis because the data are not available for the majority of the years during this time period. The regression equation is estimated in double-log form (which proved preferable to other possible functional forms after a subsequent Box-Cox power transform (Kmenta, 1986) to analyze the relationship between the dependent variable and the most significant independent variables, confirming double-log was the best functional form). The dependent variable is health care expenditure per capita converted by OECD purchasing power parities (PPPs) for GDP as done by Gerdtham et al. (1992) and others. The six independent variables are: tobacco and alcohol consumption per capita (life-style factors predicted to have a cost-inflating impact); population density (as a proxy for urbanization, whereby travel time and access are presumed to be better in nonrural areas; therefore density could have a cost-deflating impact); income as measured by gross domestic product per capita (predicted to have an additive, or cost-inflating, impact); percentage of population aged 65 and over (cost-inflating); and a trend variable for year (as a proxy for technological shifts, presumed to have a cost-inflating impact). The estimation process used the following double-log specification, with dummy variable (0, 1 for each foreign country), country i, year y, and error term e:

$$Ln\$CAPITA_{iy} = \beta_i COUNTRY + \beta_1 LnTOBAC_{iy} + \beta_2 LnALCOHOL_{iy}$$
$$+ \beta_3 LnDENSITY_{iy} + \beta_4 LnGDCAPITA_{iy}$$
$$+ \beta_5 LnAGED_{iy} + \beta_6 YEAR + e$$

To test the impact of the national health system and global budgeting on costs per capita, dummy variables for each nation are entered into the double-log regression equation. It is expected that the nations with global budgets will have a cost-deflating (negative) impact on cost per capita. The data analysis involves two steps: (1) estimation of regression coefficients from a set of original data points from 15 nations and (2) computation of predictions and prediction errors for one additional country (the United States) if it had the cost experience of the nation with the best cost-containment track record (as estimated in equation one).

The OLS (ordinary least squares) equation one exhibits evidence of autocorrelation, so the coefficients are estimated utilizing a maximum likelihood procedure for a time series of cross-sections (Kmenta, 1986). The results are listed in Table 7.1. The independent variable with the highest t-statistic is gross domestic product per capita. The income elasticity for GDP, greater than 1.0, agrees with previous studies as reported in Getzen (1990) and Gerdtham et al. (1992). All variables in the equation have the correct coefficients sign except alcohol consumption per capita (statistically insignificant negative sign). The estimates for the dummy variables are significantly different (at the 0.05 level) for six nations. Five nations with global budgets have significant negative, cost-deflating coefficients (the sixth country, Sweden, has the correct sign). The nation with the most rapid growth in the health sector, the Netherlands, began to implement a program of tight global budgets for hospitals in 1992 (Eastaugh, 1992c). The country with the most effective cost-containment experience is Ger-

Table 7.1
Estimated Health Care Costs per Capita Estimated Equation 1971–1991 Annual Time Series (t-statistic in parentheses)

	Dependent Variable Cost per Capita	
LIFESTYLE FACTORS		
1) Tobacco Consumption per Capita	0.158**	(2.94)
2) Alcohol Consumption per Capita	-0.082	(0.73)
ENVIRONMENTAL FACTOR		
3) Population Density	-0.511	(1.30)
ECONOMIC & DEMOGRAPHIC FACTORS		
4) Gross Domestic Product GDP per Capita	1.192**	(6.68)
5) Percent Population 65 and over	0.396	(1.48)
TECHNOLOGY FACTOR (PROGRESS OVER TIME)		
6) Years 1-21 (1971-1991)	0.549**	(9.21)
COUNTRY VARIABLE (n=number of years data available)		
Germany, n=14 years	-2.91**	(3.06)
Norway, n=16	-1.72**	(2.38)
Canada, n=17	-1.64*	(1.79)
Finland, n=19	-1.02*	(1.84)
Australia, n=15	-0.96*	(1.87)
Sweden, n=17	-0.715	(0.92)
Greece, n=12	-0.180	(0.70)
Spain, n=11	0.256	(0.43)
Austria, n=16	0.379	(0.44)
Denmark, n=13	0.545	(1.25)
United Kingdom, n=15	0.618	(1.18)
Italy, n=14	1.093	(1.62)
Belgium, n=18	1.271	(1.60)
Netherlands, n=16***	1.306*	(1.81)
Adjusted R^2	.921	
RHO	.80	(.05)
Durbin-Watson Test against Autocorrelation	1.79	

*Significant at 0.05 level.
**Significant at 0.01 level.
***All 16 years' data are prior to initiating global budgeting for hospital.

many. Over the time period 1971–1991, for every 10 percent expansion in GDP, health sector costs inflated only 6 percent in Germany, 25 percent in the Netherlands, and 27 percent in the United States. The best fit was double-log. Other functional forms considered include: exponential, linear, and semi-log.

SAVINGS FROM THE GERMAN APPROACH

Decentralization and budgetary control of both hospitals and physicians may be the key structural design attributes of the German health care system. American medical costs—hospital and physician services—grew by 54 percent in real terms from 1979 to 1991. Under a global-based budgeting system, however, German medical costs declined 5.3 percent in real terms over those twelve years (Eastaugh, 1992b). In Germany negotiations on hospital budgets and physician fees include the sickness funds, businesses, representatives of the doctors' associations, and other providers who meet once or twice a year in the global budgeting board forum of the Konzertierte Aktion (KA). Future research should study endogeneity, and the suggestion by Glaser (1993) that GBB is an index of political will to control costs.

The KA has 64 members, is staffed by the Ministry of Labor, and is assisted by a steering committee of university professors who report on the economy, business conditions, and medical spending. The KA recommends economically prudent increases in spending for hospital and physicians' services, and the negotiators in each state follow the guidelines to set the local global amount available. The providers can press for more, but the dispute would then go to an arbitrator, who would follow the KA's spending targets.

Each year German hospitals fill out prospective budget and retrospective cost reports for analysis by the bargaining committee of sickness funds. Hospitals send their prospective budgets to the local offices of the sickness funds as well as to the national government. The funds' managers will complain if utilization was predicted too high or the numbers of employees seem high relative to low productivity. Each hospital meets with a committee drawn from the sickness funds and selects the hospital's per diem prices close to the KA guidelines. If the hospital and global budgeting board disagree, they select a special joint subcommittee to arbitrate. Since the arbitration process tends to be stingy, hospitals typically accept price hikes within KA guidelines. The global budgeting board process of the KA reinforces the global budgeting incentive at the local level. German hospital rate setting is closer to the Maryland state system, because it allows planners to visit each hospital and suggest changes.

The KA has one basic goal: tax rate stability (do not overspend your resources). The average payroll-deduction rate in Germany increased from 11.1 percent in 1976 to only 12.4 percent in 1993 (Konzertierte Aktion, 1992). This payroll-deduction rate stability should not be described as a rigid limitation of revenues and expenditures in the statutory health care system. Rather, it should be viewed as revenue-oriented budgeting. Fixed payroll-deduction rates allow considerable increases in revenue as incomes rise. Fluctuations and trends in sickness fund memberships (volume and demographics) also have an effect on budgets. Therefore, anticipated revenues are based on the expected nominal growth rate of the gross national product. In 1992 the anticipated nominal growth rate for the GNP was 6.3 to 7.1 percent or, in real terms, 1.1 to 1.9 percent. Germans have given up free bargaining among health care participants to purchase cost containment through global budget setting. Whereas Germans will expand benefits into long-term care and still spend only approximately 8.5 percent of the GNP on health care in 1993, Americans will spend 14 percent of the GNP on health care and still leave 35 million citizens uninsured.

Nations with global-based budgeting spend proportionately one-third less of the GNP on health care than does the United States. this simple comparative statistic is confounded by the more difficult to serve population mix in the United States. Adjusted multivariate statistics shrink the apparent cost saving of global budgeting to 2.2 fewer points GNP spent on health care in Germany and 1.3 fewer points in Norway and Canada. Germany provides the best analogous comparison with the United States (hundreds of insurance funds, fee-for-service physician payment, decentralized planning, and business coalition involvement in setting health policy). Assuming the German level of GBB effectiveness, implementation of global budgeting will not cause the United States to spend 5 percent less of the GNP on health care, but it will free up 2.2 percent of the GNP. These funds may be necessary to make health care coverage more affordable for uninsured and underinsured Americans. Global budgeting also has the potential to reduce the need for explicit rationing (e.g., the Oregon Medicaid program; Strosberg, Weiner and Baker, 1993). The distributional impact of global budgeting may yield more funding for primary and long-term care.

HOW TO DO IT HERE

In the American context the GBB might better be labeled the "federal reserve board" (FRB) for setting health care spending caps. An American FRB should not be a "socialist system for planned payment" or a form of rigid price control. It should be a fundamentally different organism in both structure and intent from the American Economic Stabilization Program in effect from August 1971 to April 1974. The ideal global budgeting board for health care would have the consensus building focus that the former program lacked, and the real power that American health planners have always lacked. The board need not encroach on the economic integrity of successful, semi-competitive market participants. The efficient provider may not feel any pressure from the board's activities. Through the allocation of capital and operating funds, the local global budgeting boards would provide incentives for enhanced efficiency.

The second alternative is that GBBs be set up by each state. One state has already started down this road. In 1992 physician-governor Howard B. Dean (1992) was successful in passing the Vermont global health budget Act 160, capping both public and private spending. Preliminary expenditure targets will be set in 1993, and these targets will serve as a baseline for creating the 1994 global budget. Rather than a 64-member German KA, the Vermont system will be run by a three-member, governor-appointed authority to direct all regulation, data collection, and planning. Vermont's leadership has committed itself to health care reforms to be applied uniformly to all Vermonters, a critical policy distinction relative to other states which trim care for Medicaid only.

In 1991 Vermont passed a surcharge on hospitals and nursing homes to finance Medicaid plus landmark small-group insurance reforms that require community rating and guaranteed acceptance. In 1993 the Vermont lawmakers will select either a German-style, multi-payer negotiated system or a Norwegian/Canadian single-payer approach. Judging by the regression analysis, a sufficiently tight German-style global budgeting approach would produce an optimal amount of cost control and consumer sovereignty.

HEALTH CARE REFORM

Many Americans are a bit ambivalent about health care reform. We envy nations that have universal coverage and accept social limits on expenditures through a public global budget process. The ambivalence comes in thinking we can contain costs without containing hospital revenues and physician incomes. One cannot adopt global coverage without accepting global budgets that prevent excessive medical cost inflation. The dream of limitless coverage, limitless technology, and limitless income growth for physician specialists is an impossibility. The system requires income redistribution to primary care, prevention, and promotion, and away from surgeons, medical specialists, drug companies, and hospital equipment firms. Global budgets create the fiscal necessity to develop technology that is cost-decreasing (i.e., that has the capacity to lower or prevent future spending). For example, the adage "necessity is the mother of invention" was the motto for German hospitals that pioneered our new radiological and lab equipment for the past two decades. An MRI is cost-decreasing as it prevents more invasive exploratory surgery. Whereas, in real dollar terms, American hospitals have inflated spending per capita 46.9 percent for the period 1983–1991, German hospitals deflated spending 6.8 percent over the same period (Konzertierte Aktion, 1992).

In America, because there is a prospective payment cap on only a small portion of patients, there has been less incentive to implement or develop cost-decreasing technologies and little incentive not to purchase unproven technologies or redundant hospital equipment. Moving American hospital payment to global budgets should restrict the inappropriate and unnecessary aspects of our American tunnel of technology.

If global budgets can enhance efficiency and stimulate cost-effective innovation, what impact do they have on the caring function and the patient? One recent article suggests that patient service improves markedly. According to noted health economist Victor Fuchs (1992), "Germany provides more than twice as many physician contacts and hospital days per capita as the U.S.A.," and much of the additional care goes to help self-limiting chronic illness and disabled and incurable patients. Global budgets result in a cut in costs—but not in the benefits—of health care services. America may have the best system in the world to maximize specialist's incomes, to provide maximum hospital equipment per bed, and to maximize administrative paperwork costs. However, Germany provides better service for the vast majority of the public with lower infant mortality, higher life expectancy, 40 percent less paperwork expense (Eastaugh, 1992c), and 2.2 percent less of the GNP going to the health sector.

The American public seems to be on the verge of realizing the cost-decreasing potential of global budgets (less hospital waste), universal entitlement (fewer claims forms and paperwork expense), and containment of specialists' fees. The savings in these three areas could equal 2.2 percent of our $7 trillion general economy, funds that could be rechanneled to public health, education, and the environment. There is a quantifiable trade-off between taking money from paper pushers at commercial insurance companies, rich specialists, and hospital supply firms and giving it to those with AIDS, or Alzheimer's, or students with insufficient funds to go to school. Redistributing income from fat cats to the less powerful would produce a more equitable and efficient America.

Future research should address four political economy questions in the American context. (1) With one payment process nationally, would there be less administrative expense, as one would predict? (2) Is global budgeting a quid pro quo for reducing administrative expense incurred by providers? (3) Is global-based budgeting expected to make national health care affordable? (4) Can a GBB discern public interest and promote health services that offer both good economics and good quality?

INNOVATION OR STAGNATION— UNBALANCED GROWTH

Americans want incompatible goals: unlimited access to the best care at an affordable price. Compared with other countries, America has a schizophrenic attitude concerning the production and financing of medical services where one can demonstrate that the society as a whole earns more if the coworkers are kept healthy through preventive medicine (Eastaugh, 1987; Cahill, 1993). Most medical dollars go to curing and caring, not prevention. Some liberals would go so far as to argue that medical services are a merit good, so crucial to preserving the general welfare of society that they should be financed by government even if they are not cost-beneficial. Such an attitude is maintained in the Netherlands and Norway, where medical care is produced and financed as if it were a public good—a social service too important to be rationed on market principles.

The United States has one of the most inconsistent policies toward medical service: we produce it as a consumer good, finance it as a public good, and complain when providers react in a rational way, promoting excess demand and behaving in an inflationary "quality is all important" style of care for the subsidized service. A decade ago American health care providers were best described as a fragmented group of fiercely independent organizations. Over 90 percent of the physicians were independent operators in private practice and hospitals engaged in cost-increasing fierce competition for prestige and the newest equipment. Now physicians and hospitals are being subjected to a cost-decreasing mode of competition which is both consumer- and payer-driven.

The nature of health services delivery is changing. We can no longer deny that health care is a blend of art, business, life-style, and science. Providers' traditional objectives have been expanded to include consumer-sensitive service in a more economical style, advocating patient compliance and health promotion while offering the best technical quality of care. Overemphasis on any one aspect may spell disaster for the provider. Providers who pursue only business interests will be no more protected or respected than a used-car dealer. Likewise, those who disrespect business skills, marketing, and consumers' shifting tastes may face early retirement in the 1990s.

Changes in payment systems occur so rapidly that providers and medical suppliers are hard put to keep pace and react, much less plan proactively. There is still room for improved efficiency in a health sector that spends $1 billion every 11 hours. Some of the resources do little good, but the majority of the care averts death, pain, and erosion of functional health status. However, we must be careful not to discount quality or access in the name of economic efficiency. There is a delicate balance to maintain between health care as a social good and health care as a consumer good.

If one includes tax subsidies, health care services in America are 55 percent financed by federal and state government. Health care is subject to many of the same problems as other groups in the domain of public finance. For example, the stereotypical liberal asks: "This is what government must do, so how do we get the funds from a combination of taxation and borrowing?" The stereotypical conservative asks: "This is how much money the government has, so how do we spend it?" Global budgeting attempts to reconcile both attitudes. Global budgets offer honest realization that society must stop blank check reimbursement; but conservatives feel uneasy placing one-sixth of the economy under price controls. The global budget–setting process allows more public accountability for wise health care investments; but liberals fear that the spending targets will get too low within a few years.

The paradox is that to bring about effective cost control one also has to run the risk that we may erode the biomedical capacity of the nation. There is no painless approach. For example, if we trim administrative expenses from $230 billion to $92 billion annually (in 1994) we do damage to clerks earning $25,000 and commercial insurance executives earning $130,000. But these people can find a new position elsewhere in the American economy, at the bedside or in education. Trimming administrative costs has an intrinsic benefit: less ineffective and irksome micromanagement of claims forms, which are detrimental to patient and provider. With national health care we would have fewer forms and fewer intrusive, Byzantine rules of eligibility. Health care is a right, and everyone should be eligible.

REFORMING MEDICAID, MEDICARE, AND THE TAX CODE

The most rapidly growing public program is Medicaid, dispensing $187 billion in federal and state funds to 28 million poor Americans in 1993. Medicaid pays for half of nursing home patients, some 260,000 citizens at an average annual cost of $40,000. However, the most rapidly inflating segment of the Medicaid budget is hospital care, and 35 million Americans are uninsured but not sufficiently poor to qualify for Medicaid. With a program of national health insurance the $10 billion of paperwork concerning eligibility rules could be eliminated. With a program of global budgeting resources could be redistributed away from the hospital and into chronic care and ambulatory care. *POLICY PROPOSAL No. 37:* Pass a German-style system of global budgeting board for health care spending control, making care more affordable for private patients (saving $99 billion federally on the care of public patients over the period 1994–1997).

The GBB process would establish fees and total annual expenditures for physicians, nonphysician providers, hospitals, and freestanding centers through a formal negotiating structure. The Clinton GBB of Health Standards would determine an annual health budget for the nation, with a separate budget for each state. The board would be made up of consumers, health care providers, and representatives from business, labor, and government. States would be allowed to set health care prices if costs threatened to exceed the limit. Health care needs the discipline of staying within a budget.

Providers cannot set their own fees due to the obvious conflict of interest, but their input is vital because they understand their product better than the typical civilian. However, the decision to implement a GBB or pass a national health plan rests in the hands of a larger political community. That community should have a place on the national GBB and on state GBBs. The nature of the GBB at some level may be corporatist: closed to all but the principal players. But at a national level and at periodical local GBB meetings the process must be public. A consensus building process cannot be secretive. American experience with rate setting involves fewer consensus building activities and less concern for efficiency than in most industrial nations. Our nonfederal payers rarely have the resources to evaluate economic and operational efficiency of their health care providers. State and regional reimbursement methodologies have generally been static in nature, concentrating on arraying the cost of health care providers by some definition of allowable costs, and setting the reimbursement rate at a prescribed percentile based on the array. Some states sort providers into "peer groups," but these groupings often ignore quantitative indicators of provider efficiency, and instead focus on size, general care levels, or geographical location. In addition, these groupings tend to become static over time and do not allow the changing dynamics of both the provider and its beneficiaries to influence future reimbursements.

The federal government will spend $83 billion on Medicaid services for the poor in 1993. Federal support for state Medicaid programs has skyrocketed by 87 percent in the last three fiscal years, accounting for 70 percent of the increase in federal aid to state and local government since 1990. If Medicaid is a direct program for funding care for the poor, the Medicare disproportionate payment system (MDPS) offers an additional subsidy for hospitals that care for the poor. However, the MDPS would no longer be relevant under a comprehensive system of national health care reform and global budgeting. In 1994 MDPS is estimated to pay 1,550 hospitals $2.4 billion. Data on hospital cost per admission suggest that MDPS funds are only justified in the 136 Academic Medical Centers, according to the Congressional Budget Office (1993). *POLICY PROPOSAL No. 38:* Restrict the Medicare disproportionate payment share for low-income patients to the 136 Academic Medical Centers (thus saving $9.6 billion over 1994–1997).

The federal government will spend $138 million on Medicare services in 1993 for 34 million elderly Americans and 3.4 million disabled citizens. The Medicare program is not means-tested—that is, it provides the same benefits to the poor, frail elderly as to the rich elderly. In the interest of equity, limit the premiums for Medicare's Supplementary Medical Insurance program by *POLICY PROPOSAL No. 39:* Set the premium for physicians' services to 100 percent of costs for the rich elderly with income for couples over $110,000 and income for singles over $80,000 (saving $12 billion over the years 1994–1997). The rich would still get basic Medicare benefits, but they would have to pay their fair share of costs for supplemental physician services. Administratively, premiums could be more cost effectively collected by the Internal Revenue Service, and rates could be set in proportion to income. In the interest of equity, the coinsurance rate paid by the elderly consumer at point of service could be made uniform, thus *POLICY PROPOSAL No. 40:* Set uniform coinsurance rates at 20 percent for all Medicare services (including lab, home health care, and nursing home services). This would save $15.3 billion over the period 1994–1997 and make the coinsurance system easier to explain to the elderly ("you pay one-fifth of your bill"). By 1997 the elderly would still be spending only 29 percent of total cost in out-of-pocket expenses, which is 21 points less than the 50 percent stipulated by the original law for patient cost sharing when Medicare was passed in 1966.

If we pass global budgeting for hospitals in the mid-1990s, the Medicare program can also trim indirect payments to teaching hospitals. Studies of hospital costs by the Congressional Budget Office suggest that teaching payments could be trimmed by 50 percent. *POLICY PROPOSAL No. 41:* Restrict indirect Medicare adjustment payments to a 3.9 percent bonus for each 0.1 increase in the ratio of interns and residents per bed (saving $7.8 billion over the period 1994–1997).

Congress could change the tax code to stimulate more cost sensitivity among consumers in shopping for health insurance annually. Currently, employees do not pay taxes on employer-paid health care coverage, resulting in a net loss in revenues to the federal treasury of an estimated $68.4 billion in 1994. The richest 20 million Americans receive $1,800 per family in tax breaks, while 10 million poor families and 30 million working

Table 7.2
Health Care Statistics in the United States, Japan, and Korea, 1992

	United States	Japan	Korea
1. Life expectancy at birth			
Male	72	77	68
Female	79	83	73
Manpower ratios			
2. Physicians per 100,000 population	230	161	89
3. Surgeons per 100,000 population	60	39	22
4. Dentists per 100,000 population	16	55	62
5. Hospital personnel per occupied bed	2.9	1.0	0.8
Hospital sector			
6. Acute-care beds per 1,000 population	4.1	5.5	2.3
7. Hospital costs as percentage of GNP	4.7	2.8	1.6
8. Percentage of beds that are for-profit	16	64	74
9. Annual admissions per 1,000			
population	114	82	69
Total health care spending			
10. Spending per capita ($)	2,634	1,320	315
11. Health as a percentage of GNP	12.2	7.7	5.8
Service allocation (percentage of total			
health spending going to a given age			
group)			
12. Ages 0-14	19.8	21.2	19.0
13. Ages 65+	42.4	39.3	33.0

Sources: OECD Data Bank, 1993; Eastaugh, 1993; World Bank, *World Development Report,*
1993, Washington, DC: World Bank.

poor will receive an average tax break of only $390 in 1993. *POLICY PRO-
POSAL No. 42:* Tax as income insurance benefits exceeding $375 a month
for family coverage and $150 a month for individual coverage (in 1994 dol-
lars, indexed to inflation). This proposal would raise income tax revenues
by $50 billion and payroll tax revenue by about $34 billion over the period
1994–1997.

GENERAL ECONOMY AND THE HEALTH SECTOR

An interesting comparison can be drawn between the United States and
two other decentralized health care systems with superior economic growth:
Japan and Korea. Comparisons among the three countries are offered in
Table 7.2. The United States spends the highest fraction of resources on

the elderly (line 13). However, because Japan has the most rapidly aging population in the world, it will exceed our figure during the 1990s. Japan spends only 7.7 percent of the GNP on health care, offers no apparent surgical queues or other forms of rationing (unlike Canada; Rachlis and Kushner, 1990), yet leads the world in life expectancy and low infant mortality (Powell and Anesaki, 1991). The Japanese staffing ratio per bed (line 5) is superior to the American figure for all types of hospitals because of superior labor productivity and because Japanese (and Korean) patients receive feeding and some basic nursing care from family members in large hospital wards. The Japanese fraction of the GNP going to health care is probably underestimated by 2.4 percentage points because official government statistics exclude personal expenditures for medical care and preventive medicine (Powell and Anesaki, 1991; this is also true for the Korean statistics; Eastaugh, 1992d).

Korea finished the decade-long process of implementing national health insurance by signing up the last uninsured market segment, one in six citizens, during 1989. Japan has had universal entitlement for three decades (Ikegami, 1991). However, if we factor out the higher rate of economic growth in the two Asian countries, both nations would spend over 11.5 percent of the GNP on health care if they had experienced the sluggish American growth rate during the period 1970–1991.

The critical point is that health care cost inflation is a worldwide problem. No nation, including Canada, offers a magic formula to resolve the worldwide problems of access and cost control. It is easy to put down the American system with glib lines like, "We have no health care system; rather, we have a disjointed, sickness-care nonsystem." A disjointed American delivery system experiences as much health care cost inflation as a government-planned delivery system.

COMPETITION AND SERVICE DELIVERY

Mandatory employer-based health insurance will not cover all uninsured Americans and will introduce a new set of problems. Korea mandated health insurance by employer group, phased in over 12 years (1977–1989), and has the most rapid rate of medical cost escalation. Germany has 11 decades of experience with social insurance, but its health care system appeared to be in severe trouble even prior to reunification in 1990 (Iglehart, 1991). The German economy is concentrating high-risk patient groups in local sickness funds, many of which are in severe economic trouble. Wysong and Abel (1990) reported that the growing segmentation of risk groups in Germany threatens the concept of solidarity on which the system is founded.

From a macroeconomic viewpoint the key issue is how much the health

Table 7.3
Elasticity of per Capita Health Expeditures Relative to per Capita Gross
Domestic Product, 1975–1992

Nation	Nominal Elasticity	Real [a] Elasticity
Korea	1.58	1.61
Japan	1.29	1.41
United States	1.29	1.15
Netherlands	1.22	1.09
Switzerland	1.18	1.04
Canada	1.16	.94
Iceland	1.14	1.45
Sweden	1.10	1.03
United Kingdom	1.08	1.02
Australia	1.08	.94
Germany [b]	1.06	.93

[a] Health-price-deflated per capita health spending relative to GDP-deflator-adjuster per capita GDP.

[b] Germany has the lowest growth rate in health expenses and spends 4.3 percent less of GDP on health care compared to the United States.

Source: Government of Republic of Korea (1993), OECD (1993).

economy grows as a multiple of general economic growth. For example, in Table 7.3 Korea has the highest rate of health-sector economic growth for two primary reasons: the "catch-up" phenomenon of a large volume of unmet health care needs and a doctor-dominated, monopolist/laissez-faire delivery system that tightly restricts nonphysician providers (e.g., there is only one small home health care agency in the nation; Eastaugh, 1991b). The nominal elasticity of 1.29 for Japan and the United States in Table 7.3 indicates that for every 10 percent increase in nominal per capita GDP since 1975, each nation experienced a 12.9 percent increase in nominal per capital health care spending.

Throughout the 1980s the Korean people put pressure on the firmly entrenched conservative government to enact a comprehensive national health plan. Citizens of all political viewpoints felt personally threatened by uncontrollable medical care costs. By 1987 almost 50 percent of Koreans had employer-based health insurance and 9 percent of the population had Medicaid-eligibility access to government hospitals and clinics. The conservative central government allowed 18.5 percent of the population to join the national health insurance system from January 1988 to June 1989. The remaining uninsured 23 percent were mandated to join the national plan in July 1989. Cost inflation averaged 22 percent annual growth in real terms, 1989 to 1993. Korea spent $21 billion dollars on health care, or $490 per capita in 1991. The Korean health economy is riding the tide of a cost explosion. Many physicians and hospital managers see this cost inflation as a "go signal of necessary growth" (Eastaugh, 1992c).

The Korean experience suggests that the passage of national health insurance in the United States will be costly but popular with the public. American policymakers should draw two positive lessons from the Korean experience. Small businesses were not harmed by the employer mandate. Korea phased in political support for national health insurance by first mandating employer-based health insurance for all firms with over 500 workers in 1977, extending the law to firms with over 300 workers in 1979, over 100 in 1981, and over 5 in 1988–1989.

The political consensus builder in Korea assisting with the passage of national health insurance was the reliance on a financing mechanism of progressive social insurance. The rich pay a premium for the same insurance coverage that is threefold higher than that of the working poor. Employed urban citizens pay 3 to 8 percent of monthly wages to the insurance fund, and the employer makes an equal contribution. In the case of the self-employed and rural residents, the health insurance contribution varies widely, with 15 rate classifications determined by a family's income and assets. This funding mechanism is more popular with the public than suggesting a rise in the payroll tax or income tax.

Will mandated health benefits increase wages and small business failures and raise unemployment? Korea thrust the mandates on 24 percent of the population, and no such negative results occurred. Therefore, should we expect the results to be different if America thrusts the mandate on 7.6 percent of the population in 1994?

Rather than dooming calls for national health insurance with calls for a big tax increase, responsible health professionals should suggest a more progressive, Korean-style system of a wealth-based national insurance premium. It might be good economics and good medicine to have Ross Perot pay a health insurance premium that is five times the national average for single adults. The rich may not like progressive financing, but employers are increasingly advocating national global budgets for health care. Employer health care costs will average over 10.9 percent of American payrolls in 1993 (Eastaugh, 1992b).

The three major ingredients in understanding the recent cost inflation in Korean health care are obvious: the growth in health insurance, the diffusion of new technology, and the growing supply of physician specialists. For example, a demand-pull hospital cost inflation manifests in terms of increased admissions, patient days, and spending by the hospitals. An increasingly insured population demands more care, so the hospital can collect higher revenues and use the profits to purchase more beds and more equipment per bed, driving up the cost of care by additional increments. Economists seek the rate-limiting step: did more insurance allow patients to demand more care (at a slightly lower effective price to them), or did doctors order more hospital services and force the government and hospital managers to expand access to health insurance and invest more in hospital capital (beds and equipment)?

The basic policy issue involves how society should enhance economic efficiency by slowing this demand-pull inflation. Fee-for-service providers breed rapid cost inflation following an expansion in health insurance (it is in their economic self-interest to bill more and order the hospital to purchase more tests and procedures).

The Japanese and Korean economies expect that continued high economic growth will finance more health care spending, but American policymakers tend to talk of rationing services (Ginzberg, 1991). Americans witness the anomaly of increased discussion of rationing while the number of empty hospital beds exceeds 300,000. Global budgeting should make such trade-offs as implicit rationing explicit for public review (e.g., Oregon's Medicaid program).

In visiting Chinese hospitals, the author was interested to discover that an ancient proverb, "May you live in interesting times," was often misinterpreted by Caucasian visitors as a curse. The opportunity for substantial reform is best in just such times of stress and strain. In fact, the Chinese term for "crisis," *wei ji*, has a simultaneous dual interpretation: opportunity and danger. Over the next ten years our health system will face immense opportunity and danger in a reformation on four fronts: access, efficiency, effectiveness, and quality of life.

The challenge for providers and managers during this period of unparalleled opportunity will be to win a clear victory on all four fronts and not erode either access or quality in the name of efficiency. This is a clear challenge for both managers and policymakers. The job is doubly tough for our physicians. The challenge to physicians will be to carry on one shoulder lifesaving technology and the concomitant financial burden and, on the other shoulder, the will and imagination to apply modern management techniques.

KOREA LOOKS TO GERMANY

Health policy is the politician's dilemma. How do we reform the system before injecting more funds into it? This chapter has looked at the most recent convert to national health insurance, but policymakers from Korea to the Netherlands are studying the only nation with one century's worth of experience with national insurance, Germany. Like Korea, Germany has a large number of sickness funds and a tradition of fee-for-service medicine. The Germans have a system of global budgets by consensus which many analysts credit for their success at capping health care spending at 8.5 percent of the GNP in 1993.

In the decentralized German system, fee negotiations between hospitals and sickness funds require final approval from the state governments, but the overall management of policy is typified by compromise and consensus building. Federal and state governments, sickness funds, labor unions, hospitals, and physicians' associations (geographic-based councils known as the *Arztekemmern*, with an average membership of 7,000 doctors) annually agree on fees and annual expense targets in each sector of the health economy. If physician fees exceed their target in one time period, they are reduced in future periods to penalize providers for unplanned volume shifts.

In the jargon of accounting, this political process is described as variance analysis under a limited budget (the global pie of dollars for local health care). If the budget variance is unfavorable (over budget) the fees are deflated in proportion to the "unnecessary part of the increase in volume." Therefore, the global budget is a flexible cap.

LESSONS LEARNED

Global-based budgeting is not a technical exercise whereby provider rates are automatically set according to a multiyear rolling average economic index. It is a political process whereby payers, providers, and consumers sit down and negotiate overall hospital budgets or physician fee conversion factors. Civil servants are not directly involved in GBB negotiations in Germany, and the spending targets are set by a 64-member committee, the Konzertierte Aktion (KA). The KA recommends increases in spending for hospital and physicians' services that only keep pace with general economic growth.

The secondary lesson of the German experience is that GBB proves most effective if done for both hospitals and physicians (KA). Nominal increases in German costs per admission averaged 3.5 percent in the 1980s, and physician expenditures declined to 4.7 percent inflation (from an annual rate of 14.3 percent in the 1950s; Eastaugh, 1992a). In contrast to the Korean demand-side approach (cost-sharing strategy to hold down costs), the Germans have succeeded in bringing their health care expenditures under control as a direct result of managing sector capacity and budgets—that is, a supply side strategy. Centrally imposed regulation need not equal the imposition of arbitrary political, social, or technocratic values derived from cost-benefit ratios, but would entail public consultation in a process of argument, persuasion, and consensus building.

AMERICA LOOKS TO KOREA AND GERMANY

The defining moment in the October 1991 campaign of Pennsylvania Senator Harris Wofford came in a television commercial. Wofford sat in a hospital and said to the public: "If criminals have a right to a lawyer, why don't citizens have an equal right to see a doctor?" It has been suggested that Wofford's 50 point rise in the polls made him "health care's new hero" (Tokarski, 1992). Unbeknownst to Wofford, the analogy between legal rights and the right to health care has been around for years. In the last century, Lewis Schooler, writing in the February 4, 1899, *Journal of the American Medical Association*, asked "why the state pays attorneys for defending the vilest criminals, and also pays the cost of appeals to the Supreme Court, but makes scant provision for medical attendance upon the poor" (226).

Policymakers should pay attention to how other nations implemented the concept of a right to health care. There is no free lunch—one cannot pay for national health insurance by just trimming administrative expenses. Covering the uninsured will require more funds (witness the 1989–1993 experience in South Korea). National health insurance brought a doubling in the health sector because Korea lacked global budget cost controls (Eastaugh, 1992b). A fresh look at the much belabored cost-access interaction may bring us closer to the nature of the problem. Rather than look to Canada as a prototype for passage of national health insurance, we might do better by looking to Germany and Korea for a more appropriate analogy. Each nation has a bias for the best available "microquality" for the individual by running patients through a tunnel of technology.

The dedication of the Korean people to expand access, implementing universal national health insurance by July 1989, and also expand available technology is truly impressive. However, the expansion in insurance coverage has created ongoing dilemmas: (1) a rapid demand-pull inflation in medical costs (22 percent in 1989–1990), stimulated by the fee-for-service payment system and (2) a widening maldistribution of available resources. Health care claims are a growing percentage of the national budget. Health care spending as a percent of the Korean gross domestic product has grown from 3.7 percent in 1975 to 5.2 percent in 1985, 6.6 percent in 1989, and an estimated 7.8 percent in 1992 (Eastaugh, 1992d).

Drawing an analogy among nations over time is a hazardous undertaking. Lord Acton summarized this hazard: "the same, and always different." For example, few economists argue that Canada could implement national health insurance as efficiently in the 1990s as it did in the early 1970s. Moreover, it is hard to tell whether the Korean rate of cost escalation would be higher or lower if translated to the American context. There is ample evidence that high patient cost-sharing can dampen the rate of medical cost escalation (Manning and Newhouse, 1987). Yet the Korean economy has experienced a high level of insurance-induced inflation in a land with 30 to 55 percent coinsurance rates and $20 to $25 deductibles. On the up side, American medicine has experience with utilization review and quality-control activities unheard of in Korea.

For ethical and economic reasons, our society should be concerned that short-shrifting 35 million uninsured Americans only makes their care more expensive in the long run. If health care is a necessary basic commodity like food, society should underwrite a minimum basic-needs policy for all. Currently, the uninsured poor suffer from "reverse targeting" of preventative care; this population at the highest risk is least likely to be screened or treated. Korea passed national health insurance despite having the same four barriers to action that Fuchs (1991) outlined: distrust of government, heterogeneity of the population, a robust voluntary sector, and less sense of noblesse oblige.

IMPLEMENTING A GBB IN THE U.S.

In the spirit of democracy and pluralism, implementing a GBB in America would subject each interest group to public scrutiny. Four years with the Physician Payment Review Commission suggests the potential benefits of public scrutiny. The hope is that this process will yield a more efficient, effective, and equitable health care system. One final caveat should be considered. The consensus building for a GBB is a bit more difficult in the American context of separation of powers. By contrast, GBB is more easily created in parliamentary systems with inherent consensus between legislative and executive branches.

However, just because a GBB is more difficult to initiate does not mean that it will be any less effective at cost control. All nations with a GBB spend one-third less of the GNP on health care than the United States. Moreover, creation of a GBB might be the catalyst that breaks the gridlock against national health care reform for the 35 million uninsured Americans and those otherwise squeezed by the current approaches. Implementation of a GBB will not allow the United States to spend 2.2 percent less of the GNP on health care in one year, but it will free up the resources necessary to make health care coverage more affordable.

Where and when will the administrative cost reduction occur? Judging by the German experience, after three years of reform we can save 70 percent in insurance administration (down from a peak of $56.1 billion in 1994) with fewer clerks and sales staff, 28 percent in physician office administration (down from a peak of $67.9 billion in 1994) with fewer clerks and review staff, and 27 percent in hospital administration and overhead (down from a peak of $129.8 billion in 1994; Eastaugh, 1992c). With national health insurance, benefit management costs are trimmed by 90 percent, and accounts receivable follow-up costs are reduced by over 80 percent.

With one form for physician visits and one for hospital visits, the average teaching hospital will not have to employ 150 clerks to track the constantly changing rules of the 400 smallest insurance companies. Therefore, transaction-related paperwork costs at each patient visit will be substantially less. The $230 billion cost of medical care administration and overhead in 1994 could be trimmed by 40 percent, or $90 to $92 billion, within the initial three years of national health reform.

Simplified billing forms and computerized patient identification cards are keys to trimming administrative costs. The ID cards would be coded with personal medical information. Consequently, providers would not waste resources repeating baseline medical history information. In the initial six years of global budget setting, the Clinton plan could save businesses $157 billion and reduce federal spending by $131 billion (in 1993 constant dollars). Administrative costs are the critical ones to trim in the health economy.

South Korea has passed a national health insurance plan and initiated a GBB process for 1993. America should pass a global budget process prior to national health insurance. In our context, a more just distribution of health care resources is possible if we accept two basic facts: we currently need national health insurance, and this requires a GBB. Over the next decade our health care system will face both immense opportunity and danger in a reformation on four fronts: access, efficiency, effectiveness, and quality of life. The challenge for policymakers during this period will be to win a clear victory on every front and not erode access or quality. A GBB will ensure that the results are good economics and good medicine.

CONCLUSIONS

What does each additional dollar invested in our $3 billion dollar per day health care system seem to buy? No visible improvements in life expectancy or quality of care for the average (nonrich) patient. Indeed, each additional dollar poured into our inefficient system buys 15 cents of additional administration and overhead, 46 cents of additional biomedical technology inflation, and only 39 cents of additional necessary services (Eastaugh, 1993). Global budgeting overcomes the American habit of thinking that our health care problems are a list of discrete defects. Some 77,000 internists and 40,000 family physicians officially endorsed global budgets in 1992. Physician morale could improve as practice becomes administratively less complex.

The Congress is clearly familiar with the general concept of global budgets. Medicare Volume Performance Standard has a goal of reducing projected 1993 growth in the number and intensity of physician services by 3 percentage points (from 8.3 to 5.3 percent). Some physician groups would fight the concept of tighter global budgets by asking Congress to prohibit the Health Care Financing Administration (HCFA) from applying any behavioral offset. Other provider groups (e.g., nurses) and consumer groups (e.g., the disabled) will have various nonmonetary reasons for not trusting global budgeting (i.e., the fear of not getting their fair share).

The consensus development process will not be easy, but a federal board for setting health care spending caps is not "a socialist system for planned payment" or a form of rigid price control. The efficient hospital or physician need not feel any pressure from GBB activities. By allocating capital and operating funds the local GBBs will provide incentives for enhanced efficiency. Efficient providers could be rewarded in semiannual budget adjustments. In summary, the budget process is a proven approach for minding our Ps and Qs. We need to control both the Ps (prices) and the Qs (quantity or volume of service) to cap the Es (expenditures). A GBB is superior to price controls because it manages both Ps and Qs.

Government-imposed expenditure limitations frequently raise the specter of inflexible, highly bureaucratic regulatory agencies. Both public officials and health care personnel have come to view global budgeting processes as anything but immobile, and the systems are actually far more dynamic and are applied with greater flexibility than had been expected. However, the flexibility is exercised within an overall national expenditure goal. Budget pass-throughs and methods to deal with overruns are common, so long as the national spending targets are reasonably well met. The systems are able to come remarkably close to achieving their overall fiscal targets even while tolerating a substantial degree of variability at the state or local level. On the national level budget limits are viewed more as targets than as fixed ceilings. On the provider level hospitals are subject to expenditure caps in the form of a government-determined budget, which could theoretically cause serious problems for those that exceed their budget. In practice, however, hospitals are generally allowed to increase expenditures through a justification process. When government tried to implement harsh expenditure limitations, political pressure from provider groups and regional interests forced a modification of the budget. The health industry pushed hard, but it realizes that its political influence runs out at the point at which the costs of the requests cause major disruptions. Thus, the commitment to universal access shared by both government and the health industry acts as a force to counterbalance the power of both groups.

Global budgeting is no more regulatory an approach to health care reform than the Hillary Clinton task force approach of managed competition. Enlightened global budgets as exercised in Germany are an improvement on the American 1971–1974 approach to health care. The Clintons' Health Plan Insurance Purchasing Cooperatives are nothing but federally sponsored cartels. President Roosevelt tried this same approach in the 1930s in hopes of revitalizing industry through government-sponsored, but not government-operated, cooperatives (the New Deal). In the 1990s context government-sponsored, nonprofit co-ops would act in each state or city as price negotiators between consumers and accountable health plans. If the resulting managed competition proves a failure, as it did with federal employees in managed care plans that experienced 13.8 percent inflation from 1986 to 1993, then global budgets would become the cost containment strategy of last resort. The regression analysis in this chapter suggests that global budgets will contain health care costs.

REFERENCES

Aaron, H. (1991). *Serious and Unstable Condition*. Washington, DC: Brookings.
Anderson, G., Heyssel, R., and Dickder, R. (1993). "Competition versus Regulation: Its Effect on Hospitals," *Health Affairs* 12:1, Spring, 70–80.
Angell, M. (1993). "How Much Will Health Care Reform Cost?" *New England Journal of Medicine* 328:24, June 17, 1778–79.
Baumol, W., Blackman, S., and Wolfe, E. (1985). "Unbalanced Growth Revisited: Asymptotic Stagnancy and New Evidence," *American Economic Review* 75:4, September, 806–17.
Cahill, K. (1993). *Imminent Peril: Public Health in a Declining Economy*. Washington, DC: Brookings.
Dean, H. (1992). "Vermont Approach to Negotiate Expenditure Targets," *American Medical News*, May 11, 39.
Eastaugh, S. (1993). "Global Budgets for Health Care in Europe and Australia," Washington, DC; GWU Health Policy Institute, Unpublished Report to Robert Wood Johnson Foundation.
———. (1992a). *Health Care Finance: Economic Incentives and Productivity Enhancement*. Westport, CT: Auburn House.
———. (1992b). *Health Economics: Efficiency, Quality and Equity*. Westport, CT: Auburn House.

————. (1992c). "Impact of National Health Insurance in Korea," *Hospital Topics*, Fall, 18–24.

————. (1992d). "Lessons from the First and Last Nations to Pass National Health Insurance," *American Health Policy* 2:6, 19–22.

————. (1991a). "Economic Issues in Defining Stable Funding Levels for AIDS," *Journal of Health Administration Education* 10:1, Winter, 139–49.

————. (1991b). "Impact of National Health Insurance on Korean Health Care Expenditures," Consultant report to World Bank, Washington, DC.

————. (1987). *Financing Health Care, Economic Efficiency and Equity.* Dover, MA: Auburn House.

Fuchs, V. (1992). "The Best Health Care System in the World?" *JAMA*, 268, August 19, 916–17.

————. (1991). "National Health Insurance Revisited," *Health Affairs* 10:4, Winter, 7–16.

Gerdtham, U., Sogaard, J., Andersson, F., and Jonsson, B. (1992). "An Econometric Analysis of Health Care Expenditures: A Cross-Section Study of the OECD Countries," *Journal of Health Economics* 11:1, August, 63–84.

Getzen, T. (1990). "Macro Forecasting of National Health Expenditures," In *Advances in Health Economics and Health Services Research*, ed. R. Scheffler. Greenwich, CT: JAI, 27–47.

Ginzberg, E. (1991). *The Contribution of Health Services Research to National Health Policy.* Cambridge, Ma: Harvard University Press.

Glaser, W. (1993). "How Expenditure Caps and Expenditures Targets Really Work," *Milbank Quarterly* 71:1, Spring, 97–128.

Henke, K. (1992). "Cost Containment in Health Care." In *Health Economics Worldwide*, eds. P. Zweifel and H. Frech. Amsterdam; Kluwer Academic Publishers, 245–65.

Iglehart, J. (1991). "Germany's Health Care System," *New England Journal of Medicine* 324:7, February 14, 503–08.

Ikegami, N. (1991). "Japanese Health Care: Low Cost Through Regulated Fees," *Health Affairs* 10:3, Fall, 87–109.

Kassenarztliche Bundesvereinigung (KBV). (1992). *Grunddaten zur Kassenarztlichen Versorgung in der Bundesrepublik Deutschland.* Cologne, Germany: KBV.

Kirkman-Liff, B. (1991). "Health Insurance Values and Implementation in the Netherlands and the Federal Republic of Germany," *JAMA* 265:19, May 15, 2496–2502.

Kmenta, J. (1986). *Elements of Econometrics*, 2nd ed. New York: Macmillan.

Konzertierte Aktion (KA). (1992). *Understanding Advice for the KA in Health Care: Building on in Germany.* Baden-Baden, Germany: KA.

Lave, J., Jacobs, P., and Markel, F. (1992). "Transitional Funding Within Ontario's Global Budgeting System," *Health Care Financing Review* 13:3, 77–84.

Manning, W., and Newhouse, J. (1987). "Health Insurance and the Demand for Medical Care: Evidence from a Randomized Experiment," *American Economic Review* 77:3. March, 251–77.

Office of National Cost Estimates, HCFA. (1993). "Trends in National Health Expenditures," Washington, DC: Department of Health and Human Services.

Office of Technology Assessment. (1993). *Pharmaceutical R&D: Costs, Risks and Rewards*. Washington, DC: U.S. Congress.

Organization for Economic Cooperation and Development (OECD). (annual, 1972–1992). *Labor Force Statistics*. Paris: OECD.

Organization for Economic Cooperation and Development (OECD). (annual, 1972–1992). *National Accounts*. Paris: OECD.

Physician Payment Reform Commission (PPRC). (1993). *Annual Report to Congress*. Washington, DC: PPRC.

Powell, M., and Anesaki, M. (1991). *Health Care in Japan*, New York: Routledge, Chapman, and Hall.

Rachlis, M., and Kushner, C. (1990). *Second Opinion: What's Wrong with Canada's Health-Care System and How to Fix it*. Toronto; Collins.

Sachverstandigenrat fur die Konzertierte Aktion (SVRK). (1992). *Das Gesundheitswesen im Vereinten Deutschland: Ausbau in Deutschland und Aufbruch nach Europa*. Baden-Baden, Germany: SVRK.

Salkever, D. (1976). "Use of Dummy Variables to Compute Predictions, Prediction Errors, and Confidence Intervals." *Journal of Econometrics* 4:4, April, 393–97.

Strosberg, M., Weiner, J., and Baker, R. (1993). *Rationing America's Medical Care: The Oregon Plan and Beyond*. Washington, DC: Brookings.

Tokarski, C. (1992). "Wofford-Thornburgh: A Turning Point for Health Reform," *American Health Policy* 2:1, January-February, 17–20.

Torry, B., and Jacobs, E. (1993). "Spending in the U.S. and Canada," *Health Affairs* 12:1, Spring, 126–31.

U.S. Government. (1993). *U.S. Industrial Outlook: Health Care Spending*. Washington, DC: U.S. Government Printing Office.

Wennberg, J. (1990). "Outcomes Research, Cost Containment, and the Fear of Health Care Rationing," *New England Journal of Medicine* 323:17, October 25, 1202–4.

Wysong, J., and Abel, T. (1990). "Universal Health Insurance and High-Risk Groups in West Germany: Implications for U.S. Health Policy," *Milbank Quarterly* 68:4, Winter, 527–60.

8

Social Security: Sacred Cow or Third Rail in American Politics?

The new morality says the young should forget the old. But any politician that tries to cut Golden Agers' benefits will get a shock from the third rail of American Politics, Social Security. The elderly vote in greater numbers, and will punish the cost cutters.
—House Speaker Tip O'Neill, 1982

Politics is the art of looking for trouble, finding it everywhere, diagnosing it incorrectly and applying the wrong remedy.
—Groucho Marx, 1952

The year 1983 was proclaimed the one in which Congress saved the Social Security (SS) system from financial bankruptcy. By raising taxes in 1983 the SS trust fund went from a $7.9 billion deficit in 1982 to a $54 billion surplus in 1983. However, the system faces a demographic time bomb that will require frequent restructuring over the coming decades. It will need to be saved again, maybe in the year 2003 and again in 2023. One must address three basic truths concerning Social Security. *Fact no. 1:* Social Security is not an insurance fund, but rather a political pay-as-you-go program whereby the taxes paid by workers today go out in the mail as retiree benefit checks and pay for current government spending next week. Social Security taxes have grown from 30.5 percent of all federal taxes in 1980 to 37 percent in 1990 and 38.1 percent in 1993. The average young family of three with $36,000 in salary pays five times more federal taxes than a retired elderly couple with a $36,000 annual income. The elderly have a great deal whereby their benefits are reduced at a rate of $1 for every $3 in earnings over $9,720 (the so-called earnings test). This discount of benefits is not a penalty, but a realization that *Social Security benefits aren't rewards for attaining older age, but insurance against income lost during retirement.* No retirement, no benefit check. *Fact no. 2:* With fewer workers per retired

American Congress will have to hit the young with higher taxes to finance the life-style of the elderly. For example, workers, will be taxed over 15.4 percent for Social Security in 1994, when we will have 3.38 workers per retiree. Workers have declined as a proportion of the population since 1949, when we had 13.2 workers per retiree. In 2023 Social Security taxes may have to rise to 25 to 34 percent, because the nation will only have 2.07 workers per retiree. *Fact no. 3:* On paper, the Social Security tax is paid equally by the employer (7.7 percent) and the employee (7.7), but all econometric evidence suggests the worker bears the full 15.4 percent tax burden through reduced wages (see Brittain, 1972; Moon, 1984). In 1993 over 76 percent of working Americans pay more in Social Security taxes than in federal income tax. Social Security is more specifically known as the mandatory Federal Insurance Contributions Act (FICA) of payroll taxes on wages. Employees and their employers each pay a FICA tax of 6.3 percent of the first $55,000 for Social Security and 1.45 percent for medical health insurance for the elderly.

FUND OR FICTION?

Social Security overspending to ease our geriatric years creates the ominous problem of paying the future bills. For the American public, the financing problem is vaguely far off, like a hurricane building over Aruba. The typical retiree will receive $3.50 to $4 in the coming three decades for every dollar contributed to Social Security, even after adjusting for inflation. The young will be lucky to get 50 cents on the dollar. The elderly should not forget their easy tax burden in their working years. The maximum Social Security contribution was $30 in 1937, $45 in 1950, $94 in 1958, $374 in 1969, $1,000 in 1977, and $3,605 in 1989. This chapter will survey the short-run American solution to the financing crisis, before surveying alternative solutions, generational conflict, and experience from other countries.

In 1983 Congress implemented the Greenspan Commission recommendation that the Social Security trust fund raise revenues from payroll tax hikes until the fund equals $11.8 trillion, or 28 percent of the gross national product, by 2031. The trust fund should slowly liquidate over the next 20 years before entering the red in the year 2051. The problem with such actuarial forecasts is that they may markedly underestimate the ability of medicine to extend life, in which case the funds would be insufficient sooner.

In 1993 the trust fund represents a little over 2.5 percent of the GNP. Is the trust fund a pile of money or bonds that any worried voter can come visit? No. The funds exist on paper only, and whether the fund is an accounting fiction or a reliable IOU from Uncle Sam (based on "the security of legislative intention") depends on your political point of view.

If one trusts the liberals' claim, fund surpluses must, by definition, lead to reduced borrowing by the federal government, which in turn represents an increase in national savings. For example, if a surplus of $50 billion is used to pay federal government salaries and benefits, the federal deficit is reduced by $50 billion. Therefore, the government borrows $50 billion less, leaving $50 billion more in the hands of private savings. This liberal argument has weak points. Educated citizens are not happy to learn that their economic future is an accounting fiction in the ledger books of the richer America at some future date. The trust fund is not in some safe haven like a Swiss bank. Instead, the fund is in the hands of American politicians, and they spend every dollar each year. The 1985 and 1990 rewrites of the Budget Enforcement Laws labeled Social Security "off-budget," but the trust fund surpluses are still used (until 1994) to make it easier for Congress to meet deficit reduction targets. When the trust fund in fact goes off-budget in 1994, the deficit will balloon by over $63 billion. Politicians interested in expanding programs will fight for creative ways to raid the trust fund again after 1994. Politicians letting the off-budget surplus remain above politics, and grow to $12 trillion, is like expecting a dieter to put off food consumption while observing a neighbor eating 12 pounds of cake and ice cream. Self-control has yet to become an adjective for describing Congress.

Conservatives argue that the Social Security trust fund should remain solvent, intact, and self-financing. They argue that surpluses earned from 1984 to 1993 are in fact expenditures by federal bureaucrats, providing only a thin disguise for a much higher deficit in current accounts. Consequently, $50 billion in trust fund surplus yields zero dollars of increased private savings. The evidence on sluggish American savings rates in chapter 3 suggests that the conservative viewpoint is closer to reality. The illogic of the liberal viewpoint suggests a curious form of arithmetic: tax the payroll by $1,000, and the worker has room to save $1,000 more in private accounts plus forced savings from Social Security has been increased by $1,000. This leads to a useful functional definition of a liberal: a person who can make $1,000 sound like $2,000.

The temptation to spend the trust fund on other special programs, from medical care to nursing home care or defense, will be strong among both Republicans and Democrats. As the trust fund increases $900 million per week in the mid-1990s, will Congress have the self-control to resist spending the money on other programs? Can Congress keep the Social Security surplus high and ignore the opportunity to spend this fund for special interest groups? Under the self-interest theory outlined in chapter 2, members of Congress can be expected to sell chunks of the trust fund to special interest groups. The special interest groups that help raid the trust fund after 1993 will be spending in current accounts what the nation needs for Social Security in the 21st century. Politicians, unless controlled by a more active and informed public, will take this attitude: Why care about 2043 if they will not be running for reelection in the distant future?

Under a worst case scenario, Congress would: (1) cut payroll tax increases planned for the future to please the young and (2) spend the reduced trust fund surplus on new programs. A better case scenario would involve: paying our future pension bill, maintaining the planned growth in the trust fund, and continuing to borrow from the trust fund to cover deficits in the rest of the budget. It is less expensive to borrow from the trust fund than pay higher interest in the marketplace.

The best case scenario would involve controlling the federal deficit so that the trust fund can remain an intact and fully funded "sacred cow," sufficient to finance any future demographic bubble caused by unexpected improvements in life expectancy among retirees. The only raid on the trust fund surplus that might be justified involves the proposed inclusion of Part B of Medicare into Social Security. The elderly complain about paying a mere 25 percent of the cost of Part B coverage for physicians' services and other nonhospital programs, while general tax revenues pay 75 percent ($50 billion in 1993). If general revenue accounts are to be kept separate from the trust fund, why should the payroll tax for the elderly not finance this 75 percent share of the Medicare Part B program? If the program were subsidized by the trust fund, the fund would still build to $11 trillion by 2028. Thus, the fund would own the entire national debt ($8.6 trillion) and still have 2.4 trillion to invest elsewhere in the economy. Such a rosy scenario is predicated on substantial cost containment in the Medicare program, so that the year in which Medicare outlays will surpass those of Social Security is deferred from the year 2009 to 2038. To paraphrase former Congressman William Gray (D–Pa.): "The country is in hock, and the question is who has the pawn ticket." Perhaps Social Security has most of the pawn ticket, with 10 percent of the ticket owned by Japan and 4 to 6 percent owned by six other developed nations.

SOLUTIONS

Proposed solutions to financing future Social Security pensions involve either extending the working life, via later retirement and more part-time employment to reduce cash outflow and increase cash inflow, or a simple reduction of benefits. The reason why substantial cuts in benefits represents the inferior strategy can be documented in Ronald Reagan's ten-year approach to Social Security. In 1982 President Reagan proposed a 39 percent reduction in benefits for those retiring at 62 and a 23 percent reduction in benefits for all other retirees. The resulting political storm caused a swing in the president's position. By 1983 President Reagan withdrew to his 1980 position as a presidential candidate: "to save and strengthen Social Security." From 1972 to 1978, however, Reagan advocated that Social Security be made voluntary so that citizens could opt for a private pension. To win the presidency, though, the pragmatic Reagan realized that he had to back a fully funded Social Security.

What would a fair system look like? Under fair insurance, an individual born in 1960 earning a modest $24,000 a year for life (in 1990 dollars) could receive either a $942 Social Security check per month at retirement in 2026 or, if allowed to invest privately the money presently withdrawn for SS, receive a one-time annuity of $1.12 million.

The 1983 Social Security salvation bill raised the retirement age for those born after 1942 to 66 years and those born after 1967 to 67. However, the age for receiving full benefits may have to rise an additional three to five years to keep the program solvent. The basic problem is that the elderly are increasingly experiencing a better physiological age relative to their chronological age. A 97-year-old George Burns looks in 1992 like a typical 60-year-old man of 1935. With longer, healthier life-styles come more prolonged withdrawals from the pension fund. The elderly are increasingly taking part-time jobs, and Social Security is a decreasing fraction of their income. People aged 65 and older in 1993 receive only 44 percent of their income from Social Security. The other 56 percent comes from working, investments, and private pensions. In 1993 an estimated 38 percent of elderly males will receive private pensions ($6,900 on average), in contrast to only 18 percent of elderly females (only $4,000 on average). Any tax scheme that gives people an incentive to continue working may erode the relative economic standing of the sick elderly who are incapable of working after retirement age. The poor and the elderly often work for the less mobile elderly. Some 100,000 poor women over age 65 and another 200,000 nonelderly poor care for 1.2 million severely ill elderly with conditions such as Alzheimer's, strokes, and crippling arthritis through home care. In addition there are 1.4 million male and 2.2 million female nursing home residents in 1993.

GENERATIONAL CONFLICT

The nonelderly as a group are not well positioned to have private pensions substitute for Social Security. Currently only 39 percent of Americans are covered by private pensions, a decline from 50.2 percent in 1980, ac-

cording to the National Planning Association. A worker aged 25 has a vastly
different economic viewpoint of retirement and Social Security (SS) than a
75-year-old retiree. The young think: (1) that they will collect 1 to 2 dollars
for every $4 they contribute to SS and (2) the elderly don't care if the
young must forfeit home ownership, a new car, or education to feed the SS
fund/monster. One person's monster is another's "great deal." Over the
initial 55 years of Social Security, the average beneficiary received from the
trust fund in 21 months what he paid in payroll taxes over his entire working life. The elderly don't care if they receive $3 to $9 for every dollar paid
into Social Security because: (1) "it compensates our generation" for having
a "harder life" and (2) social justice demands a pension capable of financing
a better-than-tolerable life-style, even if (3) life was better in the past. The
elderly sometimes reflect on the contradiction between their bipolar views
(it was better/worse during their simpler times), but they clearly worked in
a booming economy, with job security and no foreign competition.

Each generation forgets the socioeconomic history of their parents or
children. The young have an AIDS epidemic that may kill 10 million over
a 25-year period, but the elderly remember a flu epidemic that killed 20
million in 1 year (1918). Many elderly citizens do not realize that their
children are paying property taxes, if they are lucky enough to own a home,
that are four times higher in inflation-adjusted dollars than they paid at the
same age. A one-worker household in 1950 spent 12 percent of its gross
income on housing, property taxes, and insurance. By contrast, a two-
worker household today spends 46 percent of its income on the same three
items. To balance the SS books and avoid substantial deterioration in the
standard of living of the young, America must produce more workers. We
can either abolish the child labor laws and have four-worker households, or
as is more likely, we can increase immigration. If we find a doubling of the
Social Security tax rates unacceptable over the period 1993–2043, one option would be to increase immigration by 50 million young (under age 40)
taxpayers over the coming decades. These immigrants will need education
to inflate the tax revenue base and maintain the current welfare state.
Many older Americans who went to college under a federal subsidy realize
the economic value of education and the need to keep younger Americans
educated, more productive, and capable of financing their monthly SS
checks.

The problems with the SS generous benefit structure is that it yields a
housing deficit, an education deficit, and a work incentive deficit among
young Americans. Americans born prior to World War II represent the first
demographic group to take more resources than they gave. After paying
higher property taxes, income taxes, and payroll taxes, along with large
student loans and much higher health insurance premiums, the standard of

living of the young suffers in comparison to past generations, even with all the new toys, from VCRs to CDs to microwave cooking. In stark economic terms, the theoretical underpinnings for SS are being undercut by the growing income disparity between workers and retirees. From 1960 to 1992 retirees' income after taxes has increased 501 percent, but workers' after-tax income increased only 216 percent. This gap between worker and retiree incomes can only widen when the 76 million "boomers" born in the demographic bulge (1946–1964) retire after the year 2012.

A 1989 Ford Foundation report, *The Common Good*, suggests that a "social deficit" of crime, illiteracy, and drug consumption will burden our nation for decades if America continues to misallocate resources to the elderly and away from the children. In view of the self-interest/special-interest paradigm introduced in chapter 1, this misallocation of resources should not be surprising. The elderly have risen as a power group and will consume 30 percent of the 1993 federal budget, compared to 16 percent in 1970. They will consume 50 percent of the federal budget by the year 2038. Which group of Americans feels the squeeze? The group with the highest poverty rate, children. Moreover, 9.5 million children have no health insurance or Medicaid eligibility, whereas all elderly have health insurance.

If the elderly remain deaf to child poverty, consider the following query. How will a generation born recently, robbed of its future, devoid of a public vision to sacrifice or share, treat its elders? Will these people vote for lower benefits per retiree and stricter eligibility rules? Will they vote to cut their payroll taxes to 1982 rates? It is deeply unifying to believe that in 1993 half of young Americans believe that Social Security is a good thing because it relieves them of some financial responsibility for the care and housing of their elders. But in the future more and more young people may come to resent their ever-increasing Social Security tax burden. The second half of this chapter shall review ways to avert a war between the young and the old and reduce the tax burden, while fairly limiting benefit checks.

Obviously, certain specific programs outside the purview of Social Security may reduce the social pressure, such as reducing the housing crunch by elder's offering their children "equity sharing" to afford the large initial down payment on a home. One generation helping the next may do something to rebuild the social contract that should make Social Security more of a pension program than a welfare program.

AVOIDING A COMING GENERATIONAL WAR

Social Security has become the economists' flypaper: they cannot seem to touch the issue without allegations that they are biased against the elderly. However, if anything, economists are older and more conservative than the general public. Most economists subscribe to Theory A: If the elderly are growing in number as a proportion of the population, their political power will get larger, and they will tax the young to finance their own retirement. The smugness in support of this theory exists on bumper stickers: "We are spending the kid's inheritance." By 2042 the number of Americans over age 80 will exceed the number of those over age 65 in 1993. Many statistics support the fact that elders are growing in number, but will voter participation among the young awaken like a sleeping giant?

An alternative Theory B suggests: As the cost to young workers skyrockets and living standards deteriorate, the political power of the young is going to get larger, not smaller. The young are not simply in search of tax relief. Many are embarrassed or outraged that while poverty rates for the elderly have declined, the rates for children are high. The elderly poverty rate was 36 percent in 1959, at which time SS taxes represented 9 percent of taxes. SS taxes are 28 percent of national tax revenues federal, state, and local in 1993. The elderly poverty rate no longer exceeds the child poverty rate. It has declined to under 12 percent, or only 8.1 percent when federal benefits (excluding health care) are included. If one includes the market value of home ownership plus health care benefits, the elderly poverty rate declines to 2.9 percent (Bureau of the Census, 1992). However, the poverty rate among children has not improved from the 16 to 20 percent range during the 1980s. To borrow an analogy from President John F. Kennedy, it appears the boat carrying the elderly is ever rising, but the children's boat is stuck in the mud. The young neither want to inflate the poverty rate for the elderly, nor do they want the elderly to live more frequently with their children. There has been no rebirth of the multigenerational family under one roof. Scholars need to remind politicians and the media of the extent to which the economic future of different age groups is interconnected. Large differentials between economic status represent a threat to the status quo. Cornell economist Alfred Kahn and S. Kamerman and others have pointed to the critical need to rechannel more resources to children.

To some extent SS robs Paul, the younger, poorer working person, to pay Peter, the retired, richer individual. The political will to upgrade SS benefits was eroded by two recent events. In 1985 the President's Council of Economic Advisers announced that the elderly are no longer a disadvantaged group because they began to exceed the annual income and new wealth of the general population. (Beneath the averages and medians, the underlying distributions still reveal significant pockets of poverty, such as single, elderly females.) The second event was the backlash during 1989 of affluent elderly citizens protesting the passage of catastrophic insurance in 1988. The new income-related premiums for this plan were much too progressive for the tastes of the richest 39 percent of senior citizens. Many in Congress came away with bitter feelings following the turbulent protest.

The taxes that finance Social Security make it hard to change the program. According to Columbia Professor Luther Gulick, President Franklin D. Roosevelt told him in 1941: "We put those 1936 payroll contributions there so as to give the contributors a legal, moral, and political right to collect their pension. With those taxes in there, no damn politician can ever scrap my Social Security program." In terms of politics he was correct, because without payroll taxes SS becomes like welfare.

TWO FRAMEWORKS FOR COMPARISON

Federal payments to an age group can be analyzed from two perspectives: (1) annual direct expense or (2) multidecade investment in human capital. From the first perspective, the elderly consume $11,800 per person in federal benefits, but we invest only $1,200 per child. The second perspective is even more interesting. Even after the "education president" George Bush reallocated some resources to schools and housing for the poor, infrastructure investment in schools and the cities will represent only $4,280 per child during 1984–1993 (1992 dollars). The incremental inflation in benefits per retiree over the budget years 1984–1993 is greater than $4,200 (1992 dollars). The elderly receive more in additional incremental funding than the children, schools, sewers, and streets receive in total funding. As a nation we are very cheap in treating children and very generous to retirees. The resulting social deficit may be a more intractable, unfunded liability than any money problem we face as a nation.

Our minimum reductionist goal as a society is that our children and the elderly live in tolerable comfort. What benefit levels will support justice between generations is the most difficult domestic public policy issue for the next century. We will live in a zero-sum world of poor alternatives unless we enhance productivity and generate more wealth, savings, and substantial private pensions. In 1992 Governor Mario Cuomo suggested that since the cost of living adjustments (COLAs) were never part of the original 1935 deal, they should be "curtailed." The macroeconomic way to reduce intergenerational inequality implicitly would involve a diet COLA, a reduction in the COLA for Social Security. The mere action of trimming the COLA for nonpoor elderly to 70 percent of the consumer price index would save $37 billion over the period 1994–2009.

According to the Congressional Budget Office, the average private pension allows an increase in benefits that covers only 30 percent of the erosion due to inflation. However, Social Security offers a 3.3-fold, risk-free better deal than private pensions: SS pays 100 percent automatic protection from inflation. *POLICY PROPOSAL No. 43:* Limit COLA adjustments for non-poor elderly to 1.5 points below the inflation rate (saving $12 billion over the period 1994–1997). This would offer the poor elderly 100 percent inflation protection and the nonpoor elderly twice the protection from inflation that private pensions offer. An alternative specification for the same general idea would be to pay a full COLA on the initial $600 of the retiree's monthly check and a 30 percent COLA on the amount above the $600 that nonpoor elderly receive each month (saving $23 billion in 1994–1997).

Federal retirees receiving a double pension from government should defer any COLAs until they have reached age 62. *POLICY PROPOSAL No. 44:* Defer COLAs until age 62 for all nondisabled employees who retire before age 61 (saving $5.1 billion in the period 1994–1997). From whom would the savings accrue? Almost 87 percent would come from former military employees. The Veterans Administration's massive social welfare system, biased against women and run independently of the Department of Health and Human Services, should also be scaled back. *POLICY PROPOSAL No. 45:* End income payments for veterans with no real disabilities and for new veterans with disabilities unrelated to military duties (saving $8.5 billion over 1994–1997).

The next two sections will survey some other options, including expansion of the retirement age and restrictions on benefit checks to the wealthy, to minimize Social Security tax hikes' negative impact on economic growth.

LESSONS FROM OTHER COUNTRIES

In creating a public pension fund, government planners can either give the first few generations a bad deal (fewer tax payments and benefits) by building up a fiscally sound insurance fund, or give future generations high taxes and overfund pension checks for the initial cohort of elderly far in excess of what they paid in their working years. Japan opted for the first alternative and built a surplus of revenues on the backs of the first two generations of workers in the mid-1990s.

America opted for the second alternative, pay-as-you-go, and hopes the fourth, fifth, and sixth generations of workers do not mind the high Social Security tax rates they pay to finance excess generosity to retirees since 1937. For policymakers, uncertainty exists in two areas: will the revenues be forthcoming from future generations and will the government dispense the benefits? Section three of this chapter outlined some reasons why young workers distrust the "security of legislative intent" and the concept that Uncle Sam's IOU is good enough to provide Social Security checks in 2023 or 2043.

Japan will have a lower worker-to-retiree ratio over the coming years than

America. But the Japanese have a better prefinanced pot of gold to meet the greater demands of future retirees. The Japanese Congress (the Diet) and treasury officials are quick to point out that their pension fund was financed during an era when Japanese labor productivity was one-third the American level. Japanese political leaders in years past were like the character Phineas Finn in Anthony Trollope's novels, legislators with respect for future generations, of scrupulous honor, totally unwilling to pander to pressure from special interest groups. American politicians like to give something for nothing, sell the future, and sail with any current hysterical popular reaction. The Japanese in 1955 were as bad off as Americans in 1937, but they structured a pension plan that would not overburden their offspring.

One other advantage the Japanese seem to enjoy is that they dislike retirement. The effective median retirement age in many Japanese towns is as high as 70 to 72, and one city the author visited had a 20 percent labor-force participation rate for 80-year-old males doing part-time work! Japanese citizens and corporations strongly believe in pay for performance, so if the individual's productivity is reduced 20 percent with age, the wage rate will reflect a 20 percent reduction. Many Japanese aged 60 to 70 take a 10 to 30 percent pay cut to continue working, with equivalent reduction in work load and responsibility. The standard retirement benefit for the third generation of Japanese pensioners has been good to the group, as the poverty rate for Japanese over age 70 has declined from 9.9 percent in 1965 to an estimated 2.6 percent in 1993. In 1993 Japan will spend 7.9 percent of its national income on Social Security pensions, in contrast to a forecasted 15.3 percent in 2035. Some countries already have a more substantial public pension burden on the economy. In 1992 Italy spent 18 percent of its national income, and Germany and France currently spend 15 percent. European countries are looking to private pensions in changing the tax laws and reducing the future expected benefit checks.

In the 1880s German Chancellor Otto von Bismarck set the retirement age at 20 years beyond the average life expectancy of 45 years, or age 65. If the current American life expectancy is 75, should the retirement age be set at 95? No, but American faces major shortages of professional and skilled labor (Bureau of Labor Statistics, 1990–1992). With such an obvious labor undersupply, our nation cannot afford to keep the retirement age under 70. Currently, an individual can qualify for partial (70 percent) Social Security benefits at age 62 and for full benefits at age 65. *POLICY PROPOSAL No. 46:* Increase the age to qualify for partial Social Security benefits to age 70 and for full benefits to age 75 by the year 2028. Today's elderly should not complain about increasing the retirement age because it would affect only future retirees. To stimulate the elderly to work part-time, even in their retirement years, pension checks could be limited and set regardless of income history. At present the richest workers get the highest Social Security checks. A preferred alternative in the interest of vertical equity across income groups would involve increasing the basic benefits for the working poor elderly and decreasing the size of the checks for the rich elderly (Eastaugh, 1987). University of Wisconsin economist Robert Haveman has suggested a standard benefit check of $6,000 a year for single elderly and $7,500 for a couple, regardless of whether they continue to work.

Ross Perot and others have suggested implementing *POLICY PROPOSAL No. 47:* Subject 86 percent of Social Security payments to income tax for those with income over $24,000 (reducing the deficit by $43 billion over the years 1994–1997). Those who depend on it for most of their income would barely be affected (the retired poor). What public finance rational is there for taxing only 86 percent? The new elderly, joining in the 1990s, get 86 percent more in benefits than what they paid in taxes (real dollars, inflation-adjusted). Given these elderly never paid taxes on their original FICA contribution as a worker, they should not be tax exempt now. Furthermore, 14 percent of the retirees' Social Security benefits represent the fiscal return of their own contributions and should be tax-free. Private pensions will continue to be underused as long as they are heavily taxed and Social Security is undertaxed (Aaron and Schultze, 1992).

BAD DEALS AND BIZARRE UNDERWRITING PRINCIPLES

The Social Security benefit structure is a crude mix of what a beneficiary pays in and what cash flow Congress allows out. Social Security is not so much a public pension plan as it is a political insurance program that pays out so much under certain circumstances. If an elderly individual does not fully retire, Social Security benefits are withheld, just as Medicare insurance benefits are withheld from the nonsick. In 1993 those aged 65 to 69 earning over $9,500 per year will receive a reduction of $1 for every $3 earned in their Social Security checks, and those under 65 earning over $7,100 per year will also have their checks reduced. The Social Security trust fund also includes some strong underwriting principles that stipulate the combination of two married individuals' lifetime contributions into one joint account that effectively ignores one spouse's tax burden. Someone should inform the Social Security administration or Congress that America is full of two-career families.

The strangest thing about Social Security for professionals is the inverse

Table 8.1
The Return on Investment in Social Security Relative to a Private Pension Investment in Chicago Municipal Bonds

Years of Schooling,	Birth Year		
Life Length (Years)	1922	1947	1972
10*, 70	-43.8%	-49.2	-52.4
20**, 70	-39.5	-45.3	-48.9
10 school, 80 life	-4.1	-12.2	-18.1
20 school, 80 life	-1.8	-10.3	-16.4
10 school, 90 life	26.7	17.9	11.4
20 school, 90 life	28.2	16.5	10.1

*For the three respective birth years, 5.4, 3.8, and 2.3 years of unemployment (during which no Social Security taxes were paid).
**Assumed working six months after finishing school.

relationship between tax contributions and rate of return. Table 8.1 provides an example of what a bad deal Social Security represents for both the professional with 20 years of schooling and the young. The median M.D. or Ph.D born after 1940 would have to live nine years beyond average life expectancy to break even and not earn a negative rate of return on Social Security. However, Social Security is a great fiscal deal for nonprofessionals born in the 1920s.

The average citizen does not realize what a bad deal Social Security represents, compared to a conservative private pension that invests perhaps in Chicago Municipal Bonds. For these obvious reasons, presidential candidates Ronald Reagan (1976) and Pierre DuPont suggested a privatization of public pensions. Workers could opt to pay all or some of their Social Security taxes into a private financial security account (FSA). This FSA would be a personal asset, so the fund would move with the worker from job to job. At death the worker would have a nest egg to leave to the family. Unlike a life insurance plan, Social Security cannot be passed down to children following the death of their parents. Social Security is more akin to welfare than to a private insurance policy or pension fund. If one in three individuals earning above-average incomes opted for this private plan, the lost tax collections might amount to $32 billion in 1995, but in theory the pension funds injected into the private sector might spur economic growth. However, with the federal deficit high and Congress unwilling to hear Reagan's clarion call to "begin the world over again" and requestion the assumptions behind SS, Americans are probably stuck with mandatory public pensions. Only an economic depression would provoke Congress to offer a voluntary private pension alternative to Social Security.

ELIGIBILITY

One technique for trimming Social Security expenses is to restrict eligibility or increase the taxes on high earners' checks. If taxes are paid on only half the Social Security benefits for couples earning over $32,000 (and singles earning over $25,000), few rich seniors will consider refusing their monthly SS checks. A better policy might be to subject 100 percent of pension income in excess of $10,000 to federal taxation (a revenue gain of $19.9 billion in 1994 from the richest 25 percent of the elderly). The elderly falsely view Social Security as an insurance program, like auto insurance, whereby the recipient does not reject cashing the check just because he or she happens to be financially better off. The selfish attitude is to suggest: "We paid out taxes; we deserve each and every check." In fact, all past taxes did not go into an insurance account. The tax contributions went to assist the life-styles of those who retired in the past. The rich elderly should not complain that they subsidize the checks for the current poor retirees; rather, they simply should receive an unfunded check from their unfunded "uninsurance" account.

All retirees' complaints about their financial situation are not unrealistic. The catastrophic health insurance plan passed in 1988, and repealed in 1989 overcharged the richest one-third of retirees to subsidize other retirees. Unwittingly, Congress in its search to hold down the cost instituted a public finance principle that only groups directly affected should pay. By this unsound logic, only parents with children in public schools should pay school tax. We all benefit from an educated populace, so all property owners should pay the local school tax. Congress at least taught the elderly lobby groups (e.g., the American Association of Retired People, or AARP) a lesson in scarce resources: do not ask for new programs or: (1) we will make your group pay their way (and give public rebuke against AARP) and (2) we will provide further examples of why we cannot afford current programs. A number of good program ideas for long-term care insurance—$10 billion for home health care or $70 billion for nursing home care—will have to be done with private funding (unlikely) or wait until a future "baby boomer" generation is born to support the elderly.

REFERENCES

Aaron, H., and Schultze, C., (eds. 1992). *Setting Domestic Priorities: What Can Government Do?* Washington, DC: Brookings.

Bernstein, M., and Bernstein, J. (1988). *Social Security; The System that Works.* Boston: Basic Books.

Brittain, J. (1972). *The Payroll Tax for Social Security.* Washington, DC: Brookings.

Bureau of Labor Statistics. (1990–1992). *Employment and Earnings.* Washington, DC: U.S. Department of Labor.

Bureau of the Census, Current Population Survey. (1992). *Money Income of Households, Families, and Persons in the United States: 1992.* Washington, DC: U.S. Government Printing Office.

Carmichael, H. (1989). "Self-Enforcing Contracts, Shirking, and Life Cycle Incentives," *Journal of Economic Perspectives* 3:4, Fall, 65–83.

Carson, R. (1990). *What Economists Know: An Economic Policy Primer for the 1990s.* New York: St. Martin's Press.

Cogan, J. (1988). "The Evolution of Congressional Budget Decisionmaking and the Emergence of Federal Deficits," Hoover Institution Working Paper in Economics E-88-33. Palo Alto, CA: Stanford University, Hoover Institution.

Committee on Ways and Means, U.S. House of Representatives. (1990). Background material and data on programs within the jurisdiction of the committee, March.

Eastaugh, S. (1992). *Health Economics: Efficiency, Quality, and Equity.* Westport, CT: Auburn House.

———. (1987). *Financing Health Care: Economic Efficiency and Equity.* Westport, CT: Auburn House, 176–206, 700–706.

Ford Foundation. (1989). *The Common Good: Social Welfare and the American Future.* Executive Panel Report, May. New York: Ford Foundation.

Grad, S. (1990). "Income Change at Retirement," *Social Security Bulletin* 53:1, January, 2–10.

Haveman, R. (1988). *Starting Even: An Equal Opportunity Program to Combat the Nation's New Policy.* New York: Simon and Schuster.

Hutchens, R. (1989). "Seniority, Wages and Productivity: A Turbulent Decade," *Journal of Economic Perspectives* 3:4, Fall, 49–64.

Johnson, P., and Thompson, D. (1990). *Aging Populations: Economic Effects and Implications for Public Finance*. Geneva: OECD, Department of Economics and Statistics, paper number 61.

Kahn, A., and Kamerman, S. (1987). *Child Care: Facing the Hard Choices*. Westport, CT: Auburn House.

Kotlikoff, L. (1989). *What Determines Savings*. Cambridge: MIT Press.

Moon, M. (1984). *Economic Transfers in the United States*. Chicago: University of Chicago Press. 327–57.

Organization for Economic Cooperation and Development (OECD). Department of Economics and Statistics. (1990). "Savings Trends and Behavior in OECD Countries," paper number 67.

Rhodebeck, L. (1993). "Politics of Greed? Political Preferences among the Elderly," *Journal of Politics* 55:2, May, 342–63.

Rice, D. (1989). "Health and Long-Term Care for the Aged," *American Economic Review* 79:2, May, 343–48.

Rivlin, A., and Weiner, J. (1988). *Caring for the Disabled Elderly: Who Will Pay?* Washington, DC: Brookings.

Schulz, J. (1976). *The Economics of Aging*. New York: Wadsworth.

Sinetar, M. (1991). *Developing a 21st Century Mind*. New York: Villard.

9

Looking to the Future

Are you a politician asking what your country can do for you or a zealous one asking what you can do for your country? If you are the first, then you are a parasite; if the second, then you are an oasis in the desert.

—Kahlil Gibran, 1919

An idealist is someone who, on noticing that a rose smells better than a cabbage, concludes that it will also make better soup.

—H. L. Mencken, 1939

Every gun that is made, every warship launched, every rocket fired signifies in the final sense a theft from those who hunger and are not fed, those who are cold and not clothed. The world in arms is spending the sweat of its laborers, the genius of its scientists, the houses of its children.

—Dwight D. Eisenhower, April 16, 1953

The point of congressional debate over the deficit or ecology is not to address the tough issues, but to appear to. Real leaders care less about appearances. The above quote by President Eisenhower could also have included "those not educated," "35 million without health insurance," "production capacity not born," and "corporations and hospitals not revitalized." The sad fact is that the peace dividend resulting from demilitarization in Europe was never a dividend paid out to social causes. The $1.1 trillion peace dividend of the 1990s was swallowed whole, fully consumed by Medicare cost inflation, the savings and loan crisis and the 1990 Saudi defense buildup. Chapters 1 and 2 outlined the dramatic federal budget problems and the problems inherent in asking bureaucrats or politicians to control spending. Weak leaders make plans for big tax increases predicated on the rose/soup assumption that the GNP will remain constant no matter what the level and incidence of taxation. The budget deficits are a step-child of Congress, a body that is political rather than economic, short-sighted rather than far-sighted.

We need an optimum blend of ecology/economy job growth (e.g., pollution controls), general economic growth, and fiscal responsibility (Gore, 1992). *POLICY PROPOSAL No. 48:* Implement a carbon dioxide stabilization tax of $34 per ton (1994 dollars) in the content of our three fossil fuels, collecting $109 billion over the period 1994–1997 and achieving the social goal of eliminating the growth in emissions. This carbon-based excise tax on fossil fuels would be $4.20 per barrel of oil, 53 cents per thousand cubic feet of natural gas, and $19 per ton of coal. This is neither a radical nor an aggressive approach. For example, the cost-benefit papers at the 1992 Rio Earth Summit suggest that America should promote carbon dioxide reductions with tax rates that are 25 percent higher than those proposed above.

Few national "leaders" care more for the national interest than for their own self-interest and reelection. We need a political body that is concerned with the national interest, not simply focused on local pursuit of the next fat government contract or pork barrel program. Special interest groups are occasionally caught in doing obvious criminal activities, as was the case in the Wedtech scandal (Traub, 1990). Special interest groups that take advantage of the national treasury are not bad people, they are just slaves to Harry Truman's maxim: "The most delicate nerve in the body is the pocketbook nerve." Our leaders must straighten out the fiscal mess while expanding the nation's sense of its ideals and purpose.

We must both preserve our fiscal future and save the renewability of the environment. Ideals must be counterbalanced by financial limitations. The ecology movement has not always been cost-beneficial in application (Boyd and Uri, 1992). Many firms made money in waste water treatment without making significant improvements in the environment. Following the lead of the 1993 Congressional Budget Office report is *POLICY PROPOSAL No. 49:* Eliminate $10.8 billion in water treatment plants over the period 1994–1997, because these grants have encouraged inefficient decisions by state and local government. The federal subsidy has done nothing to stimulate better quality waste water treatment.

The basic economic proposals (numbers 1–9, 20–29, and 37–49) offered in this book would: (1) not raise income tax rates, (2) reap a four year 1994–1997 deficit reduction of $1.02 trillion, and (3) balance the budget by 1997. Public expectations for Congress must change. Congress cannot continue to act like a group of "deadbeat dads," refusing to pay the bills. If mom (or "mother nation") receives a promissory note for future payments she has received a whole lot of nothing. The young will be burdened with double the tax rates of adults today within 30 years. The public must also stop asking for so much from government. Government can no longer continue to provide blank check funding of new or preexisting entitlements.

THE ROAD AHEAD

We need a new generation of leaders to nurture national purpose and common sense. If we give into grimness and decline, doom and gloom, we shall live in a society filled with Mahatma Gandhi's deadly sins: politics without principle, knowledge without character, wealth without work, commerce without morality, science without humanity, and pleasure without conscience. The nation has had enough of crooked bank managers, character-void leaders, bad science, low productivity, and a poor educational system. The mending process has already begun, but it needs continuous reinforcement. It is a paradox of American politics that the situation tends to improve before public interest in the topic peaks (e.g., drug usage declined three years before the public identified drugs as our number one problem). States like Florida are implementing Gold Seal Diploma programs for vocational students with high grades and a demonstrated employability in skills tests. These students are eligible for special scholarships, and the diploma is intended to tell employers that this person is work-ready (borrowing the German term). Parents in Chicago and New York are beginning to get angry as they realize that 44 percent of educational dollars never reach the classroom. Likewise, health care consumers are furious that $200 billion go toward bureaucracy and paperwork. In this context, it may become easier for the voice of the people to get through. It is good when the public gets angry, because only then do we have a chance to change things for the better. If we do not push Congress, the members will get reelected with superficial solutions that do nothing for the underlying problems. The problem with Congress is not that it ignores voters, but that it listens only to those voters who say send us more services but not the bill. The danger of the Perot idea to wire everybody electronically into the plebiscite is that it might increase pressure to enact new special interest spending programs. In this context Chief Justice Marshall was correct when he said the power to tax is the power to destroy. Voter education will minimize this problem of overexpectations. Such education should be didactic but not snobby like a PBS documentary. It does no good to tell voters that "idiot" in Greek means someone who cares nothing for issues of public life.

DOLLARS AND SENSE

Fiscal policies that overemphasized lowering unemployment distorted investment patterns and contributed to our productivity slowdown from 1973 to 1986. Many firms appear up to the challenge to enhance productivity, offering gain-sharing pay, customized flexible products, and labor-saving capital investments (e.g., McDonald's purchased two-sided grills to compensate for the decline in the supply of teenage cooks). Chapter 6 offered some practical suggestions to enhance productive investments. Tight Federal Reserve control of the money supply will curtail consumer spending and induce citizens to save more. If the suggested changes in the tax laws provided in this book are passed, even businesses facing a higher cost of funding (due to the energy crisis or tight money) will have sufficient incentive to invest and continue to grow. Our problems are substantial, but our growth capacity to mend our problems and enhance our standard of living are up to the task.

Chapter 4 provided a strong rebuke to protectionism, government-funded research as an "industrial policy," and mega-mergers. These patchwork policies will do nothing to improve the position of the American economy. Even in global markets, the domestic rivalry on product quality, productivity, and innovation are the critical issues. The Japanese have learned these lessons, which is why 25 percent of the cars manufactured in the U.S. are made in transplanted Japanese factories (Gelsanliter, 1990). Competitiveness resides within industries, not national borders. America should look within industry, not to protectionism, to improve our trade deficit. Managers must come to admit, like Cassius, that "the fault, dear Brutus, is not in the stars but in ourselves."

INEFFICIENCY IS A POOR TRADITION

Running up federal deficits has defiled our tradition of altruism. Altruism involves leaving your offspring with an endowment, not a box of bills. Cultural conservatives lament that Americans are too consumption oriented and not more Victorian in temperament. Because the Victorians acted as if they would live forever, it seems unlikely that they would have ever followed the big debt, short-run philosophy of Donald Trump or free-spending politicians. That great philosopher of rag magazines, Donald Trump, claims that a person who does not live beyond his or her means has a great lack of imagination. If debt equals imagination, then America may have an overactive one. In point of fact, investment is a Victorian concept that yields productive imagination and prosperity.

When America runs a deficit, funds flow to special interest groups plumbing for new entitlements or government contracts. When the Japanese run a deficit, the reduced tax burden on corporations tend to enhance the long-run financial health of business. In the peak years of 1989–1991,

Japan was able to spend 5.8 percent of its GNP on new product development and quality enhancement, up from 2.1 percent in 1979. The Japanese spent 5.3 percent of their GNP in 1992 on productivity improvement techniques to contend with their labor shortages. If America wants to avoid the twin problems of deep recessions and labor shortages, we must double our investment in productivity programs and improve the educational system. America needs sufficient productivity, innovation, and dedication to quality to earn a better return on capital. We also need more capital investment. If Japan can spend 23 percent of its GNP on capital investments ($810 billion by 1991), then America can spend more than 10.1 percent of its GNP on capital investments ($570 billion by 1992). We need more capital and better return on investments. We need patience rather than a focus on short-run profits. Government infected business with this fetish for short-termism. Consider one symptom: the average maturity of American government debt has shortened from 40 to 4.5 years since 1958. The quality of credit, and therefore the duration to maturity, will expand as America; puts its fiscal house in order.

If we do not save more, invest more, and enhance productivity we shall pay a high price. The bill will be a declining standard of living and diminished self-respect. Government cannot offer any new do-good, cost-beneficial programs until we regain a sense of control, a focus on the long-run national interest. We cannot regain that sense of control if our ship of state is sinking under a mountain of debt. The interest on the national debt each year is larger than total tax collections from every person and company east of the Mississippi. Productivity improvement and reduction of bureaucracy can free up the funds to improve our educational system. The process is a feedback loop, whereby improvements in education will enhance productivity in the long run and provide society with the resources to insure the uninsured and shelter the homeless. The interaction between the five deficits is outlined in figure 9.1.

CONGRESS AND THE BUREAUCRACY

The American public seems to be filled with unresolved contradictions. We hate "those politicians" but reelect members of Congress 98 percent of the time. We distrust government but expect much of it. Congress seems characterized by the terms "retrogression" and "balance." Leaders who stay in power without changing anything are retrogressing in our changing global economy. Congress has found a middle-of-the-road balance for its fiscal philosophy: it likes to spend taxpayers' money left and right. It assists special interest groups in the expropriation of wealth from the average citi-

Figure 9.1
Interaction Between the Five Basic Fiscal and Social Deficits

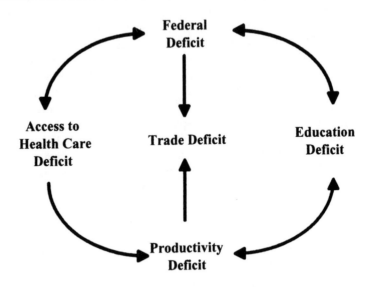

zen (which is called a crime when the president of Iraq does it). Selfishness becomes the general modus vivendi when you let special interest dominate Congress. Congress seems genetically indisposed to trimming waste and bureaucracy. In the last decade the number of federal employees has increased 9.6 percent.

The 1992 campaign of Ross Perot may not have been the ideal reform platform, but the federal government does need a major reformation. Government needs to free itself of special interest concerns and operate on a cost-benefit basis by reallocating resources out of programs with few social benefits (Seawolf submarines, bombers, organ transplants) to areas of higher yield (schools, fiber optic networks, public health). Practitioners of what Osborne and Gaebler (1992) call the new entrepreneurial government would let cost-benefit analysis guide public policy. However, as noneconomists, these two authors should be informed that we must avoid narrow cost-benefit methodology expressed only in monetary terms (net present value as computed by benefits minus expenditures). Instead, we should utilize a broad cost-benefit approach: (1) all indirect and intangible benefits must be surveyed and shadow priced (e.g., the value of incremental reductions in pain and suffering from AIDS care), and (2) the client must be society as a whole (not some influential special interest groups). This cost-benefit approach would help Congress make intelligent decisions and help educate the public.

Presidential politics can be quite unpredictable. The reader should ponder the following question in 1995: Who will be the next three presidents? No scholar in 1940 would have guessed that the correct answer then would be a meek senator from Missouri, a quiet apolitical army major, and a Catholic junior at Harvard College. Truman, Eisenhower, and Kennedy did, however, do a good job of rebuilding the American economy and infrastructure.

Barbara Tuchman (1984), in her classic book *The March of Folly*, laments the tendency of politicians and the public to persist in foolish policies. Without the prompting of armed conflict, Congress does not respond to new developments. Congressional hearings are like popcorn: seldom offensive and full of hot air. Congress will debate subsidies for high-definition TV without asking any sensible questions like: "How do we first rebuild American firms that manufacture TVs?" Defunct positions continue to hold power (e.g., "America is too rich not to do X") and previous errors are repeated (e.g., protectionism) until eventually the old paradigm (e.g., special interest politics) is totally discredited. A political vacuum then presents the disequilibrium time of danger/opportunity, which acts as a forest fire, opening up society for new growth and new paradigms.

John Stuart Mill wrote that "the despotism of custom is everywhere a standing hindrance to human advancement." The despotism of special interest politics and the hindrance of bureaucracy must be reduced or eliminated. Liberal free-spenders may fear this process presents the risk of going beyond lean, into mean and selfish. Conservatives want to coexist with compassion (the safety net) yet trim waste and excess entitlement. In the 19th century Alexis de Tocqueville observed that one special by-product of American society was restlessness amid prosperity. In the 21st century free spending will only produce more restlessness and declining prosperity. Government fiscal policy should take the moral message of the ecology movement: restraints, limits, try to balance inputs and outputs.

TRADE BIG SPENDING FOR A NEW FRONTIER

The years 1993 and 1996 may be landmark points in the saga of the federal deficit. In the year 1993 the $244 billion gross interest payment on the debt represents 42 percent of the funds on which the budgeted operations of our federal government depends. The 42 percent figure is a percentage of unobligated federal funds, excluding the 45 percent of the budget that is entitlement (nondiscretionary spending). This 42 percent leverage figure (on our discretionary spending) will also increasingly become key in evaluating the credit worthiness of Uncle Sam. The flip side of the interest cost is that the remaining 58 percent is available to cover the cost of running the government. Times were easy for those who worked in government when this "pie slice" was 62.9 percent in 1990 or 67.1 percent in 1989. If the 1989–1993 trend continues, the net interest expense will equal exactly half of unobligated funds in 1996. Our 1996 federal budget will be 25 percent gross interest expense, 50 percent entitlement, and 25 percent the cost of running the government. I hope government workers in 1996 do not mind working for departments spending 30 percent less than 1992 levels (in real dollars). To avoid this likely forecast we need some combination of reduced entitlement, reduced fraud and abuse, increased bureaucrat productivity, or higher taxes.

Another major fiscal problem for contemplation is articulated well by Ross Perot. He states that our federal system should stop financing long-term projects with short-term debt. Yet almost 70 percent of our $4.4 trillion debt (by December 1993) comes due within 60 months. We find it increasingly difficult to hope that foreigners and American banks will come to Treasury bill auctions with what used to be our money. For fiscal reasons we must stop treating the deficit as a harmless way to recycle money into the economy to pay for entitlements, "do-gooder" spending sprees, and public jobs. Trading away freedom, liberty, and the American standard of living is not good policy.

Uncle Sam has a problem. He cannot manage his finances. He is a nice guy who spends half his income on good causes. However, the good uncle has $120,000 in credit card debts and poor cash flow. His annual cash inflow is $30,000, but he spends $40,000 per year. Can we solve his problems by giving him a higher credit limit and more credit cards? No. If he stops adjusting spending to keep pace with inflation, his budget still will not be balanced for 9 years and he will not be able to pay off his credit cards for 40. One can also ask whether people from other lands will own 20 or 60 percent of his house 40 years into the future.

Readers of this story have the real problem, because we pay Uncle Sam's bills. He is our own federal government, only the dollar amounts are 40 million–fold higher. Our national debt will exceed $4.8 trillion in late 1994. Then House budget chairman, Leon Panetta (D–Calif.) suggested closing eight of the cabinet departments in October 1991. Even if we closed nine and kept open only the five major ones (Defense, Treasury, Health and Human Services, State, and Justice) the high level of federal health care spending for Medicaid and Medicare would still help make the budget difficult to balance before 2001.

Even with the record number of newly elected members of Congress in 1992, a revolution in attitudes seems slow in coming. We must stop the ideological con game. The truth is that both political parties love to spend 20 to 35 percent over budget. In the most recent 13 years (1981–1993), the difference between what congress appropriated and what the president requested is a sum total of $7.4 billion. Real spending cuts are needed. In 1993 federal, state, and local governments will spend one-tenth more of the economy's gross domestic product (34.3 percent on government) than under President Carter in 1980 (31.4 percent).

The deficit is as much a moral catastrophe as a fiscal one. Congress's objective appears to be to stay in power. This objective has been well served for three decades by following the public, claiming it is for reform, but initiating a new political business-as-usual cycle only every four to six years. To paraphrase a George Will or Ross Perot point, a political careerist is a moral slob if he or she charges $39 for every $50 worth of federal government. A growing minority in the Congress, however, dislikes the idea of leaving a negative bequest—massive debts. We can resist the impulse to live only for today. We have done it with our sex life, and we can do it with our government. We should hark back to the words of Senator John F. Kennedy spoken in July 1960:

The New Frontier of which I speak is not a set of promises—it is a set of challenges. It sums up not what I intend to offer the American people, but what I intend to ask of them. It appeals to their pride, not their pocketbook—it holds out the promise of more sacrifice instead of more security. But I tell you, the New Frontier is here, whether we like it or not.

New frontiers always receive a fire storm of criticism and disinformation. However, we need an across-the-board 10 percent cut in the administration of all federal agencies, the elimination of six to eight cabinet departments, selective cuts in some programs, and deep cuts in the defense budget. The unpopular Perot proposal of a 50 cent per gallon tax on gas at the pump would still make the price cheaper than it was in 1981. The nonpoor should receive reductions in COLAs for Social Security and other federal entitlement programs. America must stick to a course of fiscal discipline. Kennedy fans should also live by the Eisenhower principle that if people want a new government service, they have to pay for it through taxes. The deficit matters in the long run because the emphasis on consumption erodes our standard of living. The deficit matters in the short run because it absorbs hundreds of billions of dollars of investment capital that should be creating new jobs and technology.

Public policy options currently point in all different directions, similar to a pile of jackstraws. Substance has seemingly taken a back seat to image marketing. To liberals, those unsentimental conservatives put on airs about the damage that welfare programs do to the human spirit. Conservatives have an equally unflattering view of liberals and their rights agenda. After three decades of turning inward, the American public has a hunger for re-creating some sense of community, for participating in activities beyond the home front. The public is not to blame for this long period of inertia, because what they lacked was time (for work, for family, for learning new technologies). If they soon have the time to act on the general consensus that what passes for deep thought and public debate is a pile of dung and 15-second slogans, most political thinkers will be out of a job.

As we approach a new century, in what direction will the public steer the government and business community? Young leadership in both parties respects the 18th-century shining trilogy of family, work, and neighbor-hood. Hoary old salesmen of negative politics do not care about the consent of the governed, the public. Negative politics picks on compassion mongers on the left or heartless rich people on the right. Liberals harp on the lack of generosity among the public, and conservatives chatter on about the personal irresponsibility of welfare cheats. The negative malaise could lift soon if liberals rediscover responsibility and conservatives rediscover the empowerment to improve education, housing, and health care. Liberals must come to realize that certain programs must be restricted to those truly needy, and careful cost-benefit analysis can eliminate funding programs that fail to work. Conservatives must learn that the federal government might have to spend some money in the short run to save money in the long run (through neighborhood redevelopment programs, more public health clinics, more health insurance options for the 35 million uninsured Americans, more programs to allow high school graduates to continue their education, and less environmental degradation). We may need to cut spending 25 percent to finance expanding new spending one-tenth, for an effective 15 percent downsizing in the federal government. To a leader this is a challenge, but to most pols in Congress this is hell. We should reflect on President Harry S. Truman when, accused of "givin' em hell," he re-plied, "I don't give anybody hell, I just tell them the truth, and they think it's hell." The new frontier should reflect four basic principles: a cost-bene-fit orientation, individual choice, responsibility to dismantle failed pro-grams, and an investment orientation. The old frontier has poorly served the public in times of rapid change because it was consumption- and pres-ent-oriented.

The size of our federal deficit is impressive. If President Clinton were to hire 60,000 citizens to begin counting dollar bills at the rate of one a second on January 1, 1994, it would take them until November 15, 1996, to count to $5.2 trillion (the projected national debt as of that fiscal year). If the 1960s and 1970s asked "what should government do?" and the 1980s asked "how can we pay for it?," the coming years will ask "how can government assist job production while trimming bureaucracy and excessive entitlements?" We should not have $170 billion in annual federal benefits going to households with cash incomes over $60,000 in 1995. We must reform our crazy "upper middle-class welfare state" and work to target funds to the powerless (our children, the demographic group with the highest poverty rate in our society, 19 percent). Access to education and health care are key issues, but equally important are the cost-reduction efforts necessary to finance these good programs.

REFERENCES

Beer, S. (1993). "Government by the People," *The Political Quarterly* 64:2, April-June, 198–208.

Binder, A. (1987). *Hard Heads, Soft Hearts: Tough-Minded Economics for a Just Society.* New York: Addison-Wesley.

Boyd, R., and Uri, N. (1992). "Cost of Improving the Quality of the Environment," *Journal of Policy Modeling* 13:1, Spring, 115–40.

Dionne, E. (1991). *Why Americans Hate Politics.* New York: Simon and Schuster.

Eisenhower, D. (1967). *The Quotable Dwight D. Eisenhower,* ed. E. Gollagher. New York: Grosset and Dunlap.

Figgie, H., and Swanson, G. (1992). *Bankruptcy 1995: The Coming Collapse of America and How to Stop It.* Boston: Little, Brown.

Friedman, B. (1988). *Day of Reckoning.* New York: Random House.

Gelsanliter, D. (1990). *Jump Start: Japan Comes to the Heartland.* New York: Farrar, Straus & Giroux.

Gore, A. (1992). *Earth in the Balance: Ecology and the Human Spirit.* Boston: Houghton Mifflin.

Hardin, G. (1993). *Living within Limits.* New York: Oxford University Press.

Magat, W., and Viscusi, K. (1991). *Informational Approaches to Regulation.* Cambridge: MIT Press.

Markusen, A., and Yudken, J (1992). *Dismantling the Cold War Economy.* New York: Basic Books.

Offe, C., and Rolf, H. (1992). *Beyond Employment.* Philadelphia: Temple University Press.

Osborne, D. (1988). *Laboratories of Democracy.* Boston: Harvard Business School Press.

Osborne, D., and Gaebler, T. (1992). *Reinventing Government: How the Entrepreneurial Spirit is Transforming the Public Sector.* Reading, MA: Addison-Wesley.

Peters, T. (1992). *Liberation Management: Necessary Disorganization for the Nanosecond Nineties.* New York: Knopf.

Rivlin, A. (1992). *Reviving the American Dream: The Economy, the States, and the Federal Government.* Washington, DC: Brookings.

Schultze, C. (1992). *Memos to the President: A Guide through Macroeconomics for the Busy Policymaker.* Washington, DC: Brookings.

Slesnick, D. (1993). "Gaining Ground: Poverty in the Post War U.S.," *Journal of Political Economy.* 101:1, February, 1–38.

Traub, J. (1990). *Too Good to Be True: The Outlandish Story of Wedtech.* New York: Doubleday.

Truman, H. (1980). *Autobiography of Harry S. Truman,* ed. R. Ferrell, 2nd ed. Boulder: University of Colorado Press.

Trump, D. (1987). *Trump: The Art of the Deal.* New York: Random House.

Tuchman, B. (1984). *The March of Folly; From Troy to Vietnam.* New York: Random House.

Tyson, L. (1992). *Who's Bashing Whom? Trade Conflict in High-Technology Issues.* Washington, DC: Institute for International Economics.

Weaver, R., and Rockman, B. (1993). *Do Institutions Matter? Government Capabilities in the United States and Abroad.* Washington, DC: Brookings.

Appendix: The 49 Major Policy Proposals

1. Provide the president with line-item veto power.

2. Reduce federal workers' pay by 10 percent and trim pension benefits by 20 percent.

3. Down-staff the military from 1.3 million active-duty personnel in 1997 to a target of 700,000 (saving $278 billion over the period 1995–1997).

4. Eliminate the new warhead activities of the Department of Energy, cancel the Trident II (D5 missiles), terminate the Seawolf submarine program, and retire the B-1 Bomber.

5. Trim reserves from 1.04 million troops to 360,000 and reduce funds for reserve equipment by 70 percent (saving $32 billion over the four years 1994–1997).

6. Eliminate airport grants-in-aid, thus saving $8.6 billion over the period 1994–1997.

7. Reduce target prices by 4 percent a year starting with 1994 crops (saving $17.1 billion over the period 1994–1997).

8. Scale down the bureaucratic low-income home energy assistance program by $6.7 billion over the years 1994–1997.

9. Scale down Community Development Block Grants (CDBG) eligibility for non-entitlement areas (saving $12.1 billion over four years) and spend federal funds only on programs with national benefit.

10. Reallocate one-fourth of the block grant savings, or $3 billion, to rebuild Los Angeles and New York City.

11. Increase the proportion of each farmer's base acreage ineligible for farm deficiency payments from 15 percent under current law to 35 percent in 1994 (saving $7.2 billion over the years 1994–1997).

12. Require the VA system to utilize the same hospital payment system and fee schedule as Medicare, saving a minimum of $2.2 billion over the period 1994–1997.

13. Combine funding to states for welfare (AFDC), Medicaid, and food stamps into a single indexed grant, saving $5.7 billion over the period 1994–1997, according to the Congressional Budget Office.

14. Break the link between waste promotion (burning taxpayer funds) and getting reelected through public financing of elections.

15. Change the tax laws so the full value of the child tax exemption can be restored to inflation-adjusted 1960 levels.

16. Cap the home interest deduction at $15,000 a year, thus raising an additional $21.8 billion in 1994–1997 tax collections from the rich.

17. Enact a pension fund investment law based only on the 1977 Bank Community Reinvestment Act.

18. Exempt half the interest earned on savings up to $4,000 for single parents and up to $3,000 for other households from taxation.

19. Exempt half of dividends earned from taxation, up to a maximum of $4,000 for single parents and up to a maximum of $3,000 for other families, for investments held for over two years.

20. Impose a 4 percent tax on investments in pension plans and IRA accounts.

21. Tax the initial $40,000 of capital gains for job-creating assets held over six years at a 15 percent rate, and implement in 1994 a graduated capital gains tax of 18 percent for additional gains earned over five years, gradually increasing to 33 percent on gains earned in less than a year.

22. Tax capital gains held at death on the final tax return of the deceased, thus raising $16.8 billion in 1994–1997.

23. Initiate a 3 percent tax on the value of nonretirement fringe benefits (collecting $19 billion over 1994–1997).

24. Disallow deductions for half of business meal and entertainment expenses (saving $13.7 billion in 1994–1997).

25. Provide a $5.7 billion annual subsidy to new economic activity (providing no subsidy to existing capital) through a tax credit applied to the real (inflation-adjusted) change in a firm's net capital stock from year to year.

26. Levy corporate taxes on gross corporate profits, including interest expense, thus eliminating the tax advantage of debt.

27. Enact a VAT of 3 percent on items (excluding health care, food, and housing) if Congress passes an equal amount of spending cuts for each dollar of taxation.

28. Establish user fees that cover the marginal cost for air traffic control services, thus collecting $6.4 billion in 1994–1997.

29. Sell import quotas for apparel, sugar, and textiles at auction to the highest bidder (collecting $12 billion in revenues over the years 1994–1997, according to the Congressional Budget Office).

30. American companies should copy the Japanese and spend two-thirds of their research dollars on process technology and one-third on new products.

31. Make half of the productivity-based incentive pay tax-exempt.

32. Replace commercial bank loan guarantees with direct federal loans for students.

33. The new welfare reform agenda should include tripling federal government spending on job training and education by 1997, to $3.1 billion, and adding $1.7 billion in tax credits for the working poor.

34. Double the required semester hours of science and math for the average college graduate from 9 to 18.

35. American education should boost capital investment by 50 percent per employee to allow more individual-based computer learning and to stay competitive with the Japanese and Germans.

36. Fire half of the careerist education bureaucrats.

37. Pass a German-style system of global budgeting board for health care spending control, making care more affordable for private patients (saving $99 billion federally on the care of public patients over the period 1994–1997).

38. Restrict the Medicare disproportionate payment share for low-income patients to the 136 Academic Medical Centers (thus saving $9.6 billion over the period 1994–1997).

39. Set the premium for physicians' services to 100 percent of costs for the rich elderly with income for couples over $110,000 and income for singles over $80,000 (saving $12 billion over the years 1994–1997).

40. Set uniform coinsurance rates at 20 percent for all Medicare services (including lab, home health care, and nursing home services, thus saving $15.3 billion over the period 1994–1997.

41. Restrict indirect Medicare adjustment payments to a 3.9 percent bonus for each 0.1 increase in the ratio of interns and residents per bed (saving $7.8 billion over the period 1994–1997).

42. Tax as income insurance benefits exceeding $375 a month for family coverage and $150 a month for individual coverage (in 1994 dollars, indexed to inflation).

43. Limit COLA adjustments for nonpoor elderly to 1.5 points below the inflation rate (saving $12 billion over the period 1994–1997).

44. Defer COLAs until age 62 for all nondisabled employees who retire before age 61 (saving $5.1 billion in 1994–1997).

45. End income payments for veterans with no real disabilities and for new veterans with disabilities unrelated to military duties (saving $8.5 billion over the period 1994–1997).

46. Increase the age to qualify for partial Social Security benefits to age 70 and for full benefits to age 75 by the year 2028.

47. Subject 86 percent of Social Security payments to income tax for those with income over $24,000 (reducing the deficit by $43 billion over the years 1994–1997).

48. Implement a carbon dioxide stabilization tax of $34 per ton (1994 dollars) in

the content of our three fossil fuels, collecting $109 billion over the period 1994–1997 and achieving the social goal of eliminating the growth in emissions.

49. Eliminate $10.8 billion in water treatment plants over the period 1994–1997 because these grants have encouraged inefficient decisions by state and local government.

Glossary

appropriation act: A statute under the jurisdiction of the House and Senate Committees on Appropriations that provides budget authority. Enactment generally follows adoption of authorizing legislation unless the authorization itself provides the budget authority. Currently, 13 regular appropriations acts are enacted annually. When necessary, Congress may enact supplemental or continuing appropriations.

authorization: A substantive law that sets up or continues a federal program or agency. Authorizing legislation is normally a prerequisite for appropriations. For some programs, the authorizing legislation itself provides the authority to incur obligations and make payments.

baseline: A benchmark for measuring the budgetary effects of proposed changes in federal revenues or spending, with the assumption that current budgetary policies are continued without change. As specified in the Budget Enforcement Act of 1990 (BEA), the baseline for revenues and entitlement spending generally assumes that laws now on the statute books will continue. The discretionary spending projections will be based on the discretionary spending caps set by the BEA in 1994 and 1995 and adjusted for inflation in 1996 through 1998.

budget authority: Legal authority to incur financial obligations that will result in spending of federal government funds. Budget authority may be provided in an authorization or in an appropriation act. Offsetting collections, including offsetting receipts, constitutes negative budget authority.

budget deficit: Amount by which budget expenditures exceed budget revenues during a given period.

Budget Enforcement Act of 1990 (BEA): Title XIII of the Omnibus Budget Reconciliation Act of 1990. This act amended both the Congressional Budget Act of 1974 and the Balanced Budget and Emergency Deficit Control Act of 1985. The BEA provides for new budget targets, sequestration procedures, pay-as-you-go procedures, and credit reform.

budget resolution: A resolution passed by both houses of Congress that sets forth a congressional budget plan for the next five years. The plan must be carried out through subsequent legislation, including appropriations and changes in tax and entitlement laws. The resolution sets guidelines for congressional action, but it is not signed by the president and does not become law. The Congressional Budget Act of 1974 established a number of mechanisms that are designed to hold spending and revenues to the targets established in the budget resolution.

budgetary resources: All sources of budget authority that are subject to sequestration. Budgetary resources include new budget authority, unobligated balances, direct spending authority, and obligation limitations. See *sequestration.*

capital: Physical capital is the output that has been set aside to be used in production rather than consumed. According to the national income and product accounts, private capital goods are composed of residential and nonresidential structures, producers' durable equipment, and business inventories. *Financial capital* is the funds raised by an individual, business, or government by issuing securities, such as a mortgage, stock certificate, or bond. *Human capital* is a term for education, training, health, and other attributes of the work force that increase its ability to produce goods and services.

constant dollar: Measured in terms of prices of a base period, to remove the influence of inflation. Compare with *current dollar.*

consumption: Total purchases of goods and services during a given period by households for their own use. (BEA)

cost of capital: Total expected rate of return an investment must generate in order to provide investors with the prevailing market yield consistent with risk after accounting for corporate taxes (if applicable) and depreciation.

credit crunch: A significant, temporary decline in the normal supply of credit, usually caused by tight monetary policy or a regulatory restriction on lending institutions.

credit subsidies: The estimated long-term costs to the federal government of direct loans or loan guarantees calculated on the basis of net present value, excluding administrative costs and any incidental effects on governmental receipts or outlays. For direct loans, the subsidy cost is the net present value of loan disbursements less repayments of interest and principal, adjusted for estimated defaults, prepayments, fees, penalties, and other recoveries. For loan guarantees, the subsidy cost is the net present value of the estimated payments by the government to cover defaults and delinquencies, interest subsidies, or other payments, offset by any payments to the government, including origination and other fees, penalties, and recoveries.

current-account balance: The net revenues that arise from a country's international sales and purchases of goods and services, net international transfers (public or private gifts or donations), and net factor income (primarily capital income from foreign-located property owned by residents less capital income from domestic property owned by nonresidents). The current-account balance differs from net exports in that the former includes international transfers and net factor income. (BEA)

current dollar: Measured in the dollar value—reflecting then-prevailing prices—of the period under consideration. Compare with *constant dollar.*

cyclical deficit: The part of the budget deficit that results from cyclical factors rather than from underlying fiscal policy. The cyclical deficit reflects the fact that, when the GDP falls, revenues automatically fall and outlays automatically rise. By definition, the cyclical deficit is zero when the economy is operating at potential GDP.

debt restructuring: Changing the characteristics of an entity's outstanding debt, such as maturity or interest rate. Such changes can be effected by issuing long-term debt and retiring short-term debt (or vice versa) or by negotiating with creditors.

debt service: Payment of scheduled interest obligations on outstanding debt.

depreciation: Decline in the value of a currency, financial asset, or capital good. When applied to a capital good, the term usually refers to loss of value because of obsolescence or wear.

direct spending: The Budget Enforcement Act of 1990 defines this term as (1) budget authority provided by an authorization, (2) entitlement authority (including mandatory spending contained in appropriation acts), and (3) the Food Stamp program. A synonym is *mandatory spending.*

discount rate: The interest rate the Federal Reserve System charges on a loan that it makes to a bank. Such loans, when allowed, enable a bank to meet its reserve requirements without reducing its loans.

discouraged workers: Jobless people who are available for work, but who are not actively seeking jobs because they think they have poor prospects of finding any. Because they are not actively seeking jobs, discouraged workers are not counted as part of the labor force or as being unemployed. (BLS)

discretionary spending: Spending for programs whose funding levels are determined through the appropriation process. Congress has the discretion each year to determine how many dollars will be devoted to continuing current programs and funding new ones. Discretionary spending is divided among three categories: defense, international, and domestic. Compare with *direct spending.*

defense discretionary spending consists primarily of the military activities of the Department of Defense, which are funded in the defense and military construction appropriation bills. It also includes the defense-related functions of other agencies, such as the Department of Energy's nuclear weapons programs.

domestic discretionary spending includes most government activities in science and space, transportation, medical research, environmental protection, and law enforcement, among other programs. Funding for these programs is provided in ten of the annual appropriation bills.

international discretionary spending encompasses spending for foreign economic and military aid, the activities of the Department of State and the U.S. Information Agency, and international financial programs, such as the Export-Import Bank of the United States.

discretionary spending caps: Annual ceilings on budget authority and outlays for discretionary programs as defined by the Budget Enforcement Act of 1990. For fiscal years 1991 through 1993, the caps are divided among the three categories of discretionary spending—defense, international, and domestic. For fiscal years 1994 and 1995, there will be one cap for all discretionary spending. Discretionary spending caps are enforced through congressional rules and sequestration procedures.

disposable (personal) income: Income received by individuals, including transfer payments, less personal taxes and fees paid to government.

entitlements: Programs that make payments to any person, business, or unit of government that seeks the payments and meets the criteria set in law. Congress controls these programs indirectly by defining eligibility and setting the benefit or payment rules. Although the level of spending for these programs is controlled by the authorizing legislation, funding may be provided either in an authorization or in an appropriation act. The best-known entitlements are the major benefit programs, such as Social Security and Medicare; other entitlements include farm price supports and interest on the federal debt. See *direct spending.*

excise tax: A tax levied on the purchase of a specific type of good or service, such as tobacco products or telephone services.

Federal Reserve System: As the central bank of the United States, the Federal Reserve is responsible for conducting the nation's monetary policy and overseeing credit conditions.

financial intermediary: An institution that indirectly matches borrowers with lenders. For example, depository institutions, such as commercial banks or savings and loan institutions, lend funds that they have accepted from depositors. Nondepository institutions, such as life insurance companies or pension funds, lend or invest funds that they hold in reserve against future claims by policyholders or participating retirees.

financing account: Any account established under credit reform to finance the portion of federal direct loans and loan guarantees not subsidized by federal funds. Since these accounts are used only to finance the nonsubsidized portion of federal credit activities, they are excluded from the federal budget and included as a means of financing the deficit.

fiscal policy: The government's choice of tax and spending programs, which influences the amount and maturity of government debt as well as the level, composition, and distribution of output and income. An "easy" fiscal policy stimulates the short-term growth of output and income, whereas a "tight" fiscal policy restrains their growth. Movements in the standardized-employment deficit constitute one overall indicator of the tightness or ease of federal fiscal policy; an increase relative to the potential GDP suggests fiscal ease, whereas a decrease suggests fiscal restriction. The president and Congress jointly determine federal fiscal policy.

fiscal year: A yearly accounting period. The federal government's fiscal year begins October 1 and ends September 30. Fiscal years are designated by the calendar years in which they end—for example, fiscal year 1994 began October 1, 1993.

global budget: State or national cap on total health care expenditures. Designed to force providers, patients, and payers to cut costs, make hard choices. A national commission recommends budget to Congress, covering public and private spending and capital outlays.

Gramm-Rudman-Hollings Emergency Deficit Control Act of 1985: Also known as the Balanced Budget Act, it sets forth specific deficit targets and a sequestration procedure to reduce spending if the targets are exceeded. The Budget Enforcement Act of 1990 established new budget procedures as well as revised targets through fiscal year 1995, which exclude the Social Security trust funds. The president will have the option of adjusting the deficit targets for revised economic and technical assumptions when submitting the budget for fiscal years 1994 and 1995.

grants: Transfer payments from the federal government to state and local governments or other recipients to help fund projects or activities that do not involve substantial federal participation.

grants-in-aid: Grants from the federal government to state and local governments to help provide for programs of assistance or service to the public.

gross domestic product (GDP): The total market value of all goods and services produced domestically during a given period. The components of the GDP are consumption, gross domestic investment, government purchases of goods and services, and net exports. (BEA)

gross investment: Includes additions to the capital stock, but does not include depreciation of existing capital as a subtraction from the capital stock.

gross national product (GNP): The total market value of all goods and services produced in a given period by labor and property supplied by residents of a country, regardless of where the labor and property are located. The GNP differs from the GDP primarily by including the excess of capital income that residents earn from investments abroad less capital income that nonresidents earn from domestic investment.

inflation: Growth in a measure of the general price level, usually expressed as an annual rate of change.

infrastructure: Government-owned capital goods that provide services to the public, usually with benefits to the community at large as well as to the direct user. Examples include schools, roads, bridges, dams, harbors, and public buildings.

investment: Physical investment is the current product set aside during a given period to be used for future production; in other words, an addition to the stock of capital goods. According to the national income and product accounts, private domestic investment consists of investment in residential and nonresidential structures, producers' durable equipment, and the change in business inventories. *Financial investment* is the purchase of a financial security. *Investment in human capital* is spending on education, training, health services, and other activities that increase the productivity of the work force. Investment in human capital is not treated as investment in the national income and product accounts.

junk bond: A bond considered by credit rating services to be a speculative financial investment because of its relatively high risk of default or delay in meeting scheduled obligations. Junk bonds offer relatively high yields to compensate investors for their exposure to risk.

long-term interest rate: Interest rate earned by a note or bond that matures in ten or more years.

managed competition: refers to a model of health care reform that forms the basis for President Clinton's plan. It requires the government to regulate insurers so that no individual can be denied coverage and everyone buying the same health plan in the same region would pay nearly the same for it. It requires most employers and individuals to purchase health coverage through a health alliance and counts on competition among privately owned health plans to drive down the cost of health care. Many health plans would likely evolve into super-HMOs that are generally thought to be 10 percent more cost efficient.

marginal tax rate: Tax rate that applies to an additional dollar of taxable income.

means of financing: Sources of financing federal deficits or uses of federal surpluses. The largest means of financing is normally federal borrowing from the public, but other means of financing include any transaction that causes a difference between the federal (including off-budget) surplus or deficit and changes in debt held by the public. The means of financing include changes in checks outstanding and Treasury cash balances, seigniorage, and the transactions of the financing accounts established under credit reform.

means-tested programs: Programs that provide cash or services to people who meet a test of need based on income and assets. Most means-tested programs are entitlements—for example, Medicaid, the Food Stamp program, Supplemental Security Income, family support, and veterans' pensions—but a few, such as subsidized housing and various social services, are funded through discretionary appropriations.

monetary policy: The strategy of influencing movements of the money supply and interest rates to affect output and inflation. An "easy" monetary policy suggests faster money growth and initially lower short-term interest rates in an attempt to increase aggregate demand, but it may lead to a higher rate of inflation. A "tight" monetary policy suggests slower money growth and higher interest rates in the near term in an attempt to reduce inflationary pressure by reducing aggregate demand. The Federal Reserve System conducts monetary policy in the United States.

national saving: Total saving by all sectors of the economy: personal saving, business saving (corporate after-tax profits not paid as dividends), and government saving (budget surplus or deficit—indicating dissaving—of all government entities). National saving represents all income not consumed, publicly or privately, during a given period. (BEA)

net exports: Exports of goods and services produced in a country less its imports of goods and services produced elsewhere.

net interest: In the federal budget, net interest includes federal interest payments to the public as recorded in budget function 900. Net interest also includes, as an offset, interest income received by the government on loans and cash balances.

In the national income and product accounts, net interest is the income component of the GDP paid as interest—primarily interest that domestic businesses pay, less interest they receive.

net national saving: National saving less depreciation of physical capital.

nominal: Measured in the dollar value (as in nominal output, income, or wage rate) or market terms (as in nominal exchange or interest rate) of the period under consideration. Compare with *real.*

off-budget: Spending or revenues excluded from the budget totals by law. The revenues and outlays of the two Social Security trust funds and the net surplus or deficit of the postal service are currently off-budget and (except for discretionary Social Security administrative costs) are not included in any Budget Enforcement Act calculations. Medicare Hospital Insurance revenues and outlays are also designated as off-budget, but the BEA treats them as on-budget.

offsetting receipts: Funds collected by the federal government that are recorded as negative budget authority and outlays and credited to separate receipt accounts. More than half of offsetting receipts are intragovernmental receipts that reflect agencies' payments to retirement and other funds on their employees' behalf; these receipts simply balance payments elsewhere in the budget. The remaining offsetting receipts (proprietary receipts) come from the public and generally represent voluntary, business-type transactions. The largest items are the flat premiums for Supplementary Medical Insurance (Part B of Medicare), timber and oil lease receipts, and proceeds from the sale of electric power.

Organization of Petroleum Exporting Countries (OPEC): The group of oil-rich countries that tries to determine the price of crude oil (given demand) by agreeing to production quotas among its members.

outlays: The liquidation of a federal obligation, generally by issuing a check or disbursing cash. Sometimes obligations are liquidated (and outlays occur) by issuing agency promissory notes, such as those of the former Federal Savings and Loan Insurance Corporation. Unlike outlays for other categories of spending, outlays for interest on the public debt are counted when the interest is earned, not when it is paid. Outlays may be for payment of obligations incurred in previous fiscal years or in the same year. Outlays, therefore, flow in part from unexpended balances of prior-year budget authority and, in part, from budget authority provided for the current year.

pay-as-you-go: A procedure required in the Budget Enforcement Act of 1990 to ensure that, for fiscal years 1991 through 1995, legislation affecting direct spending and receipts does not increase the deficit. Pay-as-you-go is enforced through congressional rules and sequestration procedures.

personal saving: Disposable personal income that households do not use for consumption or interest payments during a given period. *Personal saving rate* is personal saving as a percentage of disposable personal income.

present value: A single number that expresses a flow of current and future income (or payments) in terms of an equivalent lump sum received (or paid) today. The calculation of present value depends on the rate of discount.

productivity: Average real output per unit of input. Labor productivity is average real output per hour of labor. The growth of labor productivity is defined as growth of real output that is not explained by growth of labor input alone. Total factor productivity is average real output per unit of combined labor and capital inputs. The growth of total factor productivity is defined as the growth of real output that is not explained by growth of labor and capital. Labor productivity and total factor productivity differ in that increases in capital per worker would raise labor productivity but not total factor productivity.

program account: Any budgetary account that finances credit subsidies and the costs of administering credit programs.

real: Adjusted to remove the effect of inflation. *Real (constant dollar) output* represents volume, rather than dollar value, of goods and services. *Real income* represents power to purchase real output. *Real data* are usually constructed by dividing the corresponding nominal data, such as output or a wage rate, by a price index or deflator. *Real interest rate* is a nominal interest rate minus the expected inflation rate. Compare with *nominal.*

receipt account: Any budget or off-budget account that is established exclusively to record the collection of income, including negative subsidies. In general, receipt accounts that collect money arising from the exercise of the government's sovereign powers are included as revenues, whereas the proceeds of intragovernmental transactions or collections from the public arising from business-type transactions (such as interest income, proceeds from the sale of property or products, or profits from federal credit activities) are included as *offsetting receipts*—that is, credited as offsets to outlays rather than included in receipts.

recession: A phase of the business cycle extending from a peak to the next trough—usually lasting six months to a year—and characterized by widespread declines in output, income, employment, and trade in many sectors of the economy. Real GDP usually falls throughout the recession.

reconciliation: A process Congress uses to make its tax and spending legislation conform with the targets established in the budget resolution. The budget resolution may contain reconciliation instructions directing certain congressional committees to achieve savings in tax or spending programs under their jurisdiction. Legislation to implement the reconciliation instructions is usually combined in one comprehensive bill. The reconciliation process primarily affects taxes, entitlement spending, and offsetting receipts. As a general rule, decisions on defense and nondefense discretionary programs are determined separately through the appropriation process, which is also governed by allocations in the budget resolution.

reserve requirements: The amount of funds that banks and other depository institutions must hold as cash or as deposits with the Federal Reserve System. The Federal Reserve System specifies reserve requirements depending on the level of deposits. Such requirements reduce the risk of bank failure and allow the Federal Reserve System to influence the money supply.

Resolution Trust Corporation (RTC): An agency created by the Financial Institutions Reform, Recovery, and Enforcement Act of 1989 (FIRREA) to close, merge, or otherwise resolve insolvent savings and loan institutions whose deposits are insured by the federal government.

sequestration: The cancellation of budgetary resources to enforce the Budget Enforcement Act of 1990. Sequestration is triggered if the Office of Management and Budget determines that discretionary appropriations breach the discretionary spending caps, that legislation affecting direct spending and receipts increases the deficit, or that the deficit exceeds, by more than a specified margin, the maximum deficit amount set by law. Failure to meet the maximum deficit amount would trigger across-the-board spending reductions. Changes in direct spending and receipt legislation that increase the deficit would result in reductions in funding from entitlements not otherwise exempted by law. Discretionary spending in excess of the caps would cause the cancellation of budgetary resources within the appropriate discretionary spending category.

short-term interest rate: Interest rate earned by a debt instrument that will mature within one year.

thrift institutions: Savings and loan institutions and mutual savings banks.

trade balance: The difference between the value of a country's merchandise exports and its imports. It can be measured on an overall basis or between two countries or regions. The United States, for example, imports more than it exports, that is, we have a trade deficit with the rest of the world. It also runs a sizable trade deficit with Japan but has a surplus with many countries. A broader measure includes all financial transactions between a country and the rest of the world and is called the balance of payments.

transfer payments: Payments in return for which no good or service is currently received—for example, welfare or Social Security payments or money sent to relatives abroad.

trust fund: A fund, designated as a trust fund by statute, that is credited with income from earmarked collections and charged with certain outlays. Collections may come from the public (for example, taxes or user charges) or from intrabudgetary transfers. More than 150 federal government trust funds exist, of which the largest and best known finance several major benefit programs (including Social Security and Medicare) and certain infrastructure spending (the highway and the airport and airway trust funds). The term "federal funds" refers to all programs that are not trust funds.

unemployment: The number of jobless people who are available for work and are actively seeking jobs. The *unemployment rate* is unemployment as a percentage of the labor force.

yield: The average annual rate of return on a security, including interest payments and repayment of principal, if held to maturity.

Author Index

Subject Index

About the Author

STEVEN R. EASTAUGH is a Professor of Economics and Finance at the School of Business and Public Management, The George Washington University. The winner of numerous awards, he is the author of six books, including *Health Care Finance* and *Health Care Economics* (Auburn House, 1992) as well as more than sixty journal articles.